AF251466

Theodoret of Cyrus
on Romans 11:26

american
university
studies

Series VII
Theology and Religion

Vol. 249

PETER LANG
New York • Washington, D.C./Baltimore • Bern
Frankfurt am Main • Berlin • Brussels • Vienna • Oxford

Joel A. Weaver

Theodoret of Cyrus on Romans 11:26

Recovering an Early Christian Elijah Redivivus Tradition

PETER LANG
New York • Washington, D.C./Baltimore • Bern
Frankfurt am Main • Berlin • Brussels • Vienna • Oxford

Library of Congress Cataloging-in-Publication Data

Weaver, Joel A.
Theodoret of Cyrus on Romans 11:26: recovering an early Christian
Elijah redivivus tradition / Joel A. Weaver.
p. cm. — (American university studies VII: theology
and religion; v. 249)
Includes bibliographical references and index.
1. Theodoret, Bishop of Cyrrhus. 2. Bible.
N.T. Romans XI, 26—Criticism, interpretation, etc.
3. Bible. N.T. Romans IX–XI—Criticism, interpretation, etc.
4. Salvation—Judaism. 5. Elijah (Biblical prophet) I. Title.
BR65.T756W43   227'.106092—dc22   2006026008
ISBN-13: 978-0-8204-8608-6
ISBN-10: 0-8204-8608-6
ISSN 0740-0446

Bibliographic information published by **Die Deutsche Bibliothek**.
Die Deutsche Bibliothek lists this publication in the "Deutsche
Nationalbibliografie"; detailed bibliographic data is available
on the Internet at http://dnb.ddb.de/.

The paper in this book meets the guidelines for permanence and durability
of the Committee on Production Guidelines for Book Longevity
of the Council of Library Resources.

© 2007 Peter Lang Publishing, Inc., New York
29 Broadway, 18th floor, New York, NY 10006
www.peterlang.com

Printed in Germany

ἐν ὅλῃ καρδίᾳ σου δόξασον τὸν πατέρα σου
καὶ μητρὸς ὠδῖνας μὴ ἐπιλάθῃ
μνήσθητι ὅτι δι᾽ αὐτῶν ἐγεννήθης
καὶ τί ἀνταποδώσεις αὐτοῖς καθὼς αὐτοὶ σοί

Sirach 7:27–28

To my parents, Mac and Judy Weaver

Contents

Acknowledgments

First and foremost, I must express my appreciation to my teacher and mentor, Dr. Charles Talbert. This project—originally presented to the Religion Department of Baylor University as a doctoral dissertation—is an outgrowth of Dr. Talbert's own work on Romans, stemming initially from his citation of Theodoret's intriguing interpretation of Romans 11:26. In addition to planting the seed, Dr. Talbert nurtured the growth by patiently providing direction and clarification. Yet his most important contribution has not been in serving as committee chairperson, but rather in providing a tangible model for what a Christian scholar should be.

I would also like to acknowledge the remainder of my doctoral committee, Drs. Sharyn Dowd and John Nordling, whose editorial eyes made the finished product much better than it would have been otherwise. I am indebted to two other professors for their aid in the beginning stages of the project. Dr. Mikeal Parsons was particularly helpful in the drafting of the prospectus, and he lent his expertise to the early work of translating Theodoret's commentary, which, at that time, had yet to be translated into English. Later on, Dr. Dan Williams was instrumental in bringing the purpose of the dissertation into focus. I would also like to express my appreciation to two of my colleagues at the George W. Truett Theological Seminary, Drs. Todd Still and Dennis Tucker. Dr. Still provided valuable advice on the restructuring of Chapter One, while Dr. Tucker graciously agreed to review the portions of Chapter Four relating to the Old Testament.

Many others have facilitated the writing of this project. Janet Jasek and her staff in the Interlibrary Services office of Moody Library proved indispensable in the procuring of research materials. Kevin Cornelius, my former graduate assistant at Baylor's George W. Truett Theological Seminary, made many pickups and deliveries on my behalf. Two of my students, Tim Buechsel and Maik Friedrich, were particularly helpful in dealing with uncertain German syntax. In addition, Candace Spain's expertise in Latin was critical as deadlines approached. Finally, a special word of thanks goes to my current graduate assistant, Drew Dabbs, for the last minute addition of indices which should serve to make the information in this text more accessible to other scholars.

I would also like to express my appreciation to those who have provided emotional support and encouragement throughout the long process of the production of this volume. I am grateful to my friends at Calvary Baptist Church in Waco for their prayers and expressions of love. My colleagues at the George W. Truett Theological Seminary have been most encouraging, especially as the end drew nigh. Moreover, I owe a great debt to my students at Truett. Their enthusiasm for learning and service has reinvigorated my own sense of calling, and their supportive words have validated my vocation. The friendship of my fellow New Testament students (Jim Oxford, Perry Stepp, and Marty Culy) made the journey more enjoyable and rewarding.

The greatest thank you is reserved for my family. Sally, you have been my partner throughout this enterprise, which began a long time ago at a school far, far away. Your steadfast love is the greatest gift I have ever been given. And as for my daughters Sarah Catherine, Anna Kay, and Becca, I owe you girls a special hug for so generously sharing your Daddy with Elijah and his numerous friends.

Abbreviations

1 En.	1 Enoch
AB	Anchor Bible
ABD	*Anchor Bible Dictionary*
ACC	Ancient Christian Commentary on Scripture
Acts Pil.	*Acts of Pilate*
ANF	*Ante-Nicene Fathers*
ANRW	*Aufstieg und Niedergang der römischen Welt*
Antichr.	*De antichristo*
Apoc. El. (C)	*Coptic Apocalypse of Elijah*
AzTh	Arbeiten zur Theologie
BEvT	Beiträge zur evanglischen Theologie
Bib	*Biblica*
BJRL	*Bulletin of the John Rylands University Library of Manchester*
BZNW	Beihefte zur Zeitschrift für die neutestamentliche Wissenschaft
CACSS	Corpus apologetarum Christianorum saeculi secundi
Carm.	*Carmen de Duobus Populis*
CBC	Cambridge Bible Commentary
CBQ	*Catholic Biblical Quaterly*
CCSL	Corpus Christianorum: Series Latina. Turnhout, 1953–
CRINT	Compendia rerum iudicarum ad Novum Testamentum
DBSup	*Dictionnaire de la Bible: Supplément.* Edited by L. Pirot and A. Robert. Paris, 1928–
DOP	*Dumbarton Oaks Papers*
DSD	*Dead Sea Discoveries*
DTC	*Dictionnaire de théologie catholique.* Edited by A. Vacant et al. 15 vols. Paris, 1903–1950
EECh	*Encyclopedia of the Early Church.* Edited by A. di Berardino. Translated by A. Walford. New York, 1992
EKKNT	Evangelisch-katholischer Kommentar zum Neuen Testament
EstBib	*Estudios bíblicos*
FB	Forschung zur Bibel
FC	Fathers of the Church. Washington, D.C., 1947–

FRLANT	Forschungen zur Religion und Literatur des Alten und Neuen Testaments
GCS	Die griechische christliche Schriftsteller der ersten [drei] Jahrhunderte
HAT	Handbuch zum Alten Testament
HTR	*Harvard Theological Review*
ICC	International Critical Commentary
Int	*Interpretation*
JBL	*Journal of Biblical Literature*
JECS	*Journal of Early Christian Studies*
JETS	*Journal of the Evangelical Theological Society*
JJS	*Journal of Jewish Studies*
JSNT	*Journal for the Study of the New Testament*
JSOT	*Journal for the Study of the Old Testament*
JSPSup	Journal for the Study of the Pseudepigrapha: Supplement Series
JTS	*Journal of Theological Studies*
Jub.	*Jubilees*
KAT	Kommentar zum Alten Testament
KEK	Kritisch-exegetischer Kommentar über das Neue Testament
KNT	Kommentar zum Neuen Testament
L.A.B.	*Liber Antiquitatum Biblicarum* (Pseudo-Philo)
LD	Lectio Divina
LW	*Luthers Werke*
LXX	The Septuagint
Mal	Malachi
Matt	Matthew
MSU	Mitteilungen des Septuaginta-Unternehmens der Gesellschaft der Wissenschaften zu Göttingen
MT	Masoretic Text
NCB	New Century Bible
NEchtB	Neue Echter Bibel
NovT	*Novum Testamentum*
NTAbh	Neutestamentliche Abhandlungen
NTD	Das Neue Testament Deutsch
NPNF[1]	*Nicene and Post-Nicene Fathers,* Series 1
NPNF[2]	*Nicene and Post-Nicene Fathers,* Series 2
NRSV	New Revised Standard Version
NTS	*New Testament Studies*
OTL	Old Testament Library

PAPS	*The Proceedings of the American Philosophical Society*
PG	Patrologia graeca [=Patrologiae cursus completus: Series graeca]. Edited by J.-P. Migne. 162 vols. Paris, 1857–1886.
PSB	*Princeton Seminary Bulletin*
PSt	*Patristic Studies*
PTS	Patristische Texte und Studien
RB	*Revue Biblique*
Rev	Revelation
RHE	*Revue d'histoire ecclésiastique*
RNT	Regensburger Neues Testament
RSPT	*Revue des sciences philosophiques et théologiques*
SAC	Studies in Antiquity and Christianity
SBLDS	Society of Biblical Literature Dissertation Series
SB	Sources bibliques
SC	Sources Chrétiennes. Paris: Cerf, 1943-
SHBC	Smyth & Helwys Bible Commentary
Sib. Or.	*Sibylline Oracles*
SJT	*Scottish Journal of Theology*
ST	*Studia theological*
StPatr	Studia patristica
SVTP	Studia in Veteris Testamenti pseudepigraphica
T. Benj.	*Testament of Benjamin*
T. Jos.	*Testament of Joseph*
T. Levi	*Testament of Levi*
TDNT	*Theological Dictionary of the New Testament.* Edited by G. Kittel and G. Friedrich. Translated by G. W. Bromiley. 10 vols. Grand Rapids, 1964–1976
TGl	*Theologie und Glaube*
ThH	Théologie historique
THKNT	Theologischer Handkommentar zum Neuen Testament
ThSt	Theologische Studien
TQ	*Theologische Quartalschrift*
TSR	*Texts and Studies in Religion*
TUGAL	Texte und Untersuchungen zur Geschichte der altchristlichen Literatur
WBC	Word Biblical Commentary
WSA	*The Works of St. Augustine:* A Translation for the 21st Century
ZNW	*Zeitschrift für neutestamentliche Wissenschaft und die Kunde der älteren Kirche*
ZTK	*Zeitschrift für Theologie und Kirche*

Introduction

This study aims to explore a particular patristic reading of Romans 11:26 that is virtually unknown to modern research despite recent interest in the question of Jewish salvation. This chapter will present a history of scholarship beginning with a treatment of Romans 9–11 in general. Then the focus will narrow to Romans 11:26 in particular, presenting the basic interpretive issues in modern study.

Few passages in the New Testament have engendered as much debate and discussion as chapters 9–11 of the Apostle Paul's letter to the Romans. One of the most persistent questions raised by modern scholars has been that of these chapters' relationship to the remainder of the epistle. The responses run the gamut from, on the one hand, seeing Romans 9–11 as the interpretive key to the letter to, on the other hand, regarding it as a nonessential interpolation. This first question essentially deals with the literary and theological integrity of the letter as a whole. A second key question engaged by commentators has been that of the theological content of Romans 9–11. In their approach to these chapters, many interpreters have focused upon a particular issue, and the discussions of the various issues have often been driven by contemporary theological debates and historical concerns. That which follows is a brief history of research on Romans 9–11 in the light of these two pivotal questions.

What is the Relationship of Romans 9–11 to the Rest of Romans?

Romans 9–11 as Central to Paul's Argument

Some scholars have asserted that the content of chapters 9–11 should guide the reading of the rest of Romans. F. C. Baur was first and foremost among these. Given his dialectical approach to early Christian history, Baur asserted that Paul wrote the epistle to combat the teaching of Jewish Christians in the Roman church. Thus, all of Romans is regarded as polemical in nature, a "systematische Streitschrift gegen das Judenchristentum."[1] The general treatment of the righteousness of God receives practical application in these chapters, which confront the matter of Jewish particularism. Bruce Corley states that "the practical outcome of Baur's view was an elevation of chapters 9–11, where the problem of Israel was engaged, to the apex of the dogmatic argument."[2]

Oscar Cullmann and Johannes Munck, two leading figures in the *Heilsgeschichtliche* approach to New Testament theology, also view these chapters as pivotal in the reading of Romans, not to mention the larger Pauline corpus. Yet whereas Baur's thesis rested upon a given historical reconstruction of the early church—namely that the Roman church was a predominantly Jewish-Christian congregation—the *Heilsgeschichtliche* approach is rooted in Paul's apostolic consciousness.[3] The proclamation of the gospel to the Gentiles is a necessary part of God's salvific plan, as it must precede the eschatological salvation of Israel. The Jewish rejection of Jesus as the Messiah opens the way for extending the proclamation to the Gentiles. Nevertheless, Jewish salvation will become a reality through the Gentile mission; the destinies of the two groups are inextricably bound. Thus, Paul becomes the central figure in the story of salvation as he plays the key role in moving the process of redemptive history towards its intended conclusion, the salvation of both groups.[4] For *Heilsgeschichtliche* scholars, Romans 9–11 provides the clearest expression of Paul's understanding of salvation history, which serves as the theological center in which all readings of Paul are to be grounded.

Krister Stendahl, an heir of the *Heilsgeschichte* school, asserts that "the climax of Romans is actually chapters 9–11, i.e., his reflections on the relation between church and synagogue...not the attitudes of the gospel versus the attitudes of the law."[5] According to Stendahl, the focus of Romans is the relation between Jews and Gentiles. The idea of justification by faith is advanced in service of the notion that Gentiles can come to God through faith in Christ, just as the initial Jewish Christians did, and be received on an equal footing. Thus, chapters 1–8 serve as a "preface" to the "central revelation" of Romans 9–11.[6]

Romans 9–11 as Peripheral to Paul's Argument

A number of scholars have seen chapters 9–11 as loosely connected or tangentially related to the rest of Romans. C. H. Dodd, sensing an interruption of the logical movement from the theological material of Romans 1–8 to the ethical application of Romans 12, declares that:

> Chaps. ix.–xi. form a compact and continuous whole, which can be read quite
> satisfactorily without reference to the rest of the epistle, though it naturally gains by
> such reference, just as other parts of the epistle gain by being read alongside Galatians
> or 1 Corinthians. It has been suggested that the three chapters were originally a
> separate treatise which Paul had by him, and which he used for his present purpose.
> There is a good deal to be said for this view.[7]

Dodd maintains that chapters 9–11 constitute a sermon that Paul must have frequently used to address the Jewish question; Paul inserts this material as an excursus in order to clear up questions inadequately addressed in the main argument.[8]

Francois Refoulé agrees with Dodd regarding the self-contained subject matter of this section of Romans and concludes that this must constitute a later addition: "les chapitres 9–11 ne peuvent avoir appartenu originellement à l'épître aux Romains."[9] Labeling these three chapters "a kind of supplement," F. W. Beare maintains that they do not form an integral part of the main argument of Romans.[10] M.-E. Boismard regards this section as a "corps étranger," possibly added by an editor.[11]

Given his existentialist presuppositions, Rudolf Bultmann reads Romans from an individualistic perspective. According to Bultmann, "Paul's view of history is not derived from his reflection on the history of Israel but from his anthropology."[12] It is the history of the individual that is significant. Thus, the salvation-history motif of these chapters proves to be an uninteresting excursus for Bultmann.[13] He even goes so far as to say that "the history-of-salvation mystery in Romans 11:25ff is derived from speculative fantasy."[14] And so Christian Müller places Bultmann on the opposite end of the spectrum from F. C. Baur.[15]

Romans 9–11 as Integral to Paul's Argument

It is best to avoid using the term consensus in the discussion of any aspect of Romans 9–11. Nevertheless, in recent decades there has been a trend towards viewing these chapters as simply one part, though an important one to be sure, of Paul's overall argument in the letter. Charles Talbert states that "this section of Romans is neither peripheral nor central, rather it is integral to Paul's argument."[16] Likewise, C. E. B. Cranfield calls these chapters "an integral part of the working out of the theme of the epistle."[17]

Such an integrated reading of Romans is even employed by scholars on different ends of the interpretive spectrum. Ernst Käsemann, standing in the Lutheran tradition, views Romans 9–11 as an illustration of Paul's doctrine of justification. The presentation of salvation-history serves to prevent an individualistic reading of chapters 1–8, against Bultmann. Käsemann goes so far as to say that "the justification of the ungodly is here again the secret theme of the problem raised."[18] Francis Watson, however, opposes any traditional Lutheran reading of Romans. He argues that the entire letter is an attempt by Paul "to persuade the Jewish Christian community in Rome to separate themselves from the Jewish community, to accept the legitimacy of the Pauline Gentile congregation in which the law is not observed, and to unite with it for worship."[19] Thus, Watson sees Romans 9–11, along with chapters 1–8, as part of a coherent argument for social reorientation.

What is the Theological Content of Romans 9–11?

In Romans 9–11 the apostle Paul presents his vision of the working out of God's salvific plan. As previously noted, commentators throughout history have disagreed as to the subject matter of the material in these chapters. While the approaches have been many and diverse, all of these treatments can be divided into two main camps according to this basic line of distinction: Is Paul discussing individuals or groups in these chapters?

Individuals

The early church Fathers initially established the direction of the discussion of Romans 9–11 along the individual line of interpretation. Romans 9 became the focus as the Fathers struggled with the issues of human freedom and divine predestination. The aim of the Greek tradition was to preserve human freedom and responsibility.[20] This reading of Romans 9 began with Origen, and his vigorous defense of freewill proved to be influential.[21] Human freedom was preserved by asserting that God's election was based upon divine foreknowledge. In discussing the choice of Jacob over Esau, Chrysostom declares that God "does not wait, as a person does, to see who is good or not from the completion of the deeds, but he even knows before these happen who is evil and who is not."[22] This line of thought reflects the predominant tradition in the East and is found in the writings of such other Fathers as Diodore, Theodore of Mopsuestia, and Cyril of Alexandria; the tradition is also evident in the West in the works of Ambrosiaster, Jerome, and Pelagius.[23]

Augustine is responsible for redirecting the Western tradition regarding the reading of Romans 9. Initially, Augustine also sought to protect freewill by means of divine foreknowledge, although he did insist that this divine foreknowledge was of human faith, not works.[24] Augustine, however, relinquished his position with respect to freewill, asserting that election must depend completely upon divine grace.[25] This focus on predestination was maintained in the West through the medieval scholastics down to the reformers.

John Calvin closely followed the line of Augustine regarding Romans 9–11 as the *locus classicus* of the doctrine of predestination. Calvin goes so far as to say on the matter, "If I wanted to weave a whole volume from Augustine, I could readily show my readers that I need no other language than his."[26] Commenting on Romans 9:10–13, Calvin makes his reading of the passage clear: "Paul's first proposition, therefore, is as follows: 'As the blessing of the covenant separates the people of Israel from all other nations, so also the election of God makes a distinction between men in that nation, while He predestinates some to salvation, and others to eternal condemnation.'"[27]

Martin Luther also followed Augustine, but Luther eschewed a theoretical doctrine of double predestination. "Indeed, Blessed Augustine shows admirably why the apostle spoke as he did, namely in order to instruct us in humility. It is plainly not the purpose of his words to lead us to the horror of despair but to induce us to praise grace and to put down all presumptuous pride." For Luther, such language serves to cause a person to recognize his or her own state of fallenness; it reminds one that humans cannot save themselves by their own power, particularly not by acts of free will. Paul Althaus declares Luther's theology at this point to be "completely untheoretical and pastoral."[28] Luther is intent not on theological speculation but on turning one's attention to the wounds of Jesus.[29]

The concerns of the Greek Fathers were also represented in the sixteenth century. Erasmus argued that God's election followed foreseen human merit, and notable reformers such as Melancthon and Bullinger both expressed reservations regarding the grounding of election in the divine will alone.[30] As the Augustinian view held sway in Calvinist circles, a reaction to this position sprang from the question of theodicy—can a God who decrees some people to eternal reprobation be viewed as truly righteous and just? The chief figure in this theological response was James Arminius who emphasized divine foreknowledge and human faith in his treatise *Declaration of Sentiments*.[31]

By the nineteenth century, three approaches to Romans 9–11—viewed as the *locus classicus* of the question of Paul's theodicy—can be seen: (1) Calvinist, (2) Arminian, and (3) a mediating (*vermittelnde*) position.[32] Charles Hodge was perhaps the leading advocate of the Calvinist position. He asserted that Romans 9 taught God's sovereign election of individuals for personal salvation, not nations or communities for external advantages.[33] F. A. G. Tholuck, a leading proponent of the Arminian position, ardently defended free will and human responsibility. Tholuck anticipated the subsequent change of approach in the interpretation of Romans 9–11 by arguing that "it is not the vocation of individuals in the kingdom of grace which is treated of, but that of entire national masses."[34] Nevertheless, within the Arminian camp, the reading of Romans 9–11 was still tied to the issues of predestination and theodicy. Heinrich Meyer was a chief figure in the development of the mediating view which attempted to allow the determinism of Romans 9 and the indeterminism of Romans 10 to stand side by side as contradictory yet valid truths.[35] This popular approach had the effect of leading many subsequent readers of Romans 9–11 to view Paul's argument as being logically inconsistent.

Groups

The line of questioning pursued by the Fathers and the reformers was based upon the premise that Paul's argument centered on God's eternal decrees with respect to individual persons. It must be noted that both the Fathers and the reformers addressed the destiny of the nation of Israel in their discussion of Romans 11; nevertheless, the aforementioned premise effectively sundered Romans 9–10 from chapter 11 as the focus was placed upon theological concepts such as predestination, reprobation, and free will.[36] Yet during the nineteenth century, scholars began to doubt whether Paul was concerned with the same questions as the Fathers and reformers. With the rise of historical approaches toward the reading of Scripture, scholars began to see all of Romans 9–11 as dealing with the relationship between Jews and Gentiles as groups.

History was the key for F. C. Baur's reading of Romans 9–11. For Baur, Paul's message was driven by the historical setting of the first century church in Rome, which, so Baur contended, was primarily Jewish. Thus, these chapters of Romans address the problems arising from the conflict of Jewish particularity in the face of the evangelization of the Gentiles.

The proponents of the *Heilsgeschichtliche* movement, a theological approach toward history, sought to eliminate the difficulties posed by the traditional treatments of Romans 9–11 by arguing that these chapters did not deal with personal election and eternal decrees but rather with a corporate election and temporal destiny that served a teleological function. During the nineteenth century, the two most influential figures of this school were J. T. Beck and J. C. K. von Hofmann.[37] Theodore Zahn was a leading advocate of this view during the twentieth century, along with the aforementioned Oscar Cullman and Johannes Munck.[38] Munck states that:

> In these chapters Paul speaks, not of individuals, but of nations. Abraham and Isaac, Edom and Pharaoh are nations. God chooses one nation and rejects another…But in this connexion, when only nations are concerned, and where at last the acute crisis in

the history of salvation is being worked out in relation to the two categories, Israel and the Gentiles, one individual, Paul, is taking part as though it were a matter of course.[39]

Regarding the *Heilsgeschichtliche* school's reading of Romans 9–11, Corley observes that "the great appeal of this exegesis was its wholistic treatment of Paul's argument. The traditional approach had often struggled with the inner relationship of the three chapters; however, the salvation-history motif perfectly accommodated the flow of thought."[40]

Dispensationalists, on the whole, belong in this category as well.[41] Dispensationalism emerged in mid-nineteenth century England among the Plymouth Brethren led by John Nelson Darby.[42] It was popularized in America by the widespread dissemination of *The Scofield Reference Bible* which was published in 1909.[43] In this system, history is divided into a number of dispensations, each of which contains a particular manifestation of God's administrative rule. The introduction of a new mode of divine governance with one group does not necessarily abrogate the requirements of previous dispensations. Thus, there can be an overlapping of the dispensations, since they deal primarily with modes of governance rather than time.[44]

A key component of Dispensationalism is the sharp distinction made between Israel and the church. Charles Ryrie claims that this distinction "is probably the most basic theological test of whether or not a man is a dispensationalist."[45] Traditional Dispensationalism asserts that there are two distinct peoples of God. The church is God's heavenly people, destined for a spiritual mode of existence in heaven. Israel, on the other hand, is God's earthly people to whom the promises were given and with whom the covenants were made; they are destined for a physical existence on earth in which these promises are literally fulfilled.[46]

For the Dispensationalist, Romans 9–11 provides the salvation history of these two distinct groups. God chose ethnic Israel first, but Israel rejected God's Messiah. God then offered salvation to the Gentiles through Christ. Traditionally, Dispensationalism has seen this as an interruption of God's dealings with Israel, with the present age of the church labeled as a parenthesis. After the Parousia of Christ, God will renew his dealings with ethnic Israel, which will then experience the fulfillment of the Old Testament prophecies on earth during the millennial kingdom. It must be noted that contemporary Dispensationalists have softened the vigorously asserted dichotomy of Darby, Scofield, and Chafer, most notably eliminating the terminology of heavenly and earthly people.[47] Despite increasing disagreement over the nature of the dichotomy between Israel and the church, an insistence on a distinction remains.[48] Therefore, Dispensationalism still clearly stands over against the idea of supercessionism, in which the church is viewed as the New Israel.

One final development under the group heading must be mentioned. In reaction to the Holocaust and the emergence of the new state of Israel, scholars have reexamined traditional readings of Romans 9–11, particularly with regard to the salvation of the Jews. The traditional notion that Jews must turn to faith in Christ for salvation has been rejected in favor of an idea that is commonly referred to as the two-covenant view. This concept of a complementary existence between Israel and the Church rests upon the premise that there are separate avenues of salvation for Jews and Gentiles. John Gager describes it as follows:

> Thus Christ and Torah remain for Paul mutually exclusive categories, though not at all as traditionally understood. He simply held that the significance of Christ was that Gentiles no longer needed to become Jews in order to enjoy the advantages once reserved exclusively for Israel. This is not to say that the Gentiles have been incorporated into God's covenant with Israel at Sinai. Rather it is the case—Abraham is the critical figure here—that God's promise of righteousness leads in two separate directions, each according to its own time. The promise to Abraham as the father of the circumcised is fulfilled through Moses at Sinai. That promise contains clear evidence, states Paul, of a promise to Abraham as the father also of the uncircumcised, a promise fulfilled at a later time through Christ. For him, Christianity is neither superior to Judaism nor its fulfillment. Nor are the two one except insofar as God's promises are one.[49]

In this approach, Romans 9–11 is seen as dealing with the problem of how Jews and Gentiles are to relate to one another; properly understood, these chapters do not espouse supersessionism with the Church as the new Israel. According to the advocates of this position, such an idea is rooted in patristic error.[50] This two-covenant view, which fits well within a post-modern framework, has been well received within the academy and has renewed interest in the question of Israel's salvation.

Romans 11:26 in Modern Research

Within Romans 9–11, Paul's statement regarding the salvation of Israel has proved to be particularly problematic. In Romans 11:25–27 the apostle states:

> 25 Οὐ γὰρ θέλω ὑμᾶς ἀγνοεῖν, ἀδελφοί, τὸ μυστήριον τοῦτο, ἵνα μὴ ἦτε [παρ'] ἑαυτοῖς φρόνιμοι, ὅτι πώρωσις ἀπὸ μέρους τῷ Ἰσραὴλ γέγονεν ἄχρις οὗ τὸ πλήρωμα τῶν ἐθνῶν εἰσέλθῃ, 26 καὶ οὕτως πᾶς Ἰσραὴλ σωθήσεται· καθὼς γέγραπται, Ἥξει ἐκ Σιὼν ὁ ῥυόμενος, ἀποστρέψει ἀσεβείας ἀπὸ Ἰακώβ· 27 καὶ αὕτη αὐτοῖς ἡ παρ' ἐμοῦ διαθήκη, ὅταν ἀφέλωμαι τὰς ἁμαρτίας αὐτῶν.

Christoph Plag has gone so far as to argue that these verses are a secondary addition which stands in discontinuity with the surrounding context.[51] His thesis has not garnered much support, yet it stands as testimony to the difficulties posed by this perplexing passage. In an effort to understand the pregnant phrase "and so all Israel will be saved" in Romans 11:26, modern interpreters have focused upon three crucial preliminary questions: (1) How is καὶ οὕτως to be translated? (2) What did Paul mean by πᾶς Ἰσραὴλ? (3) When will this salvation take place? A brief outline of modern responses to these questions follows.

How is καὶ οὕτως to be Translated?

There are four options to be considered, and these are based upon the grammatical classification of the οὕτως in Romans 11:26 as being modal, consecutive, correlative, or temporal. The predominant view has been the modal usage, which syntactically links οὕτως with the preceding clause.[52] Looking backward, the modal sense would be something along this line: "The partial hardening of Israel that led to Gentile inclusion will subside when the full number of Gentiles enters the kingdom, *and in this manner*, all Israel will be saved." Closely related is the consecutive usage, which would be: "*As a consequence of* the preceding events, all Israel will be saved."[53] Both the modal and consecutive uses of οὕτως refer back to the events that Paul described in 11:11–24 and summarized in verse 25.

The correlative usage of οὕτως links the clause in 11:26a with the adverb καθὼς, which, in this case, follows it. Thus, the οὕτως...καθὼς construction connects the salvation of Israel with the scriptural citation regarding the redeemer figure in 11:26b-27.[54] A correlative rendering of οὕτως would read: "*In the following way*, all Israel will be saved, namely, just as it is written, 'The Deliverer will come from Zion.'" The promised Deliverer is understood to be the agent of Israel's salvation.

In recent years, support has increased for the temporal usage, a reading which had long been dismissed by the majority of New Testament scholars. Fitzmyer went so far as to argue that a temporal meaning for οὕτως is "not found otherwise in Greek."[55] Pieter van der Horst, however, has demonstrated that the temporal use of οὕτως was, in fact, a widespread classical idiom.[56] A temporal reading–seen as equivalent to καὶ τότε–would be as follows: "*And then*, after the full number of Gentiles has come in, all Israel will be saved."[57] The NEB–"when that has happened"–presents such a reading. Corley prefers the temporal meaning because "it presupposes the retrospective (modal) and prospective (correlative) conditions."[58]

What Did Paul Mean by πᾶς Ἰσραὴλ?

Again, there are four interpretive options. The phrase πᾶς Ἰσραὴλ can be taken in a numerical, restrictive, spiritual, or collective sense.[59] The numerical sense of πᾶς would refer to "every Israelite" or "every living Jew."[60] The restrictive reading of the phrase would refer to "the total of elect Jews who believe Christ during the gospel era."[61] Both of these views have received limited support during the modern period.[62] The spiritual rendering of πᾶς Ἰσραὴλ would refer to the "Israel of God", that is, the church, which is comprised of both the Jews and the Gentiles who follow Christ.[63] This reading had support among the early Fathers and became particularly popular during the post-reformation period.[64] Nevertheless, support has waned during the modern period. Such an understanding of Ἰσραὴλ in 11:26 would require a shift in meaning from its use in 11:25 as well as the rest of chapter eleven.

The collective understanding of πᾶς Ἰσραὴλ has received increasing support in modern scholarship.[65] The fixed Jewish formula "all Israel" is a well-attested idiom used to refer to the nation as a corporate entity.[66] It does not have the connotation of numerical completeness. For example, *m. Sanhedrin* 10:1 states, "All Israelites have a share in the world to come;" nevertheless, this statement is followed by a list of specific Israelites who are exceptions.[67] So in Romans 11:26, the collective πᾶς Ἰσραὴλ serves as the counterpart to τὸ πλήρωμα τῶν ἐθνῶν ("the full number of the Gentiles"), which is likewise a corporate designation that does not entail numerical completeness.

When Will This Salvation Take Place?

With this question there are three basic interpretive options as to when this salvation will transpire. The first option holds that Paul envisaged here a steady flow of Jews into the church during the gospel era. This influx is to be attributed to Jewish jealousy of the Gentile inclusion plus the effects of the proclamation of the gospel. Those who favor a restrictive reading of the phrase πᾶς Ἰσραὴλ fit into this category.[68]

The second option maintains that the salvation of the Jews will transpire in a future event, yet prior to the Parousia. This salvation event will be a catalyst for the return of Christ rather than a result of that return. Talbert notes that 11:12 states that the inclusion of Israel would yield even more riches for the Gentiles, while 11:15 indicates that the acceptance of Israel will result in "life from the dead." Furthermore, the latter verse echoes the belief that the faithfulness of Israel would bring about the shift of the ages.[69] These verses seem to indicate an interval, albeit an indeterminate one, between the inclusion of Israel and the Parousia. Such an interpretation affects the reading of the Old Testament citation in verses 26-27; the Deliverer cannot then refer to the return of Christ but must refer instead to the initial coming of Jesus or an advent of God himself. While Paul does use the word ῥύομαι in 1 Thess 1:10 to refer to Christ's second coming, Fitzmyer points out that "he uses it elsewhere in a more generic sense, referring to God (15:31; 2 Cor 1:10) or Christ (7:24). Not even the future ἥξει necessarily implies the second coming."[70] There is no reference to the Parousia elsewhere in Romans 9-11.[71]

The third and final option places the time of Israel's salvation at the Parousia. Israel will be saved by an event that takes place at the return of the aforementioned Deliverer (vv. 26-27). Thus, this Old Testament citation is primarily seen as referring to the second coming of Christ.[72] This third option is the prevailing view among modern exegetes.[73]

A Fourth Question Emerges

A fourth key preliminary question has come to the fore in recent studies of Romans 11:26: who is the Deliverer to whom the Old Testament citation refers in verse 26b? Advocates of the two-covenant view have challenged the traditional Christian messianic reading of the prophecy, arguing that it will be God, not the Christ, who will serve as the eschatological agent of Israel's salvation. This question regarding the identity of the Deliverer (ὁ ῥυόμενος) in Romans 11:26b is of particular concern for this study. After an examination of Paul's citation of the Septuagint (LXX), this section will present the current lines of debate as to the identity of this figure.

Paul's Citation of the LXX

Paul's citation of the Old Testament in Romans 11:26a-27 is a composite of two LXX texts: Isaiah 59:20-21a and a clause from Isaiah 27:9. The Pauline text differs from the LXX in the following ways: the conjunction καί is omitted twice; the preposition ἐκ is used instead of ἕνεκεν before the proper noun Σιών; the noun ἁμαρτίαν and its modifiers are pluralized; and the possessive pronoun αὐτῶν is placed in final position.[74] The shift to the plural (τὰς ἁμαρτίας αὐτῶν) in Romans 11:27b is clearly a result of the conflation, bringing the clause into numeric agreement with the αὐτοῖς in 27a.

The most significant difference is the Pauline ἐκ Σιών ("from Zion") instead of the LXX ἕνεκεν Σιών ("for the sake of Zion"). Some interpreters have attributed this change to Paul himself; E. Earle Ellis states that Paul departs from the traditional reading "with a hermeneutical purpose in view".[75] The change, whether by Paul or someone else, may have arisen from the influence of the language of Psalms 14:7; 53:6; 110:2 (LXX 13:7; 52:7; 109:2), which use the phrase ἐκ Σιών.[76] Berndt Schaller argues that the reading ἐκ Σιών may have resulted from a scribal misreading of a manuscript containing the phrase εἴς Σιών, which would more accurately correspond to the Hebrew לציון ("to Zion") of the Masoretic text.[77] Christopher Stanley asserts that Paul is drawing upon an oral tradition from Diaspora Judaism in which the two Isaiah passages had already been joined. The change to ἐκ Σιών represented the hope that "Yahweh would come forth 'out of Zion' to rescue his dispersed children."[78] Deitrich-Alex Koch also sees Paul using a preexisting tradition, albeit from the pre-Pauline Christian community.[79] Regardless of the origin of the conflated citation, the interpretation of Paul's understanding of the identity of the Deliverer has significant implications for the soteriology of Israel.

Who is the Deliverer (ὁ ῥυόμενος)?

Yahweh. In the traditional Jewish reading of Isaiah 59:20, ὁ ῥυόμενος (for the גואל of the MT) certainly predicates Yahweh as the redeemer figure. The question is: does Paul eschew a typical early Christian christological reading of Isaiah here? Since the Second World War, an increasing number of exegetes have answered yes. Stendahl notes that Paul does not mention Jesus Christ throughout this entire section of Romans (10:18–11:36), not even in the final doxology (11:33–36).[80] Getty appeals to Paul's use of the verb ῥύομαι elsewhere as evidence that the referent is God (Rom 7:24; 15:31; 2 Cor 1:10).[81] The covenant mentioned in Romans 11:27 (from Isa 59:20) is understood to be the Sinai covenant, and so the omission of the qualifier 'new' is significant for these interpreters (cf. 1 Cor 11:25; 2 Cor 3:6). It indicates that Paul has in view a promise that applies only to Israel.[82] Martin Rese confirms that Yahweh is the principal in view here by stating, "So wie Gott das Subjekt ihrer Verstockung war (vv. 7–10), so wird er auch das Subjekt der Aufhebung ihrer Verstockung sein."[83] K. L. Schmidt comments that the conversion of Jews throughout history is not sufficient to elicit Paul's shout of jubilee in Romans 11:30; therefore, God himself will set the matter straight.[84]
The Returning Christ. The traditional reading of the text has been that ὁ ῥυόμενος refers to the Parousia of Christ, and this is still the position of the majority of exegetes.[85] Some commentators note a similar eschatological use of ὁ ῥυόμενος in 1 Thessalonians 1:10, in which Jesus delivers his followers from the wrath to come.[86] The future verb ἥξει ("he will come") of the citation is read as an eschatological allusion as well.[87] Advocates of this position read the ἐκ Σιών as referring primarily to the heavenly Jerusalem in keeping with the tradition reflected in Galatians 4:26, Hebrews 12:22, and Revelation 3:12;

21:2.[88] Dunn notes the possibility that ἐκ Σιών could refer to the return of Christ in Jerusalem.[89] E. P. Sanders, arguing against the reading of the Deliverer as God alone, has written a frequently cited line in favor of the traditional interpretation: "it is incredible that he [Paul] thought of 'God apart from Christ,' just as it is that he thought of 'Christ apart from God.'"[90] In Sanders' view, Paul would not make such a distinction between an act of God, on the one hand, and an act of his eschatological agent, Jesus Christ, on the other.

One further argument often presented in favor of the christological reading of ὁ ῥυόμενος is the rabbinic tradition found in *b. Sanh.* 98a of the sixth-century Babylonian Talmud. A messianic interpretation of Isaiah 59:20 is ascribed to Rabbi Johanan, a third-century Palestinian of the second generation of Amoraim: "When thou seest a generation overwhelmed by many troubles as by a river, await him, as it is written, *when the enemy shall come in like a flood, the Spirit of the Lord shall lift up a standard against him*; which is followed by, *And the Redeemer shall come to Zion.*"[91] Cranfield thinks it is "likely that Paul so understood it."[92] The rabbinic reference is certainly too late to be evidence of a first century reading. Nevertheless, it does show that some Jews felt free to read the ὁ ῥυόμενος in Isaiah as someone other than Yahweh.

The Incarnate Christ. Other scholars, while still reading the text christologically, see the referent of ὁ ῥυόμενος as the historical Jesus.[93] Marie-Joseph Lagrange asserts that "Paul a pu mettre ἐκ Σιών pour suggérer le role historique de Jésus."[94] The phrase ἐκ Σιών would allude specifically to the Davidic ancestry of Jesus or to the crucifixion and resurrection events as a whole in Jerusalem.[95] Dieter Zeller equates the phrase ἐκ Σιών with the earlier phrase ἐξ ὧν ὁ Χριστὸς τὸ κατὰ σάρκα from Romans 9:5; furthermore, he notes the use of ἐν Σιών in reference to the placement of the "stumbling stone" in Romans 9:33.[96] The purpose of the scriptural citation then is to show that the coming of the savior was foretold in the scriptures and that Zion was given as the location of this soteriological event.[97]

The Christ event as a whole. A few scholars have argued that ὁ ῥυόμενος should be understood in a more general way as referring to the Christ event as a whole. Luz asserts that the Parousia does not represent a new stage of salvation but is part and parcel of the Christ event at large.[98] H. W. Schmidt suggests that the passage should not be read in an either/or manner since it encompasses the salvific effectiveness (Erlösungswirkens) of Christ ranging from his historical appearance until his future return.[99] Finally, N. T. Wright claims that Paul sees the Deliverer, instead of Torah (cf. Mic 4:2), going out to the nations from Zion; thus, the Deliverer is, in essence, the saving gospel of Jesus Christ, i.e., the Christ event as a whole.[100]

Soteriological implications. The scholars who see Yahweh as the Deliverer generally hold some version of the two-covenant view of Israel's salvation. Yahweh will personally deliver his covenant people at the end of history, and thus Jesus Christ plays no role in the salvation of Israel. Those who hold the traditional view as to the identity of the Deliverer—Jesus at the Parousia—generally maintain that Israel's salvation will result from its recognition of Jesus as the Messiah. Moo's language is typical as he mentions "Israel's acceptance of the gospel message about the forgiveness of sins in Jesus Christ."[101] Käsemann, comparing Israel and the Church, states, "Only the time, not the salvation, is different."[102] W. D. Davies concurs that the Jewish people will accept Jesus as their Messiah at the Parousia; however, he is more guarded with his use of language, suggesting that "Paul was not thinking in terms of what we normally call conversion from one religion to another but of the recognition by Jews of the final or true form of their own religion."[103]

Franz Mussner does not fit either of the two models above. He agrees with the traditionalists that Israel will by saved by the return of Christ, but he sides with the two-covenant view in holding that Israel's salvation occurs without conversion to the Christian gospel: "Der Parusiechristus rettet ganz Israel ohne vorausgehende 'Bekehrung' der Juden zum Evangelium. Gott rettet Israel auf einem 'Sonderweg.'"[104] Similarly, H. J. Schoeps espouses a two-covenant model, yet he holds out the hope that Christ will fulfill the expectations of both groups: "But it might well be that He who comes at the end of time, He who has been alike the expectation of the synagogue and the church, will bear one and the same countenance."[105]

Finally, if one reads the Deliverer in Romans 11:26 as an allusion to the historical Jesus, then the implication is that Israel's salvation must then depend upon its response to this prior act rather than an anticipated future one. The means of salvation becomes Israel's historical response to the Christian gospel. Those scholars who see the Deliverer as referring to the Christ event as a whole fit here in this category as well. Since Israel's deliverance is dependent upon the Christ event, they similarly employ the language of proclamation and conversion.[106]

Are There Any Other Options?

Modern scholarship has reached an impasse with respect to the identity of the Deliverer in Romans 11:26. Interpreters are divided into two main camps: those who read the text theologically (Yahweh as the Deliverer) and those who read it christologically (Christ as the Deliverer). The christological camp is subdivided further among those who read the christological reference as referring to either the incarnation or the Parousia of Christ. Are these, however, the only options?

Theodoret of Cyrus, an Antiochene Father of the fifth century, provides the following commentary on this controversial passage: "And he [Paul] urges them not to despair of the salvation of the other Jews; for when the Gentiles have received the message, even they, the Jews, will believe, when the excellent Elijah comes, bringing to them the doctrine of faith. For even the Lord said this in the sacred gospels: 'Elijah is coming, and he will restore all things.'"[107] Immediately thereafter, Theodoret refers to the "prophetic witness" of the Isaiah passage. This statement of Theodoret's is striking for two reasons. First, it provides an interpretation of Romans 11:26 that is virtually ignored by the modern critical commentaries on Romans.[108] Second, it provides an unusual Christian interpretation of the Elijah tradition.

The Revival of Interest in Patristic Exegesis

Modern biblical scholarship has looked dismissively upon pre-critical readings of the biblical text. Referring to the Church Fathers, Frederic W. Farrar echoed a familiar refrain when he wrote in his *History of Interpretation* that "there are but few of them whose pages are not rife with errors—errors of method, errors of fact, errors of history, of grammar, and even of doctrine."[109] This negative depiction of the Fathers is rooted in the polemical battles of the Reformation as well as the philosophical presuppositions of the Enlightenment.

For most Protestants, the Reformation is viewed as a return to the Christianity of the New Testament era, whereas the intervening centuries represent a falling away from the pristine faith of the apostolic period. As such, the patristic sources have little to offer in terms of biblical interpretation or church doctrine. D. H. Williams asserts that this has been a "governing historical point for free church historiography."[110] To the Protestant mind, the tradition of the first five centuries of the Christian era became inseparable from the tradition of medieval Roman Catholicism. Williams demonstrates that this rejection of ancient Christian tradition was, in fact, a post-Reformation development.[111] Early reformers such as Hus, Luther, Melanchthon, Bullinger, and Calvin frequently appealed to the Fathers and early councils; their concern was to reform the church by eliminating the superfluous accretions of medieval papal decrees and canon law. Nevertheless, subsequent generations did not follow their lead. Responding in a polemical fashion to the Council of Trent's pairing of scripture with tradition, post-Reformation interpreters used the doctrine of *sola scriptura* to effectively separate the Bible and its interpretation from the history of the church.

The negative appraisal of the Fathers is equally indebted to the philosophical principles of modernity that emerged from the Enlightenment, particularly reductive naturalism and autonomous individualism. As a result, the Bible became the object of rational criticism; the independent critic was set free to discover the meaning of the text by means of scientific inquiry, unfettered by the quaint and curious readings of antiquity. As the methods of modern biblical criticism developed, so did a "modern chauvinism" that looked askance at all pre-critical exegesis.[112] Modern commentators compulsively cite one another while ignoring the opinions of those who played a role in the development of the canon, theology, spirituality, and worship of the orthodox Christian faith.

Yet change is on the horizon. Revolutions in science, philosophy, and communication theory have eroded the foundations of modernity. As a result, many are looking to classical Christianity in order to speak meaningfully to the postmodern world.[113] Therefore, in the past two decades there has been a revival of interest in pre-critical exegesis among both biblical scholars and theologians.[114] Most notably, this movement includes significant Protestant participation. This renewed patristic interest is evident in ongoing projects such as the Ancient Christian Commentary on Scripture, which provided the germinal idea for this study.[115]

A return to the writings of the Fathers is, for Robert Wilken, the answer to the absence of memory, in which autonomous reflection is performed adrift from any real connection to the Christian past.[116] A recovery of the ancient tradition returns the Bible to its historical cradle; the scriptures and the ancient tradition developed side by side. The ancient church played a role in shaping the canon and formulating the basic creedal doctrines of the church. Its councils articulated the orthodox understandings of the trinity (Nicea) and the natures of Christ (Chalcedon). It provided foundational thought on ecclesiology, sacraments, and worship, not to mention ethical issues which still trouble modern society.[117] The Fathers demonstrate that Scripture and tradition need not be arrayed against each other in an either/or format. Williams notes that the "coherence model generally evident in patristic Christianity looked upon the church's Tradition and scripture in reciprocal terms."[118] Furthermore, a return to the Fathers accents what is common to the Christian faith since they precede the subsequent divisions into Eastern Orthodox, Roman Catholic, and Protestant. Thomas Oden argues that the key to modern orthodoxy for any Christian movement is the return to what he calls "paleo-orthodoxy," i.e., the classic consensual teaching of the Church.[119] Finally, a return to the Fathers provides what Dale C. Allison Jr. calls "hermeneutical proximity." Allison notes that the Fathers had a smaller literary canon; they still read aloud and heard scripture chanted. In addition, their educational methodology emphasized memorization. As a result, reading the Fathers can help compensate for the modern reader's lack of intertextual background. "For they were, in so many ways, closer to the first century Christians than we are—for they, unlike most of us, lived and moved and had their being in the Scriptures."[120]

The Elijah *Redivivus* Tradition

The Jewish belief in a returning prophet is rooted in the promise of Deuteronomy 18:15 that God will raise a prophet like Moses. Elijah, because of his translation into heaven (2 Kgs 2:1–12a) and the mention of his sending in Malachi 3:23 (Mal 4:5 in English),[121] became a prominent figure with regard to the speculation surrounding this eschatological prophet in the literature of Middle Judaism[122] as well as the later rabbinic texts. This expectation is evident in the New Testament, as some of Jesus' contemporaries believe him to be this returning Elijah figure (Mark 8:27–28; Matt 16:13–14; Luke 9:18–19). Some scholars have even argued for a primitive Christology in which Jesus was understood in such terms by certain early followers.[123] R. H. Fuller writes, however, that "there is no evidence that the post-Easter church ever interpreted Jesus...as Elijah *redivivus*, although certain traits from the Elijah traditions were taken up into the later conception of Jesus as an eschatological prophet. Rather, in Christian tradition John the Baptist himself became Elijah *redivivus* (Mark 9:13)."[124]

Theodoret's application of the Elijah tradition in connection with Romans 11:26 is interesting because it stands in stark contrast to the established tradition that John the Baptist was the expected Elijah figure. Theodoret's reading implies that the role of the Elijah *redivivus* has yet to be fulfilled, contrary to the prevailing tradition. This divergence of opinion regarding the fulfillment of the Elijah *redivivus* role is evident within the New Testament.

The Gospel tradition is not uniform regarding the identity of John the Baptist as Elijah. Matthew 11:14 removes all ambiguity regarding the identity of the Baptist, making explicit the connection with Elijah which was implicit in Mark, thus providing an important proof-text for Jesus' messianic identity.[125] Luke, however, downplays the identification of John as Elijah, suggesting only that he will be like Elijah (Luke 1:17); the Baptist did not restore all things, since that task is reserved for Jesus at the Parousia. In the Fourth Gospel, the Elijah identification is expressly denied (John 1:21; 25); the Logos can have no forerunner.[126]

The New Testament also contains a tradition that still expects Elijah to fulfill a role in the future. Revelation 11:3–13 describes two eschatological witnesses who suffer death at the hands of the beast and are raised from the dead by God. Although the witnesses are not named, the string of Old Testament allusions strongly implies that the two figures are Elijah and Moses. James VanderKam notes that "early Christian exegetes agreed that Elijah was one of the witnesses, but the other one was identified by some as Enoch, not Moses, despite the clear hints in the text." [127] Therefore, the New Testament witness itself does not uniformly designate John the Baptist as the Elijah *redivivus* figure. Furthermore, as the Revelation 11:3–11 pericope attests, there was a late first century Christian tradition that viewed the role of the Elijah *redivivus* figure as still to be fulfilled in the future, much like the tradition evident in Theodoret's commentary on Romans 11:26.

Statement of Purpose

This study is in keeping with the aforementioned revival of interest in patristic writings. As such, it is an attempt to listen seriously to an ancient voice without prejudging its merits according to the canons of modernity. Theodoret's striking statement that Elijah will come bearing "the doctrine of faith" (τὴν διδασκαλίαν τῆς πίστεως), which will lead to Jewish belief in Christ, is certainly distinct. The purpose of this study is to survey the early Christian Elijah *redivivus* traditions in order to determine if this reading is unique. If not, an auxiliary purpose will be the marshalling of those texts that contain similar depictions of the eschatological Elijah in order to establish the larger trajectories of the Christian Elijah *redivivus* tradition. It is hoped that the recovery of such ancient Christian readings might yield a collection of data that could subsequently be used to bring an ancient yet fresh perspective to bear upon the impasse regarding the interpretation of Romans 11:26.

Methodology

The methodological approach to be undertaken in this project is basically descriptive. In that sense, the method will be eclectic, drawing upon historical, sociological, linguistic, and literary tools as needed in order to describe Theodoret's life and role in Christian history, translate his commentary on Romans 9–11, and recover the early Christian Elijah *redivivus* traditions.

Overview of Chapters

Chapter Two will present a biography of Theodoret of Cyrus, an introduction to his writings, and an analysis of his method of biblical interpretation. The aim of this chapter is to demonstrate Theodoret's significance in church history and therefore provide justification for the serious consideration of his reading of Romans 11:26. Chapter Three will provide a translation of chapters 9–11 of Theodoret's *Commentary on Romans*, which includes an introduction. The aim is to provide the reader with the full context out of which Theodoret's distinct reading emerges. Chapter Four will examine the Old Testament roots of the Elijah *redivivus* tradition in the Masoretic Text and the Septuagint. Then attention will be given to the function of the returning Elijah in the non-Christian texts of the Middle Jewish period. Having surveyed these influential texts, the focus in Chapter Five will turn to the Christian Elijah redivivus traditions, ranging from the first century to first half of the fifth century, that is, up until Theodoret. The aim of these two chapters is to determine the uniqueness of Theodoret's reading and to present the broad trajectories of the Elijah *redivivus* traditions. The study will conclude with Chapter Six, which will present a summation of the findings and offer avenues for future research.

Notes

1. Ferdinand Christian Baur, "Über Zweck und Gedankengang des Römerbriefs," *Theologische Jahrbücher* 16 (1857): 91.

2. Corley labels such approaches to Romans 9–11 as "prismatic." Bruce Corley, "The Significance of Romans 9–11: A Study in Pauline Theology" (Ph.D. diss., Southwestern Baptist Theological Seminary, 1975), 3.

3. Oscar Cullman, *Christ and Time: The Primitive Christian Conception of Time and History* (trans. Floyd V. Filson; Philadelphia: Westminster, 1950), 224. See also his Salvation in History (trans. Sidney G. Sowers; London: SCM, 1967), 118.

4. Johannes Munck, *Paul and the Salvation of Mankind* (trans. Frank Clarke; Richmond: John Knox, 1959), 43–49.

5. Krister Stendahl, *Paul Among Jews and Gentiles and Other Essays* (Philadelphia: Fortress, 1976), 4.

6. Ibid., 29. See also Stendahl's *Meanings: The Bible as Document and Guide* (Philadelphia: Fortress, 1984), 205–244. For similar views, see J. Christiaan Beker, *Paul the Apostle: The Triumph of God in Life and Thought* (Philadelphia: Fortress, 1980), 86–89; J. H. L. Ellison, *The Mystery of Israel* (Exeter, 1976), 27ff.

7. C. H. Dodd, *The Epistle of Paul to the Romans* (New York: Harper and Brothers, 1932), 148.

8. Ibid., 149.

9. Francois Refoulé, "Unité de la L'Épître aux Romains et histoire du salut," *RSPT* 71 (1987): 242.

10. Frank W. Beare, *St. Paul and His Letters* (New York: Abingdon, 1962), 97.

11. M.-E. Boismard, "Review of Franz-J.Leenhardt, L' Épître de saint Paul aux Romains," *RB* 65 (1958): 432.

12. Rudolf Bultmann, "History and Eschatology in the New Testament," *NTS* 1 (1954): 12.

13. Corley, "Significance of Romans 9–11," 5.

14. Rudolf Bultmann, *Theology of the New Testament* (trans. Kendrick Grobel; 2 vols.; New York: Charles Scribner's Sons, 1951–1955), 2:132.

15. Christian Müller, *Gottes Gerechtigkeit und Gottes Volk: Eine Untersuchung zu Römer 9–11* (FRLANT 86; Göttingen: Vandenhoeck & Ruprecht, 1964), 26.

16. Charles H. Talbert, *Romans* (SHBC; Macon, Ga.: Smyth & Helwys, 2002), 241.

17. C. E. B. Cranfield, *A Critical and Exegetical Commentary on the Epistle to the Romans* (ICC; Edinburgh: T & T Clark, 1979), 2:445. Scholars with similar views: Anders Nygren, *Commentary on Romans* (trans. Carl C. Rasmussen; Philadelphia, Muhlenberg, 1949), 353–408; C. K. Barrett, *A Commentary on the Epistle to the Romans* (New York: Harper and Brothers, 1957), 175; E. Elizabeth Johnson, *The Function of Apocalyptic and Wisdom Traditions in Romans 9–11* (Atlanta: Scholars, 1989), 116–123; Joseph A. Fitzmyer, *Romans: A New Translation with Introduction and Commentary* (New York: Doubleday, 1993), 541;

Douglas J. Moo, *The Epistle to the Romans* (Grand Rapids, Mich.: Eerdman's, 1996), 547–552; Luke Timothy Johnson, *Reading Romans: A Literary and Theological Commentary* (Macon, Ga.: Smyth & Helwys, 2001), 150–151.

18. Ernst Käsemann, *Commentary on Romans* (trans. Geoffrey W. Bromiley; Grand Rapids, Mich.: Eerdman's, 1980), 260. See also Günther Bornkamm, *Paul* (trans. D. M. G. Stalker; San Francisco: Harper & Row, 1971), 149–151; Christian Müller, *Gottes Gerechtigkeit und Gottes Volk: Eine Untersuchung zu Römer 9–11* (Göttingen: Vandenhoeck & Ruprecht, 1964); Peter Stuhlmacher, *Paul's Letter to the Romans: A Commentary* (trans. Scott J. Hafemann; Louisville: Westminster/John Knox, 1994), 142–144.

19. Francis Watson, *Paul, Judaism and the Gentiles* (Cambridge: Cambridge University Press, 1986), 173.

20. Talbert, *Romans*, 241.

21. William Sanday and Arthur C. Headlam, *A Critical and Exegetical Commentary on the Epistle to the Romans* (ICC; New York: Charles Scribner's Sons, 1896), 269–70.

22. Chrysostom, *Homiliae in Epistolam ad Romanos* 16.5–6 (PG 60 col. 155).

23. Karl Hermann Schelkle, *Paulus, Lehrer der Väter: Die altkirchliche Auslegung vom Röm 1–11* (Düsseldorf: Patmos, 1959), 346–51.

24. Augustine, *Expositio quarumdam quastionum in epistula ad Romanos* 60 (Rom 9:11–13).

25. Augustine, *De diversis quaestionibus ad Simplicianum* 1:2:5. He formally retracts his earlier position and asserts the priority of the divine call in *Retractationum* 1:23:2–3 and *De praedestinatione sanctorum*. 3:7.

26. John Calvin, *Institutes of the Christian Religion* (ed. John T. McNeill; trans. Ford Lewis Battles; 2 vols.; Philadelphia: Westminster, 1960), 2:942.

27. John Calvin, *The Epistles of Paul the Apostle to the Romans and to the Thessalonians* (eds. David W. Torrance and Thomas F. Torrance; trans. Ross Mackenzie; Grand Rapids, Mich.: Eerdmans, 1961), 199–200.

28. Paul Althaus, *The Theology of Martin Luther* (trans. Robert C. Schultz; Philadelphia: Fortress, 1966), 286. See also Gordon Rupp, *The Righteousness of God: Luther Studies* (New York: Philosophical Library, 1953), 185–191. The concept of reprobation seems to be mitigated in Luther's thought by means of his giving it a pastoral function for the sake of the elect. He does not encourage further speculation on the matter.

29. Martin Luther, *LW* 25:389.

30. Talbert, *Romans*, 242.

31. Jacobus Arminius, *The Writings of James Arminius* (vol. 1; trans. James Nichols; Grand Rapids, Mich.: Baker, 1977).

32. These categories were proposed by Willibald Beyschlag, *Die paulinische Theodicee, Römer IX–XI: Ein Beitrag zur biblischen Theologie* (Halle: Eugen Strien, 1868), 3–22.

33. Charles Hodge, *Commentary on the Epistle to the Romans* (Grand Rapids, Mich.: Eerdmans, 1950), 310.

34. F. A. G. Tholuck, *Exposition of St. Paul's Epistle to the Romans* (trans. Robert Menzies; Philadelphia: Sorin and Ball, 1844), 340–41.

35. Heinrich August Wilhem Meyer, *Critical and Exegetical Handbook to the Epistle to the Romans* (ed. William P. Dickson; trans. John C. Moore and Edwin Johnson; New York: Funk & Wagnalls, 1884), 395.

36. In the individual approach, even the relationship between Romans 9 and 10 is problematic.

37. See Johann Tobias Beck, *Versuch einer pneumatisch hermeneutischen Entwicklung des neunten Kapitels im Briefe an die Römer* (Stuttgart: C. Hoffmann, 1833); J. Chr. K. Hofmann, *Der Schriftbeweis: Ein theologischer Versuch* (2 vols.; Nördlingen: C. H. Beck, 1852). See also Beyschlag, *Die paulinische Theodice*, 24–27.

38. Theodor Zahn, *Der Brief des Paulus an die Römer* (KNT 6; 3d ed.; Leipzig: Deichert, 1925).

39. Munck, *Paul and the Salvation of Mankind*, 42–43. Cullman asserts that election is both corporate and individual; he maintains that each person, by faith, joins the "Christ-line" and thus participates in the entire redemptive process. Cullman, *Christ and Time*, 220.

40. Corley, "Significance of Romans 9–11," 28.

41. Otto Piper asserts that Heilsgeschichte became Dispensationalism in the English speaking tradition, as the two movements are separate developments of the theological ideas of eighteenth century theologian Johann Bengel. Otto Piper, "Heilsgeschichte," in Halverson and Cohen, *A Handbook of Christian Theology*, 156.

42. Peter E. Prosser, *Dispensationalist Eschatology and Its Influence on American and British Religious Movements* (TSR 81; Lewiston, N.Y.: Edwin Mellen, 1999), 183–99.

43. Cyrus I. Scofield, ed., *The Scofield Reference Bible* (New York: Oxford University Press, 1909).

44. Typically there are seven dispensations; the following is a representative list: (1) The Dispensation of Innocence (Garden of Eden); (2) of Conscience (fall to Noah); (3) of Human Government (flood to Abraham); (4) of Promise (Abraham to Sinai); (5) of Law (Moses to Christ); (6) of Grace (Christ until the Parousia); and (7) of the Kingdom (a millennium following Christ's Second Coming). Larry V. Crutchfield, *The Origins of Dispensationalism: The Darby Factor* (Lanham, Md.: University Press of America, 1992), 34–40.

45. Charles Caldwell Ryrie, *Dispensationalism Today* (Chicago: Moody, 1965), 44–5.

46. Crutchfield attributes this distinction to the application of the hermeneutical principle of literal interpretation to all scripture, including prophecy. Crutchfield, *Origins of Dispensationalism*, 31, 205. For a fuller treatment of this dichotomy, see Lewis Sperry Chafer, *Systematic Theology* (8 vols.; Dallas: Dallas Seminary Press, 1948), 4:34, 47–53.

47. Craig A. Blaising, "Dispensationalism: The Search for Definition," in *Dispensationalism, Israel and the Church: The Search for Definition* (ed. Craig A. Blaising and Darrell L. Bock; Grand Rapids, Mich.: Zondervan, 1992), 25.

48. J. Lanier Burns, "The Future of Ethnic Israel in Romans 11," ibid., 223–25.

49. John G. Gager, *The Origins of Anti-Semitism: Attitudes Toward Judaism in Pagan and Christian Antiquity* (New York: Oxford University Press, 1983), 263–64. For similar views see Lloyd Gaston, *Paul and the Torah* (Vancouver: University of British Columbia Press, 1987), 139–150; Mary Ann Getty, "Paul and the Salvation of Israel: A Perspective on Romans 9–11," *CBQ* 50 (1988): 456–469; Paul van Buren, "The Church and Israel: Romans 9–11," *PSB*, *Suppl. 1* (1990): 5–18; *A Theology of the Jewish–Christian Reality. Part I: Discerning the Way*

(New York: Seabury, 1980); *A Theology of the Jewish–Christian Reality. Part II: A Christian Theology of the People Israel* (New York: Seabury, 1987); *A Theology of the Jewish–Christian Reality. Part III: Christ in Context* (San Francisco: Harper & Row, 1988); Krister Stendahl, *Paul Among Jews and Gentiles and Other Essays* (Philadelphia: Fortress, 1976), 4, 132; *Meanings: The Bible as Document and as Guide* (Philadelphia: Fortress, 1984), 243; H. J. Schoeps, *Paul: The Theology of the Apostle in the Light of Jewish Religious History* (trans. Harold Knight; Philadelphia: Westminster, 1959), 255-58; *The Jewish–Christian Argument: A History of Theologies in Conflict* (trans. David E. Green; New York: Holt, Rinehart and Winston, 1963); Pinchas Lapide and Peter Stuhlmacher, *Paul: Rabbi and Apostle* (trans. Lawrence W. Denef; Minneapolis: Augsburg, 1984), 47–55; Franz Rosenweig, *Der Stern der Erlösung* (Heidelberg: Lambert Schneider, 1954).

50. Alan T. Davies, *Anti–Semitism and the Christian Mind: The Crisis of Conscience After Auschwitz* (New York: Herder and Herder, 1969), 69.

51. Plag asserts that there are two distinct ways of salvation for Israel presented in Romans 11: the way of conversion (verses 11–24 and 28–32) and the way of the Deliverer (verses 25–27). He sees verses 25–27 as secondary insertion, albeit Pauline, of a Jewish apocalyptic tradition that is likely borrowed from another Pauline letter. This tradition is, according to Plag, added in response to the failure of the way of conversion, Plag, *Israels Wege zum Heil*, 66. For the chief arguments against Plag, see Ulrich Wilckens, *Der Brief an die Römer* (EKKNT; Zürich: Benziger, 1978-1980), 2:252.

52. Beker, *Paul the Apostle*, 334; Lucien Cerfaux, *The Church in the Theology of St. Paul* (trans. Geoffrey Webb and Adrian Walker; Freiburg: Herder & Herder, 1959), 63–64; Cranfield, *Romans*, 2:575-76; James D. G. Dunn, *Romans 9–16* (WBC; Dallas: Word, 1988), 681; André Feuillet, "Le plan salvifique de Dieu d'après L'Épitre aux Romains. Deuxieme Partie: Le plan salvifique de Dieu et le sort d'Israel," *RB* 57 (1950): 504; Hans–Martin Lübking, *Paulus und Israel im Römerbrief: Eine Untersuchung zu Römer 9–11* (Frankfort am Main: Peter Lang, 1986), 123; F. W. Maier, *Israel in der Heilsgeschichte nach Röm. 9–11* (Biblische Zeitfragen 12.11-12; Münster in Westfalen: Aschendorff, 1929), 525–27; Moo, *Romans*, 720; Handley C. G. Moule, *The Epistle of St. Paul to the Romans* (New York: A. C. Armstrong & Son, 1905), 199–200; François Refoulé, *"... et ainsi tout Israël sera sauvé": Romains 11, 25-32* LD 117 (Paris: Editions due Cerf, 1984), 71–74; Sanday and Headlam, *Romans*, 335; Wilckens, *Römer*, 2:255.

53. Marie-Joseph Lagrange, *Saint Paul: Épitre aux Romains* (Paris: J. Gabalda, 1950), 284;Fitzmyer, *Romans*, 623; Otfried Hofius, "Das Evangelium und Israel. Erwägungen zu Römer 9-11," *ZTK* 83 (1986): 314-16.

54. Gaston, *Paul and the Torah*, 143; C. Müller, *Gottes Gerechtigkeit und Gottes Volk*, 43; Ulrich Luz, *Das Geschichtsverständnis des Paulus*, (BEvT 49; München: C. Kaiser, 1968), 293–294; Christoph Plag, *Israels Wege zum Heil: eine Untersuchung zu Römer 9 bis 11*. AzTh 1, 40 (Stuttgart: Calwer, 1969), 37; Peter Stuhlmacher, "Zur Interpretation von Römer 11:25-32," in *Probleme biblischer Theologie: Gerhard von Rad zum 70. Geburtstag* (ed. Hans Walter Wolff; München: Chr. Kaiser, 1971), 559–61; Frederick William Danker, ed., *A Greek-English Lexicon of the New Testament and other Early Christian Literature* (Chicago: University of Chicago Press, 2000), 742.

55. Fitzmyer, *Romans*, 622.

56. He also argues that Acts 7:8; 20:11; 27:17; 1 Thess 4:16-17; 1 Cor 14:25 are other temporal examples of οὕτως found in the NT. Pieter van der Horst, "'Only Then Will All Israel Be Saved': A Short Note on the Meaning of καὶ οὕτως in Romans 11:26," *JBL* 119 (2000): 521-525.

57. Ibid.; Käsemann, *Romans*, 313-14; Barrett, *Romans*, 223; Talbert, *Romans*, 264; Otto Michel, *Der Brief an die Römer* (KEK; Göttingen: Vandenhoeck & Ruprecht, 1963), 281; Paul Althaus, *Der Brief an die Römer* (NTD 6; Göttingen: Vandenhoeck & Ruprecht, 1959), 107-08.

58. Corley, "Significance of Romans 9-11," 204-05.

59. This terminology is used by Corley. Ibid., 205-207.

60. Dodd, *Romans*, 182-86; Ernst Kühl, *Der Brief des Paulus an die Römer* (Leipzig: Quelle & Meyer, 1913), 392-393; Karl Ludwig Schmidt, *Die Judenfrage im Lichte der Kapitel 9-11 des Römerbriefes* (ThSt 13; Zollikon-Zurich: Evangelischer, 1947), 31-41; Heinrich August Wilhelm Meyer, *Critical and Exegetical Handbook to the Epistle to the Romans* (New York: Funk & Wagnalls, 1884), 448-52; W. S. Plummer, *Commentary on Romans* (Grand Rapids, Mich.: Kregel, 1971), 553.

61. R. C. H. Lenski, *The Interpretation of St. Paul's Epistle to the Romans* (Columbus: Wartburg, 1945), 725-27; William Hendriksen, *Israel in Prophecy* (Grand Rapids, Mich.: Baker, 1968), 48 51; C. M. Horne, "The Meaning of the Phrase 'And All Israel Will Be Saved' (Romans 11:26)," *JETS* 21 (1978), 331-34; Refoulé, *tout Israël*, 135-43, 179-81; G. C. Berkouwer, *The Return of Christ* (Grand Rapids, Mich.: Eerdmans, 1972), 349.

62. The restrictive sense was advocated by some Greek Fathers; see Schelkle, *Paulus, Lehrer der Väter*, 401.

63. This was the position of Calvin, and it proved influential in Reformed circles. John Calvin, *The Epistles of Paul the Apostle to the Romans and the Thessalonians* (eds. David W. Torrance and Thomas F. Torrance; trans. Ross Mackenzie Grand Rapids, Mich.: Eerdmans, 1961), 255; See also Karl Barth, *The Epistle to the Romans* (trans. Edwyn C. Hoskyns; Oxford: Oxford University Press, 1968), 46; Millard Erickson, *Christian Theology* (3 vols.; Grand Rapids, Mich.: Baker, 1985), 3:1043; Nygren, *Romans*, 399-400; Lucien Cerfaux, *Une Lecture de l'épître aux Romains* (Tournai: Castermann, 1947), 104-105.

64. Moo, *Romans*, 720-21.

65. Dunn, *Romans*, 2:681; Michel, *Römer*, 281; Otfried Hofius, "'All Israel Will be Saved': Divine Salvation and Israel's Deliverance in Romans 9-11." *PSB, Suppl* 1 (1990): 35-36; Cranfield, *Romans*, 2:576-77; Zahn, *Römer*, 524; Fitzmyer, *Romans*, 623; Käsemann, *Romans*, 313; Talbert, *Romans*, 264; Stuhlmacher, *Romans*, 172; LaGrange, *Romains*, 285.

66. See 1 Sam 25:1; 1 Kgs 12:1; 2 Chr 12:1; Dan 9:11; *Jub.* 50.9; *T. Levi* 17.5; *T. Jos.* 20.5, *T. Benj* 10.11; *L.A.B.* 22.1; 23.1.

67. Herbert Danby, ed., *The Mishnah* (Oxford: Oxford University Press, 1933), 397.

68. Lenski, *Romans*, 725-27; Hendriksen, *Israel in Prophecy*, 48-51; Horne, "And All Israel Will Be Saved", 331-34; Refoulé, *tout Israël*, 135-42, 179-82; Berkouwer, *The Return of Christ*, 349.

69. Talbert, *Romans*, 265.

70. Fitzmyer, *Romans*, 625.

71. Deitrich-Alex Koch, "Beobachtungen zum christologischen Schriftgebrauch in den vorpaulinischen Gemeinden," *ZNW* 71 (1980): 187.

72. Some interpreters see here a final advent of God himself instead of Christ. This will be addressed in the following section.

73. Käsemann, *Romans*, 314; Cranfield, *Romans*, 2:578; Wilckens, *Römer*, 2:256; Dunn, *Romans*, 2:683; Stuhlmacher, *Romans*, 172; Hofius, "'All Israel Will be Saved'," 36-37; Johannes Munck, *Christ & Israel: An Interpretation of Romans 9-11* (trans. Ingeborg Nixon; Philadelphia: Fortress Press, 1967) 137. The dispensationalists would also be classified here; it must be noted that their notion of Israel's salvation, generally speaking, is confined to the establishment of an earthly millennial kingdom which is the literal fulfillment of Old Testament prophecy. This kingdom is inaugurated by the return of Christ. Ryrie, *Dispensationalism Today*, 146-48; Erich Sauer, *From Eternity to Eternity: An Outline of the Divine Purposes* (trans. G. H. Lang; Grand Rapids, Mich.: Eerdmans, 1957), 185-194; Robert H. Gundry, *The Church and the Tribulation* (Grand Rapids, Mich.: Zondervan, 1973), 24-25.

74. Christopher D. Stanley, "'The Redeemer Will Come ἐκ Σιών': Romans 11:26-27 Revisited," in *Paul and the Scriptures of Israel* (ed. Craig A. Evans and James A. Sanders; Sheffield: JSOT, 1993), 121-22.

75. E. Earle Ellis, *Paul's Use of the Old Testament* (Edinburgh: Oliver and Boyd, 1957), 140; Dunn, *Romans*, 2:682; Moo, *Romans*, 728; Stuhlmacher, "Zur Interpretation," 561.

76. Cranfield, *Romans*, 2:577; Fitzmyer, *Romans*, 624; Johnson, *Reading Romans*, 184.

77. Berndt Schaller, "HΞEI EK ΣION O PYOMENOΣ: Zur Textgestalt von Jes. 59.20-21 in Rom. 11.26-27," in *De Septuaginta: Studies in Honour of John William Wevers on his Sixty-Fifth Birthday* (ed. A. Pietersma and C. Cox; Missisauga, Ontario: Benben, 1984), 201-206.

78. Stanley, "The Redeemer," 135.

79. Koch, "Beobachtungen," 188-89. Barrett suggests that Paul may have drawn the composite quotation from a Testimony Book. Barrett, *Romans*, 224.

80. Stendahl, *Meanings*, 243. So also Gager, *The Origins of Anti-Semitism*, 261; Getty, "Paul and the Salvation of Israel," 464; Stanley, "The Redeemer," 137.

81. Getty, "Paul and the Salvation of Israel," 461.

82. Gaston, *Paul and the Torah*, 143; Getty, "Paul and the Salvation of Israel," 461.

83. Martin Rese, "Die Rettung der Juden nach Römer 11," in *L'Apôtre Paul* (ed. A. Vanhoye; Leuven: University Press/Peeters, 1986), 428. See also Bernhard Mayer, *Unter Gottes Heilsratschluss: Prädestinationsaussagen bei Paulus* (FB; Würzburg: Echter, 1974), 291-93.

84. For him, die *Judenfrage* is an issue of how to relate to the Jews in this world (Germany in particular), for their ultimate salvation by God can be taken as a given. K. L. Schmidt, *Die Judenfrage im Lichte der Kapitel 9-11 des Römerbriefes*. ThSt 13. Zollikon-Zurich: Evangelischer, 1947, 31-33.

85. E. P. Sanders, *Paul, the Law, and the Jewish People* (Minneapolis: Fortress, 1983), 194; Käsemann, *Romans*, 314; Cranfield, *Romans*, 2:578; Fitzmyer, *Romans*, 624; Wilckens, *Römer*, 2:256; Stuhlmacher, *Romans*, 172; Hofius, "'All Israel Will be Saved'," 37; Munck, *Christ and Israel*, 137; *Paul and the Salvation of Mankind*, 285; Dunn, *Romans*, 2:682; Moo, *Romans*, 728; Burns, "The Future of Ethnic Israel," 214; John F. Walvoord, *The Nations, Israel, and the Church in Prophecy* (Grand Rapids, Mi.: Academie, 1988), 113.

86. Stuhlmacher, "Zur Interpretation," 561; Käsemann, *Romans*, 314; Wilckens, *Römer*, 2:256; Moo, *Romans*, 728.

87. Wilckens calls the verb a "futurum propheticum," *Römer*, 2:257, n. 1155.

88. W. D. Davies, "Paul and the People of Israel," *NTS* 24 (1977-78): 27; Joachim Jeremias, "Einige vorwiegend sprachliche Beobachtungen zu Römer 11:25-36," in *Die Israelfrage nach Röm 9-11* (ed. Lorenzo De Lorenzi; Rome: Abtei von St Paul von den Mauern, 1977), 200.

89. Dunn, *Romans*, 2:682.

90. Sanders, Paul, the Law, and the Jewish People, 194.

91. *Sanhedrin* 98a (Freedman, Soncino).

92. Cranfield, *Romans*, 2:578.

93. Heikki Räisänen, "Römer 9-11: Analyse eines geistigen Ringens," *ANRW* II 25.4:2920; John Murray, *The Epistle to the Romans: The English Text with Introduction, Exposition and Notes* (2 vols.; Grand Rapids, Mich.: Eerdmans, 1965), 2:99; Ernst Kühl, *Der Brief des Paulus an die Römer* (Leipzig: Qeulle & Meyer, 1913), 393; Lenski, *Romans*, 729.

94. Lagrange, Romains, 286.

95. Koch, "Beobachtungen, 189.

96. Dieter Zeller, *Der Brief an die Römer* (RNT; Regensburg: Pustet, 1985), 199; *Juden und Heiden in der Mission des Paulus: Studien zum Römerbrief* (FB; Stuttgart: Katholisches Bibelwerk, 1973), 261. Räisänen notes that other than these two references (Rom 9:33; 11:26) "Zion" is not used by Paul. Räisänen, 2920.

97. Koch, "Beobachtungen, 189.

98. Luz, *Geschichtsverständnis*, 295.

99. Hans Wilhelm Schmidt, *Der Brief des Paulus an die Römer* (THKNT; Berlin: Evangelische, 1966), 199.

100. Moo classifies Wright as understanding the Deliverer as referring to the historical Jesus, but Wright's conception is broader than that. N. T. Wright, *The Climax of the Covenant: Christ and the Law in Pauline Theology* (Minneapolis: Fortress, 1991), 250-51.

101. Moo, *Romans*, 729.

102. Käsemann, *Romans*, 314.

103. Davies, "Paul and the People of Israel," 27.

104. Franz Mussner, *Traktat über die Juden* (München: Kösel, 1979), 60.

105. Schoeps, *Paul*, 258.

106. Luz, *Geschichtsverständnis*, 295; H. W. Schmidt, *Römer*, 199.

107. Theodoret of Cyr, *Interpretatio in xiv epistulas sancti Pauli* (Migne, PG 82:180).

108. The reading is listed in the catena style commentary of the Ancient Christian Commentary on Scripture's volume on Romans; Gerald Bray, ed. *Romans* (ACC; New Testament, vol. 6; Downers Grove, Ill.: InterVarsity, 1998). Charles Talbert also cites it in his commentary, *Romans*, 242. Otherwise, I know of no modern commentary that refers to it. The initial idea for this study stems from Dr. Talbert's observation.

109. Frederic W. Farrar, *History of Interpretation* (London: Macmillan, 1886), 162-63.

110. D. H. Williams, "Reflections on *Retrieving the Tradition and Renewing Evangelicalism*: a response," *SJT* (2002): 108.

111. D. H. Williams, "Scripture, Tradition, and the Church: Reformation and Post-Reformation," in *The Free Church & the Early Church: Bridging the Historical and Theological Divide* (ed. D. H. Williams; Grand Rapids, Mich.: Eerdmans, 2002), 101–126.

112. The term "modern chauvinism" is used by Thomas C. Oden in "The Long Journey Home," *JETS* 34 (1991): 82.

113. Robert Webber, *Ancient-Future Faith: Rethinking Evangelicalism for a Postmodern World* (Grand Rapids, Mich.: Baker, 1999), 20–24.

114. See Brevard Childs, "The *Sensus Literalis* of Scripture: An Ancient and Modern Problem," in *Beiträge zur Alttestamentlichen Theologie* (ed. Herbert Donner et al.; Göttingen: Vandenhoeck & Ruprecht, 1977), 80–93; David Steinmetz, "The Superiority of Pre-critical Exegesis," in *A Guide to Contemporary Hermeneutics* (ed. Donald K. McKim; Grand Rapids: Eerdmans, 1986), 65–77; François Bovon, *Luke 1: A Commentary on the Gospel of Luke 1:1–9:50* (trans. Christine M. Thomas; Minneapolis: Fortress, 2002); Ulrich Luz, *Matthew 1–7: A Commentary* (trans. Wilhelm C. Linss; Minneapolis: Fortress, 1989); Brian E. Daley, "Is Patristic Exegesis Still Usable? Some Reflections on Early Christian Interpretations of the Psalms," in *The Art of Reading Scripture* (ed. Ellen F. Davis and Richard B. Hays; Grand Rapids, Mich.: Eerdmans, 2003), 69–88; David Burrell, *Knowing the Unknowable God: Ign-Sina, Maimonides, Aquinas* (Notre Dame: University of Notre Dame Press, 1986); Ellen T. Charry, *By the renewing of your minds: the pastoral function of Christian doctrine* (New York: Oxford University Press, 1997); Bruce D. Marshall, *Trinity and Truth* (Cambridge: Cambridge University Press, 2000); John Milbank, *The Word Made Strange: Theology, Language, Culture* (Oxford: Blackwell, 1997); Rowan Williams, *Chrisitan Spirituality: A Theological History from the New Testament to Luther and St. John of the Cross* (Atlanta: John Knox, 1980); Thomas C. Oden, *Systematic Theology* (3 vols.; San Francisco: Harper & Row, 1987–1992); Robert L. Wilken, *Remembering the Christian Past* (Grand Rapids, Mich.: Eerdmans, 1995); James S. Cutsinger, ed., *Reclaiming the Great Tradition: Evangelicals, Catholics and Orthodox in Dialogue* (Downers Grove, Ill.: InterVarsity, 1997); Robert Webber and Donald Bloesch, *The Chicago Call* (Nashville: Nelson, 1979); Charles Colson and Richard John Neuhaus, *Evangelicals and Catholics Together: Toward a Common Mission* (Dallas: Word, 1995); Paul Lakeland, *Post Modernity: Christian Identity in a Fragmented Age* (Minneapolis: Fortress, 1997); Bradley Nassif, ed., *New Perspectives on Historical Theology: Essays in Memory of John Meyendorff* (Grand Rapids, Mich.: Eerdmans, 1996); Hans-Georg Gadamer, *Truth and Method* (New York: Continuum, 1995); Christopher A. Hall, *Reading Scripture with the Church Fathers* (Downers Grove, Ill.: InterVarsity, 1998).

115. Thomas C. Oden, ed., Ancient Chrisitan commentary on Scripture (Downers Grove, Ill.: InterVarsity, 1998–). Other English language series include: the Fathers of the Church (Catholic University of America Press), Ancient Christian Writers (Paulist), Cistercian Studies (Cistercian Publications), The Church's Bible (Eerdmans), Message of the Fathers of the Church (Michael Glazier, Liturgical Press), and Texts and Studies (Cambridge).

116. Wilken, *Remembering*.

117. Webber, *Ancient-Future Faith*, 28.

118. Williams, "Reflections," 107.

119. Oden identifies this ancient consensual teaching as "the seven leading ecumenical councils received by patristic, medieval, Lutheran, Calvinist and Anglican consent, and

supplementary early synods that came to be decisively quoted as effectively representing the mind of the believing Church; and the four great doctors of the eastern church tradition (Athanasius, Basil, Gregory Nazianzen, John Chrysostom) and of the West (Ambrose, Jerome, Augustine, Gregory the Great), as well as others who have been perennially valued for accurately stating certain points of general lay consensus: Cyril of Jerusalem, Cyril of Alexandria, Hilary, Leo, [and] John of Damascus." Oden, "Long Journey," 82.

120. Dale C. Allison Jr., from a lecture delivered at the Billy Graham Center, Wheaton College, for the first annual meeting of the Society for the Study of Eastern Orthodoxy and Evangelicalism, September 28, 1991, quoted in Hall, *Reading Scripture*, 39.

121. The English chapter and verse divisions of Malachi differ from those of the Septuagint and Masoretic text. This study will employ the numbering of the MT. The LXX reverses the order of the epilogues in Malachi, placing the Elijah epiloge in 3:22-23 and the Moses epilogue in 3:24.

122. I am using the terminology advocated by Gabriele Boccaccini in *Middle Judaism: Jewish thought, 300 B.C.E.–200 C.E.* (Minneapolis: Fortress, 1991).

123. John A. T. Robinson suggests that there was an early Christology which saw Jesus as Elijah first and then the Christ second upon his eschatological return. Yet by the time the gospels were written, John the Baptist had become, through the influence of the words of Jesus, the designated Elijah figure in Christian tradition. See John A. T. Robinson "Elijah, John, and Jesus: An Essay in Detection," *NTS* 4 (1958): 263-281. J. Louis Martyn concludes that in the Fourth Gospel the evangelist suppresses an Elijah Christology which was present in his source; J. Louis Martyn, "We Have Found Elijah," in *Jews, Greeks and Christians: Religious Cultures in Late Antiquity. Essays in Honor of William David Davies* (ed. Robert Hamerton–Kelly and Robin Scroggs. Leiden: E. J. Brill, 1976), 218.

124. R. H. Fuller, *The Foundations of New Testament Christology* (London: Collins, 1965), 126-27.

125. Walter Wink, John the Baptist in the Gospel Tradition (Cambridge: Cambridge University Press, 1968), 32-33, 40-41; Markus Öhler, Elia im Neuen Testament: *Untersuchungen zur Bedeutung des alttestamentlichen Propheten im frühen Christentum* (BZNW 88; Berlin: Walter de Gruyter, 1997), 299.

126. Wink, *John the Baptist*, 42-45, 105; Öhler, *Elia im Neuen Testament*, 293-295.

127. James C. VanderKam, "1 Enoch, Enochic Motifs, and Enoch in Early Christian Literature," in *The Jewish Apocalyptic Heritage in Early Christianity* (ed. James C. VanderKam and William Adler; CRINT; Minneapolis: Fortress, 1996), 90-92; Jerome Walsh states that this identification is "presumably because both had been miraculously translated to heaven." Jerome T. Walsh, "Elijah," *ABD* 2:466.

CHAPTER TWO

Theodoret of Cyrus

Among the leaders of Christian antiquity, Theodoret of Cyrus has not received a level of attention commensurate with his accomplishments. This fifth century Antiochene bishop was a key figure in the christological debates leading up to the Council of Chalcedon. A voluminous writer, Theodoret has been praised particularly for his role as an apologist. In addition to his ecclesiastical histories, Theodoret penned numerous commentaries on Scripture, including the Pauline corpus. This chapter will provide an introduction to his life, works, and exegetical method with an eye toward providing justification for the serious consideration of his particular reading of Romans 11:26.

Biography

Theodoret himself provides a great deal of information about his life in his own writings. His historical work entitled *Historia religiosa seu ascetica vivendi ratio* includes biographical data related to his early years,[1] and the extant collection of his letters covers significant periods of his tenure as Bishop of Cyrus.[2] The polemical and apologetic nature of many of his writings also point to the key conflicts, both within the church and without, that shaped his life and career.

Antioch on the Orontes

Theodoret was born, raised, and educated in the city of Antioch. Ancient Antioch—located on the Orontes River in the southwestern corner of the Amuk plain—was founded as a Greco-Macedonian *polis* on non-Greek soil. Antioch grew in power and prestige as the Romans developed it into one of the two chief centers, along with Alexandria, of administrative and military power in the eastern half of the empire. The city, which had served as the initial base for the Gentile mission, also became a center of Christian ecclesial power. By the end of the fourth century, Antioch possessed a diverse population composed primarily of Syrians, Romans, Greeks, and Jews.[3] Glanville Downey states that "a number of factors—mixed population, strategic position, wide commercial connections, especially with the East, and political importance as first a Seleucid and then a Roman administrative center—all combined to make Antioch a natural focus for both the collection and the diffusion of ideas."[4]

The famous fourth century sophist Libanius extols the virtues of his native city in his *Oration in Praise of Antioch*, which was written in the year 360. In addition to praising Antioch's location, climate, trade, agricultural fertility, and public buildings, he likewise notes the cosmopolitan character of the city. "Indeed, if a man had the idea of traveling all over the earth, not to see how the cities looked, but to learn their ways, our city would fulfill his purpose and save him his journeying. If he sits in our market place he will sample every city."[5] Yet throughout his work, Libanius clearly indicates that, in his view, Antioch's greatest virtue lies in its role as a center for learning. He goes so far as to set it on par with Athens: "Indeed these two cities have held high the torch of eloquence, the one illuminating Europe, the other Asia."[6] Labanius reinforces this reputation again in his conclusion:

> What city can we say is worthy to be compared with this? More fortunate than the oldest, it is superior to some in size, surpasses others in the nobility of its lineage, and others in its all-producing territory. By one it may be excelled in walls, but it is greater than this in the abundance of its water and in the mildness of its winter, in the refinement of its inhabitants and in its pursuit of learning; and it is more fair than that city which is even larger, because of that fairest thing, Hellenic education and literature.[7]

Higher education was subsidized by the state, and Antioch was one of the cities that funded a municipal chair from the civic revenues. Spurning an offer from Athens, Libanius returned to his hometown to teach, and his celebrity made Antioch a rival to Athens and Alexandria during his tenure.[8] While the theoretical aim of Greek higher education was a general education (ἐγκύκλιος παιδεία), the *de facto* program consisted primarily of grammar and rhetoric. The aim of this linguistic and literary program was to teach classical Attic diction, to instill appreciation of the form and content of classical literature, and to train the student in the writing and oration of elegant rhetorical compositions.[9] The adoption of this Greek παιδεία during the Roman period also continued a process of Hellenization that assured uniformity among the ruling elite.[10]

Theodoret's Birth

Theodoret presents a good amount of autobiographical information about his early years in the *Historia religiosa*.[11] The date of Theodoret's birth, though uncertain, is generally given as *circa* 393.[12] Theodoret's story, however, begins seven years prior to that with his mother, whom Frances M. Young describes as a "flashy socialite."[13] She visited a hermit named Peter the Galatian who lived in an unoccupied tomb on the outskirts of Antioch in search of healing for an eye ailment. Peter not only cured her but also converted her to what Theodoret called the "devout life," in which she rejected the ornate dress, jewelry, and cosmetics of her former lifestyle.[14] She continued to visit Peter who provided cures for other family members,[15] and she became the client of other local holy men as well.[16]

Theodoret's father also sought the help of the local monks with regard to his wife's barrenness. An ascetic named Macedonius the Barley-Eater promised that the couple would have a son provided that he be devoted to the service of God.[17] Theodoret's mother eventually became pregnant, and the intervention of Macedonius was required again in order to avert a potential miscarriage in the fifth month of the pregnancy.[18] Again, Macedonius insisted that the child, as God's gift, must be dedicated to the one who had given him. And so the parents consecrated him to the service of God and named him Theodoret (Θεώρδορητος), meaning "gift of God." In an apologetic letter to the Consul Nomus *circa* 449, Theodoret defends himself by providing a litany of proofs of his devotion and service to God, which can be traced prior to his birth. "Even before my mother's conception, my parents promised to offer me to God, and from infancy they dedicated me according to this promise, and deemed it fitting to provide an appropriate education."[19]

Theodoret's Education

Theodoret was the recipient of a dual education encompassing both sacred and secular training. Although it cannot be proved, Pierre Canivet has suggested that Theodoret's first language was Syriac.[20] Nevertheless, Theodoret maintained regular contact with the Syrian monks throughout his childhood. His mother sent him once a week to receive a blessing from Peter,[21] and he often accompanied his mother on her visits to other celebrated holy men.[22] He frequently visited Macedonius as well, who provided encouragement while continually reminding Theodoret of his dedication to God.[23]

As Theodoret grew into an adolescent, he developed an interest in the ascetic lifestyle of the local monks. He mentions in particular a visit with the hermit Zeno in which he questioned the monk regarding his philosophy.[24]

Theodoret also tells of a weeklong visit, accompanied by friends who shared his ascetic inclinations, to the monastery at Teleda founded by Ammianus and Eusebius;[25] in addition, he notes repeated visits to another monastery in Teleda that had been home to Symeon the Stylite shortly before.[26] The Syrian holy men surrounding Antioch played a large role in Theodoret's religious education. Nevertheless, Peter the Galatian noted that an ascetic life was not to be for Theodoret, given the attachment that his parents had for him.[27] Price comments that Theodoret's parents viewed his dedication to God as involving an ecclesiastical career in Antioch rather than the isolated monastic life which would have required his separation from them.[28]

At the time of his blessing by Zeno—when he had just received his first growth of whiskers—Theodoret mentions that he had already been appointed to the office of lector in Antioch.[29] Brought up in the Antiochene tradition, Theodoret refers to Diodore of Tarsus and Theodore of Mopsuestia as his teachers,[30] "though certainly the former and probably the latter he can only have known through books."[31] John of Antioch and Nestorius have traditionally been mentioned as fellow students of Theodoret at Antioch, yet there is no evidence to corroborate this claim.[32]

Theodoret does not mention his classical education. His silence on the matter might be attributed to the tenuous relationship between Christianity and the pagan educational curriculum during this period. A. H. M. Jones notes that within Christianity there was a fundamentalist current of thought which viewed the pagan classics as sinful. This viewpoint is found in the Canons of the Apostles, "which though not official was widely accepted as authoritative in the Eastern churches in the fourth, fifth and sixth centuries. It expressly commands all the faithful to abstain from all pagan books, and declares that the scriptures contain all that is necessary not only for salvation but for culture."[33] Despite their reservations regarding the curriculum, many conceded that such a classical education was necessary for boys, and the basic syllabus remained unchanged throughout the fourth, fifth, and sixth centuries.

Given the social status of his parents and his location in a city that served as an educational center, Theodoret would almost certainly have followed the classical παιδεία. John Chrysostom and Theodore of Mopsuestia had done likewise as students of Libanius himself. Despite his silence regarding the matter, Theodoret's writings provide clear evidence of his classical training. He corresponds with contemporary sophists such as Aerius and Isokasius, and his letters contain quotations from Homer, Sophocles, Euripides, Aristophanes, Demosthenes, Thucydides, Pittacus, and Cleobulus. [34] Other works demonstrate his knowledge of Plato, Isocrates, Herodotus, Hesiod, Aristotle, Apollodorus, Plotinus, Plutarch, and Porphyry.[35] Theodoret's apologetic works are universally held in high regard, and M. M. Wagner asserts that his epistles are the best examples of the Byzantine letter form.[36] His Attic style and vocabulary alone are enough to demonstrate the quality of his education.[37]

Theodoret as Bishop

Theodoret inherited his parent's wealth while in his early twenties. No longer bound by familial obligations, Theodoret distributed his wealth to the poor and embarked upon a monastic life. In response to his later condemnation, Theodoret would defend himself by asserting that "during my tenure as bishop, I did not acquire for myself a house, a field, a penny, or a tomb, but I embraced poverty voluntarily after immediately distributing what I received from my parents after their death."[38] And so having been greatly influenced by the Syrian holy men of his youth, Theodoret entered a monastery near Apamea.[39] He stayed there writing until 423 when, around the age of thirty, he was elected Bishop of Cyrus.[40] Theodoret notes that he received this elevation in office against his wishes, preferring instead the quiet life.[41]

The small city of Cyrus was two days journey northeast of Antioch, about halfway to the Euphrates River. Theodoret's diocese belonged to the Metropolitan see of Hierapolis, which was the capital of the Cyrestica (Κυρρηστική), a rough and mountainous region.[42] Theodoret writes that his diocese is 40 milestones in length and width, containing many high mountains.[43] Young refers to Cyrus as a "little backwater,"[44] and it certainly paled in comparison to his native Antioch. Nevertheless, Theodoret's diocese was well populated and contained 800 parishes.[45]

Theodoret was an ardent defender or orthodoxy. Cyrus and its environs, in addition to containing many pagans and Jews, were home to a number of Christian heretics. Gustave Bardy notes that the oldest errors preserved followers in such remote regions.[46] As Bishop, Theodoret claims that he "freed more than a thousand souls from the malady of Marcionism, and led many others from the company of Arius and Eunomius to the Lord Christ...not one tare remains, but our flock has been freed from every heresy and error."[47] Glenn Chesnut observes that the Arian movement was the principle object of Theodoret's theological attack.[48] Theodoret also mentions eliminating more than 200 copies of Tatian's Diatessaron from churches within his diocese.[49] In addition, the bishop also targeted the local pagans and Jews with his apologies. Theodoret was also known for his homilies, and he recalled receiving standing ovations from the patriarch John during his regular visits to preach in Antioch.[50]

Theodoret was deeply concerned with the welfare of his city and its citizens, and as a result, he used his office for public benefaction rather than personal gain. Theodoret allocated significant amounts of ecclesiastical revenues for public works; he was responsible for building porticoes, baths, bridges, an aqueduct, and other public buildings.[51] The bishop also brought the necessary skilled laborers and physicians to live and work in Cyrus.[52] Furthermore, Theodoret acted as an advocate for economic reform on behalf of his people. Because peasant farmers were losing their land due to inordinately high taxes, Theodoret wrote imperial civil servants imploring the state to lower the assessment and reduce dues.[53] Finally, Theodoret's bishopric was characterized by administrative integrity. He was able to write that neither he nor his subordinates had been involved in bribery nor had any charges or lawsuits been brought against them.[54]

The Christological Controversies

Theodoret spent most of his tenure as bishop embroiled in the decades of christological controversy leading up to the Council of Chalcedon. In 430 Cyril of Alexandria sent a letter to Nestorius, Patriarch of Constantinople, demanding his subscription to an appended list of twelve anathemas. Nestorius sent the letter to John of Antioch who viewed Cyril's position as being Apollinarian. John gave Theodoret, along with Andrew of Samosata, the responsibility of refuting Cyril and defending the Antiochene position with regard to the humanity of the Christ. The Antiochenes were further concerned with Cyril's use of the title Mother of God (θεοτόκος) for Mary without sufficient explanation.[55]

Theodoret responded in 431 with *Refutation of the Twelve Anathemas of Cyril of Alexandria against Nestorius*.[56] The Third Ecumenical Council at Ephesus was called in 431 to settle the dispute between the Antiochene and Alexandrian factions. Theodoret arrived first and served as the spokesman for the Antiochenes. Nevertheless, the Alexandrians succeeded in opening the debates before John of Antioch and the majority of his party arrived. Thus, Cyril's supporters were able to depose Nestorius and condemn his doctrine without granting Nestorius the opportunity to defend and clarify his position. Theodoret led a delegation of eastern protesters that met with the emperor, but they left empty handed.[57] As a result, Theodoret returned home and renewed his attack against Cyril through speaking and writing.

Meanwhile, in an effort to preserve the unity of the church, John and Cyril reached an accord in 433 known as the Symbol of Union. Most scholars agree that the christological formula within this document was written by

Theodoret himself.[58] Still, Theodoret remained intractable, refusing to subscribe to the instrument of agreement. Obviously Theodoret had no problems with the doctrinal formulation, but he felt that Cyril had not sufficiently addressed the heretical concerns related to his letter of anathemas against Nestorius. John of Antioch had relented to the Alexandrians regarding the deposition of Nestorius, but Theodoret was resolute in his refusal to sign the decree of condemnation; Theodoret commented that he would have his two hands cut off first.[59] Theodoret would eventually sign the accord, *circa* 434, after John dropped his insistence that Theodoret disassociate himself from Nestorius.[60]

The Antiochene battle with Arian theology was at the heart of Theodoret's vociferous reaction to the one-nature christological language promulgated by Cyril and the Alexandrian school. The two-natures language employed by the Antiochenes had proved to be a useful apologetic tool in combating the subordinationism of the Arian position. When the Arians appealed to scripture as the basis for applying non-divine attributes to the Logos, the Antiochenes would argue that such attributes were to be attributed to Christ's human nature.[61] Therefore, Theodoret tenaciously defended the distinction between Christ's humanity and divinity in an effort to preserve the hard-won victory over the followers of Arius and Eunomius.[62]

Theodoret enjoyed a decade of peace following his agreement with Cyril on the formula of the Symbol of Union. After Cyril's death in 444, however, Cyril's Alexandrian supporters renewed their attacks on the two-natures doctrine in general and Theodoret, the leader of the Antiochene school, in particular. Cyril's successor, Dioscorus, launched a campaign to reassert the one-nature doctrine.[63] In 447 Dioscorus complained to Domnus, who had replaced his uncle as the new patriarch in Antioch, that Theodoret was preaching in the city of Antioch itself that there were two sons. Theodoret responded with an eloquent letter to Dioscorus explaining his christological position, and he ended the letter by condemning all those who did in fact divide the Son in two.[64]

In the year 448, Dioscorus managed to arrange an imperial decree confining Theodoret to his diocese and thus prohibiting him from preaching in Antioch. The pretext for this ban was that Theodoret had been disturbing the ecclesiastical peace by summoning too many synods. The Alexandrians followed their initial ploy by convening a church council in Ephesus in 449. A further imperial edict prohibited Theodoret from attending unless invited by the council. Theodoret, of course, was not invited, so he was deposed, along with Domnus and a number of other Antiochenes associated, however remotely, with Nestorius, including Flavian, the Patriarch of Constantinople.[65]

Sent into exile, Theodoret returned to the monastery near Apamea. He appealed to Pope Leo for help, but it could not arrive in time. Like Nestorius, Theodoret was outraged at being denied an opportunity to be tried in person so that he could respond to the charges. He laments in a letter that even murderers, tomb-robbers, and adulterers have the right to defend themselves at trial, whereas he has been tried and convicted in absentia.[66]

The general council at Ephesus even prohibited the legates of Pope Leo from reading his *Tome*, which expressed his hostility to the one-nature doctrine. Controlling the proceedings, the Alexandrian faction formally set aside the statement of the Symbol of Union and subsequently anathematized any confession of Christ having two-natures. The decisions of the prior council of Ephesus (431), which had been led by Cyril, were reaffirmed. Pope Leo would dub this latest council the *Latrocinium* of Ephesus (the Robber Synod).[67]

Theodoret returned to monastic life and engaged in writing.[68] Theodoret's cause gained renewed hope with the death of the emperor Theodosius in 350. The Antiochenes were blessed with a more sympathetic emperor, Marcian, who quickly restored Theodoret to his see as Bishop of Cyrus. Both Theodoret and Pope Leo pushed for a new general council in order to address the grievances arising from the Robber Synod;[69] this new council convened in Chalcedon in 451. Marcian's charge that Theodoret take part caused great protestations from the Alexandrians. Before he was allowed to take his place, Theodoret had to defend his views. Furthermore, the condemnation of Nestorius was demanded, to which Theodoret finally consented. Thus, on October 26, 451, at the eighth session of the council, Theodoret declared, "Anathema to Nestorius and to all those who refuse the title Mother of God to the holy Virgin Mary and to those who divide into two sons the unique Son, the only-begotten."[70] As a result, the council acknowledged Theodoret as an orthodox doctor of the church and allowed him to take his place among the bishops. Commenting on the christological settlement of Chalcedon, Kelly asserts that "in its final shape the Definition is a mosaic of excerpts from Cyril's two Letters, Leo's *Tome*, the Union Symbol and Flavian's profession of faith at the Standing Synod (of Constantinople, 448)."[71] Since Theodoret is reputed to be the author of the christological statement in the Symbol of Union, he must be viewed as a key figure in the shaping of the two-natures formula of the Council of Chalcedon.

Theodoret's Final Years

There is not much data by which to chronicle the last years of Theodoret's life. Much of the correspondence, though not all, is driven by the polemical concerns of the christological debates. Following Chalcedon, Theodoret returned to his post, and thereafter he seems just to have faded from view. For a long time it was assumed that he died shortly after Chalcedon. Ernst Honigmann has countered this argument from silence, demonstrating that he was probably alive after 460 and that the year 466 is not out of the question.[72] Thus, most recent works give the date of Theodoret's death as *circa* 466 as opposed to the earlier date of *circa* 457.[73] Nevertheless, the last certain date in Theodoret's life is June 11, 453, the date of a letter written to him by Pope Leo.[74]

Writings

Theodoret was a prolific writer, and his body of work is more varied than that of any of his fellow Antiochenes. Theodoret writes in the year 450 that he has written thirty-five books interpreting the scriptures and combating heresies,[75] and his literary output certainly continued beyond that date. Unfortunately, a number of his works have not survived, but due to the sheer volume of the *corpus*, a significant selection remains extant.[76] Theodoret's writings can be divided into the following categories: exegetical works, apologetic works, dogmatic works, historical works, sermons, and letters.

Exegetical Works

Theodoret produced a number of commentaries on scripture. The only exegetical work he wrote on the New Testament was his commentary on the letters of Paul, from which the passage being examined in this study comes.[77] It is interesting to note that Theodoret did not write a commentary on the four gospels, given his career long involvement in the ongoing christological controversy. He did, however, write extensively on the Old Testament. The majority of his commentaries consist of a verse by verse format, and Theodoret's comments upon the text are generally clear and concise. His initial work was an interpretation of the Song of Songs, which he viewed as an allegorical treatment of the relationship between Christ and the Church.[78] Theodoret also penned a series of commentaries on the prophets which include works on Daniel,[79] Ezekiel,[80] the twelve Minor Prophets,[81] Isaiah,[82] and Jeremiah;[83] the latter work also covers Baruch and Lamentations. Perhaps the most famous of his works in this genre is his commentary on the Psalms.[84] Finally, there are two works in this category which Theodoret produced in a question and answer format. One addresses a series of questions on the Pentateuch, as well as Joshua, Judges, and Ruth,[85] while the other continues the questions through the books of Kings. The section in the latter book dealing with Chronicles returns to the verse by verse commentary format. [86] More will be said regarding Theodoret's hermeneutical methodology later in this chapter.

Apologetic Works

Aided by his classical education, Theodoret excelled in the area of apologetics, and there are four known works of his that are generally classified in this genre.[87] Theodoret wrote a refutation of the objections of the Persian magi to the Christian faith;[88] this work is not extant, with the exception of brief excerpts from his own quotations of it. His apology entitled *adversus Judaeos* (*Against the Jews*) has also been lost, although some scholars believe a fragment found in the di Medici library in Florence to be a part of that document.[89] Theodoret's *Ten Discourses on Divine Providence*, though delivered as sermons in Antioch, is generally placed in this category.[90] The discourses are proofs of divine providence from the natural, moral, and social orders. The most significant of the apologies is *The Cure of Pagan Maladies or The Truth of the Gospels Proved from Greek Philosophy.*[91] In this work Theodoret juxtaposes in twelve discourses the Christian and pagan answers to the fundamental religious and philosophical questions. In so doing he cites over 100 pagan philosophers in approximately 340 different passages. *The Cure of Pagan Maladies* is generally regarded as the finest example of the Christian apologies that respond to the paganism of the Greco-Roman culture.[92]

Dogmatic Works

Several of these works arose from the christological controversy associated with the initial defense of Nestorius and the subsequent Council of Ephesus in 431. The first was *Theodoret's Refutation of the Twelve Anathemas of Cyril of Alexandria against Nestorius.* This work was condemned by the Fifth Ecumenical Council at Constantinople in 553 and thus not preserved. Nevertheless, much of the text can be reconstructed from Cyril's surviving response.[93] Following the first Council of Ephesus, Theodoret wrote five books, the *Pentalogium*, attacking Cyril and the council's actions. Also condemned at Constantinople, it survives only in fragments.[94] Two other books from the same period—*On the Holy and Vivifying Trinity* and *On the Incarnation of the Lord*— have recently been shown to be a composite work of Theodoret.[95] Ironically, they have been preserved as works of Cyril, against whom they were written.[96] Theodoret's major christological treatise is the *Eranistes* (*Beggar*), which he wrote *circa* 447.[97] He presents the one-nature Christology as a poor doctrine that has been collected, as if by a beggar, from a litany of the church's infamous heretics. A final christological treatise, of uncertain date, on the unity of the two-natures is *That there is One Son, Our Lord Jesus Christ.*[98]

An early dogmatic work of Theodoret was preserved under the name of Justin Martyr. This work, the *Expositio rectae fidei*, predates the Nestorian controversy.[99] The *Quaestiones et responsiones ad orthodoxos* of Pseudo-Justinian has been restored to Theodoret as well.[100] Given that Theodoret frequently mentions his efforts at eradicating the heresies of Arius, Eunomius, Apollinarius, Marcion and the like in his letters, it is likely that he wrote additional dogmatic works of which no record remains.

Historical Works

Theodoret played a significant role as a church historian. His *Ecclesiastical History* is an intentional continuation of the work of Eusebius.[101] It covers the years 323 to 428, ending with the death of Theodore of Mopsuestia. The work does not deal with Theodore's successor in Antioch, Nestorius. Nevertheless, the *Ecclesiastical History* is certainly relevant to the christological debate of Theodoret's lifetime. Chesnut comments that the document could have been subtitled "An Account of the Arian Controversy."[102] The previous century's battle against Arianism and its offshoots provided the subtext for all of Theodoret's exchanges with the Alexandrians, since Theodoret felt their one-nature Christology threatened to open the door again to subordinationist error.

Theodoret made another significant contribution with his *History of the Monks in Syria.*[103] This work provides a glimpse of the ascetic life in the region of Syria through the eyes of an ecclesiastical figure that had an intimate personal acquaintance with a number of the principals. Theodoret also wrote a five-book *History of Heresies* which runs the gamut from Simon Magus to Theodoret's time, concluding with the polar opposites Nestorius and Eutyches.[104] The last book is a systematic presentation of the church's teaching which, according to Quasten, "is unique in Greek patristic literature and very valuable for the history of dogma."[105] Finally, Theodoret is reputed to have written a historical review of the Council of Chalcedon, but it has not survived.[106]

Sermons and Letters

The *Ten Discourses on Divine Providence* has already been mentioned. Although renowned as a preacher,[107] few other examples of his homilies remain. One can be found at the end of his *History of the Monks in Syria*, while fragments of a few others remain in Latin.[108] As for his correspondence, Nicephorus Callistus claimed to have over 500 letters of Theodoret in the 14th century.[109] Only 232 of them, however, are extant.[110]

Exegetical Method

As has been noted above, Theodoret penned many works of biblical commentary, a number of which have survived. Since he is frequently hailed as the last significant theologian or exegete of the Antiochene School, most discussions of his exegesis are placed within the context of the competing methodologies of the schools of Antioch and Alexandria. As a result, the state of scholarship on Antiochene biblical interpretation must be addressed briefly.

The Antiochene School

Generally speaking, Antiochene exegesis is presented in the patrologies and histories of interpretation as the foil of Alexandrian exegesis. Whereas the Alexandrian School employed allegory as a key interpretive tool, the Antiochene School favored a grammatical-historical method that emphasized the literal meaning of the text. While this basic dichotomy is true, it needs to be pointed out that scholars have recently argued that such generalizations and oversimplifications do not do justice to the diversity within the Antiochene School itself[111] nor to the common ground shared by the two schools.[112] While the complexities of the Antiochene School are beyond the scope of this study, two important developments in the arena of Antiochene research will be addressed.

First, Christoph Schäublin and Frances Young have demonstrated that the roots of Antiochene methodology are to be found in the ancient Alexandrian grammatical tradition.[113] Influenced by the rhetorical schools, the Antiochenes applied the conventions of classical grammatical analysis, rhetoric, and historiography to their reading of biblical texts. Referring to these canons, John O'Keefe states that "biblical exegesis that seemed to break these rules and destroy narrative integrity was rejected. Allegorical reading of the Bible seemed to break these very rules. Second, the Antiochenes linked theological mistakes to methodological mistakes. Hence, the controversy surrounding the work of Origen figures prominently in the emergence of the Antiochene resistance to allegory."[114]

Second, the key concept of θεωρία (*vision, insight, contemplation*) within the Antiochene tradition has been clarified through a series of studies in the last century. Heinrich Kihn first pointed out the distinction made by the Antiochenes between θεωρία and ἀλλεγορία.[115] Alberto Vaccari then identified four general properties of the concept of θεωρία, which the Antiochenes used to balance both a historical and christological reading of the biblical text: (1) θεωρία presupposes the historical reality of the event described by the author. (2) θεωρία embraces a second object in the future which is ontologically related to the initial historical event. (3) The first object is related to the second as small to great, image to person, or sketch to finished portrait. (4) While both events are the object of θεωρία, the first is the means through which the more significant second event is conveyed.[116] Vaccari classified θεωρία as one of two kinds of typology, with the distinctive feature of θεωρία being the prophet's foreknowledge of both objects. Paul Ternant subsequently argued that θεωρία could also apply to the work of a redactor as well.[117]

Bertrand de Margerie asserted that, according to the Antiochenes, prophetic activity consisted of history and contemplation (θεωρία), both of which were consistent with the literal meaning of the biblical text. "There is a single prediction only, which is twice fulfilled: the first time partially, the second time fully."[118] Thus, both historical events are aspects of the literal sense of the text. Yet the significance of de Margerie's study was his shifting of the discussion of θεωρία from prophetic intention to fulfillment: "What interested them [the Antiochenes] was not so much the subjective awareness of the biblical writers as the objective fulfillment of what they announced."[119] John Breck has recently built upon this shift; while focusing on the role of the Holy Spirit, he locates θεωρία in "the intuitive perception of spiritual meaning not by the author, but by the later interpreter."[120]

The Antiochene method of θεωρία was an attempt to navigate between the extremes of Alexandrian allegory and Jewish literalism. While the foregoing discussion serves to provide an outline of this Antiochene exegetical program, a caveat is warranted. There is great diversity within the Antiochene tradition. Francisco Seisedos notes that the Antiochenes were often terminologically imprecise, and the resulting subtle distinctions led to confusion amid the ranks.[121] Bradley Nassif concludes that "the diverse ways in which θεωρία was employed as a *terminus technicus* in Antiochene exegesis makes it impossible to construct a single model of the hermeneutic that was uniformly applied."[122] Nevertheless, this cursory treatment of Antiochene methodology will suffice to provide a rough graph on which to plot Theodoret's exegetical method.

Theodoret's Exegetical Method

Theodoret viewed himself as an heir of the Antiochene tradition, and he generally refers reverentially to his well-known predecessors. In the preface to his Pauline commentary Theodoret notes that critics "will perhaps find me presumptuous and audacious for being so bold as to interpret the apostle following this person and that, the luminaries of the world."[123] He goes on to comment that it is not unreasonable for him, "like some kind of gnat, to buzz around the apostolic meadows with those bees."[124] While Theodoret has often been characterized as lacking in originality,[125] Jean-Noël Guinot warns against regarding Theodoret "merely as a clever compiler."[126] Theodoret frequently distances himself from his Antiochene forebears.[127]

Theodoret's careful regard for grammatical-historical exegesis is seen in his consistent application of textual criticism throughout his commentaries.[128] His Old Testament commentaries were based upon the Antiochene text of the Septuagint.[129] While Theodoret considers the LXX to be divinely inspired, he still compared his exemplar with a number of other sources. The LXX versions of Aquila, Symmachus, and Theodotion—"the three interpreters"—are the most frequently cited. In addition, Theodoret consulted Origen's *Hexapla* as well as other unnamed Greek copies. He even compares his text with Hebrew and Syriac versions.

Guinot suggests that Theodoret's method can be understood in terms of three levels of interpretation: literal, figurative, and typological.[130] At the first level of interpretation, the literal, Theodoret viewed his role as explanatory in nature. The goal, in essence, was to provide a paraphrase of the text in order to make the "plain sense" (πρόχειρος) more readily accessible to the reader. At this level of interpretation, Theodoret employed tools such as grammar, style, history, and geography.[131] Of these, grammatical analysis proves to have received the majority of Theodoret's attention. He was concerned with the divisions of the text, in terms of sentences and clauses as well as larger sections of the text.[132] In addition, Theodoret addressed issues of verbal mood, syntax, lexical meaning, idiom, and style. Historical concerns were also an important element of literal interpretation. With respect to prophecy, history served as the means of verification of fulfillment. Theodoret stands out in relation to his Antiochene predecessors by establishing a number of messianic prophecies by means of literal exegesis.[133]

The second level of Theodoret's interpretation is the figurative (τροπικός or πνευματικός) reading. For Theodoret, this level is still a literal sense in that it addresses the literal function of metaphorical or figurative language.[134] Such use of language is common in scripture; therefore one is able to establish the meaning of recurring figurative expressions. Building upon his premise of the harmony (συμφωνία) of scripture, Theodoret established a finite domain of equivalences for such figures, preventing the exegete from engaging in flights of fancy. Quotations within the biblical text often serve as the means "to elucidate the 'symphony' of figurative interpretations and, beyond that, the harmony of all Scripture."[135] For Theodoret, there is no mingling of literal and figurative readings, since the figurative reading serves as the literal sense of certain modes of expression. Thus, Theodoret's metaphorical readings are subjected to certain methodological rigor.

Guinot labels the third level of Theodoret's interpretation broadly as typological. This level corresponds to the Antiochene principle of θεωρία,[136] although Theodoret never formally addresses his understanding of the term.[137] Guinot states that "its goal is not so much to assure immediate comprehension of the text as to disclose its larger significance, which almost always means establishing its ultimate purpose with respect to the Messiah and the New Testament."[138] Theodoret speaks of prophecies with double fulfillments; the initial realization is the "type" or "figure," with the latter fulfillment being the "antitype." He follows the standard Antiochene line by describing the relationship of the former to the latter as small to great, image to person, or sketch to finished portrait. For Theodoret, what is realized "figuratively" (τυπικῶς or κατὰ τύπον) in the Old Testament is subsequently fulfilled "properly and truly" (κυρίως καὶ ἀληθῶς) in the New Testament. Guinot concludes that the basic process remains the same at all three levels: "to safeguard the 'reality' and historicity of the text by demonstrating its truth with the testimony of facts (τὰ πράγματα), and by specifying its significance through determining the end (τέλος) which genuinely fulfills the prophecy."[139]

Despite his adherence to Antiochene methodology, Theodoret stands out from his Antiochene predecessors. He has traditionally been heralded as the exegete who took the middle road between Alexandrian allegory and Antiochene literalism.[140] Theodoret says much the same thing regarding himself in the preface to his commentary on the Psalms:

> Having consulted various commentaries, I found some which had given way fully to allegory, while others had adapted the prophecies to certain historical events, thus advocating an interpretation that was more for the Jews than for the pupils of the faith. I have made it my practice to avoid both extremes. All that is relevant to ancient history needs to be recognized. But predictions concerning Christ our Savior, the church of the Gentiles, the gospel way of life, and the preaching of the apostles should not be applied to other things, which is exactly what it pleases the Jews to do, as they construct a defense of their unbelief.[141]

Modern scholars with differing perspectives on Antiochene exegesis share this view of Theodoret as a mediating figure in the history of exegesis. Young, who looks favorably upon Antiochene exegesis, suggests that in the preceding quotation, Theodoret had Theodore of Mopsuestia in view.[142] Unlike Theodore, Theodoret perceived a unity between the Old and New Testaments. Therefore, without sacrificing the historical context of the Old Testament books, the Bishop of Cyrus was able to see Christian content within the Old Testament texts. Applying θεωρία more frequently than his predecessors, Theodoret allows Old Testament texts to have two ends in view (σκοποί): a historical reference and a future messianic reference.[143] Metropolitan Demetrios Trakatellis contends that Theodoret's works exhibit a christocentric exegesis—which was not fully operative in the Antiochene school—that represents a remarkable synthesis of Antiochene and Alexandrian traditions. While likely influenced by figures such as Cyril and Eusebius, Theodoret did not "allow his christocentric exegesis to produce an interpretation loaded with heavy and elaborate theological language. His christocentric exegesis is presented in a precise and concise language, controlled by and integrated with the other major exegetical methods."[144]

O'Keefe, on the other hand, has a negative opinion of Antiochene exegesis as a whole. He concludes that it failed because it was a backward-looking program that severed the links between the Old and New Testaments, between the story of Israel and the story of Jesus.[145] Nevertheless, in comparing Theodoret to his predecessors Diodore and Theodore, O'Keefe notes that "Theodoret, while operating within the same basic tradition, seems to realize the mistake of his teachers and allows for more robust and more frequent figural interpretations. Because of this, Theodoret's exegesis possesses a more explicit Christian content."[146] So for O'Keefe, Theodoret demonstrates an attempt to move beyond the inadequate Antiochene approach through his recognition of Christ as a hermeneutical key. Thus, a wide-ranging group of scholars have agreed that Theodoret possessed an exegetical approach that was marked by balance and moderation.[147]

While discussing Theodoret's exegetical method, a brief word needs to be made regarding his style. Modern commentators have noted the clarity and conciseness of his style.[148] Theodoret addressed the issue himself in the preface to his Pauline commentary: "My particular concern is for conciseness: I am aware that brevity encourages even those inclined to easy ways to do some reading."[149] The ancient critic Photius, writing in the ninth century, assessed Theodoret' ability as follows:

> His style is particularly suited to the writing of commentaries. He reveals the meaning of what is obscure by his pure and lucid language. By his agreeable quality, which adds something pleasant, he increases the reader's enthusiasm. Furthermore, he never allows himself to digress or become irrelevant; he does not exhaust the reader. He

makes the examination of the problems clear, coherent and accessible to students of his book. The language and the composition of the sentences do not conceal their origin in the good qualities of Atticism...As a whole, he is classed among the best commentators, and it is not easy to find any better interpreter...The combination of plain language, concise explanation of all the essentials, avoidance of digressions or demonstrations of epideictic skill, which might be valuable in other respects but deflect one from the question at issue, this is the achievement which distinguishes the excellent Theodoret from others.[150]

Guinot points out that the frequency with which Theodoret is quoted in the *catenae* reflects the high regard in which his exegetical ability and readable style were held.[151] Price declares that "he had a clear perception of what in any topic was really at issue; his reasoning is sharp and incisive, his exposition lucid and uncluttered. Add to this the verve and elegance of his style, and Theodoret emerges as the most attractive writer of his generation."[152]

Theodoret's Lasting Reputation

Theodoret's reputation among the Fathers has suffered due to the lasting stigma caused by his close association with Nestorius. In addition, the Fifth Ecumenical Council at Constantinople in 553 condemned Theodoret's writings against Cyril and the Council of Ephesus.[153] Given these two factors, Theodoret's exegetical works and apologies have not received the level of attention that they deserve.

Theodoret's vociferous and steadfast defense of Nestorius has been noted. Theodoret objected in particular to the manner of Nestorius' deposition, in which the Patriarch of Constantinople was tried in absentia and thus denied an opportunity to defend and clarify his views. Furthermore, Theodoret—who had endured similar charges and treatment—likely felt that Nestorius did not in fact hold the positions attributed to him by his enemies. Since the discovery of the *Bazaar of Heracleides*, a number of modern historians have contended that Nestorius himself was not what has been traditionally labeled as "Nestorian."[154] It must be mentioned that other factors were also at work; the christological debates of the period cannot be separated from the social and political conflicts of the period.[155] After two decades of obstinacy, Theodoret reluctantly pronounced anathema upon Nestorius at Chalcedon in the interest of securing church unity.[156] Nevertheless, he would remain suspect in the eyes of many due to his association with the name Nestorius and the traditional heresy attached to it. The posthumous condemnation of certain writings of Theodoret at Constantinople served to reinforce that suspicion, despite the fact that his exegetical works were not repudiated.[157] Price laments this state of affairs thusly, "The modern age that has rehabilitated Theodore and Nestorius naturally looks on Theodoret with a kindlier eye; but the crude, if useful, schematization that sees the Council of Ephesus as a duel between Cyril and Nestorius, and Chalcedon as the victory of Leo over Eutyches, has kept Theodoret at the rear of the stage."[158]

Conclusion

This chapter has established that Theodoret was a significant figure in early Christian history. As the leading thinker of the Antiochene school, he was in the vanguard of the fight to defend the christological concept of Christ's two natures. He, along with Pope Leo, was instrumental in bringing about the Council of Chalcedon in 451 in order to address the problem of the deposed eastern bishops, and Theodoret's formula from the Symbol of Union was incorporated into the final Chalcedonian christological statement. Furthermore, in terms of literary activity, Theodoret produced "an *oeuvre* unequaled in range by any of his contemporaries."[159] In addition to his contributions as a historian, he wrote what is regarded by many as the finest of Christian apologies, *The Cure of Pagan Maladies*. Perhaps most significantly, this chapter has demonstrated that Theodoret was a careful and balanced interpreter of scripture, adhering to Antiochene methodology while also allowing for the existence of a christological harmony between the testaments. Finally, his clear and concise style was not given to eccentric or speculative readings of texts. Thus, given his place within church history and his practice as an exegete, his most unusual application of the Elijah tradition should not be treated dismissively by modern scholarship.

Notes

1. For the most recent critical edition, see Theodoret, *Théodoret de Cyr, Histoire des Moines de Syrie* (SC 234, 257; ed. Pierre Canivet and Alice Leroy-Molinghen; Paris: Editions du Cerf, 1977–1979); for an English translation, see Theodoret, *A History of the Monks in Syria* (trans. R. M. Price; Kalamazoo, Mich.: Cistercian Publications, 1985).

2. 232 letters of Theodoret's correspondence have survived. 147 were first published in *Opera omnia in quatuor tomos distributa, quorum plurima, Graece, quaedam etiam Latine nunc primum prodeunt: Graeca cum manuscriptis exemplaribus...collata, Latinae versiones ad Graecorum normam exactae & recognitae* (ed. Jacques Sirmond; Paris: Sumptibus S. Cramoisy, 1642). Subsequent critical editions of his correspondence have included additional letters, and some letters are to be found in separate conciliar collections. The most recent critical edition is that of Sources chrétiennes: *Théodoret de Cyr, Correspondance* (SC 40, 98, 111; ed. Yvan Azéma; Paris: Editions du Cerf, 1955–1965). Volumes 98 and 111 consist of the 147 letters of the Collectio Sirmondiana, and volume 40 presents 52 additional letters. An English translation of the correspondence is available in NPNF[2] 3:250–348.

3. Phyllis Rodgerson Pleasants, "Making Antioch Christian: The City in the Pastoral Vision of John Chrysostom" (Ph.D. diss., The Southern Baptist Theological Seminary, 1991), 29.

4. Glanville Downey, *A History of Antioch in Syria: from Seleucus to the Arab Conquest* (Princeton: Princeton University Press, 1961), 11–12.

5. Libanius, *Oration in Praise of Antioch*, trans. Glanville Downey, *PAPS* 103 (1959), 670.

6. Ibid., 672.

7. Ibid., 681.

8. A. H. M. Jones, *The Later Roman Empire, 284–602: A Social, Economic, and Administrative Survey* (2 vols.; Norman: University of Oklahoma Press, 1964), 2:998.

9. Ibid., 2:1002–03.

10. Francesco Cordasco, *A Brief History of Education* (Paterson, NJ: Littlefield, Adams, 1963), 15.

11. Secondary authors have generally not questioned the historical reliability of Theodoret's material, e.g. Philippe Escolan, *Monachisme et Eglise: Le monachisme syrien du IVe au VIIe siècle, un ministère charismatique* (ThH 109; Paris: Beauchesne, 1999). Theresa Urbainczyk, however, notes that Theodoret's history is part of the larger Antiochene-Alexandrian confrontation, and the positive portrayal of Theodoret within it serves several purposes. It demonstrates that Syria is the equal of Egypt in producing ascetics and holy men. The text depicts these rural monks as deferential to Theodoret and his office, thereby bringing them under the purview of the church's ecclesiastical structure and enhancing Theodoret's reputation of power. Buttressing his personal power was important in the face of the open attack of the Alexandrians. Urbainczyk, *Theodoret of Cyrrhus: The Bishop and the Holy Man* (Ann Arbor: The University of Michigan Press, 2002).

12. Gustave Bardy, "Théodoret," *DTC* 15:299; Johannes Quasten, *Patrology* (3 vols.; Utrecht: Spectrum, 1950–1960), 3:536.

13. Frances M. Young, *From Nicaea to Chalcedon* (Philadelphia: Fortress, 1983), 266.

14. Theodoret, *Historia religiosa seu ascetica vivendi ratio* 9.5–8 (SC 234:414–22).

15. Theodoret, *Historia religiosa* 9.9, 10, 14, 15 (SC 234:422–26, 430–34)

16. Theodoret, *Historia religiosa* 6.14 (SC 234:364)

17. Theodoret, *Historia religiosa* 13.16 (SC 234:502)

18. Theodoret, *Historia religiosa* 13.17 (SC 234:504)

19. Theodoret, *Letter* 81 (SC 98:196).

20. Canivet asserts that the purity of his Greek is indicative that Greek was an acquired literary language for Theodoret. Yet given his families wealth and social status in a city such as Antioch, Greek could just as easily have been his first tongue. At any rate, Theodoret clearly grew up in a bilingual environment. See Pierre Canivet, *Histoire d'une enterprise apologétique de Ve siècle* (Paris: Bloud & Gay, 1958), 25.

21. Theodoret, *Historia religiosa* 9.4 (SC 234:414).

22. Theodoret, *Historia religiosa* 8.15 (SC 234:402).

23. Theodoret, *Historia religiosa* 13.18 (SC 234:506–08).

24. Theodoret, *Historia religiosa* 12.4 (SC 234:464).

25. Theodoret, *Historia religiosa* 4.10 (SC 234:312–16)

26. Theodoret, *Historia religiosa* 26.4 (SC 257:164–66)

27. Theodoret, *Historia religiosa* 9.4 (SC 234:414).

28. R. M. Price, "Introduction," in Theodoret, *A History of the Monks in Syria*, xii.

29. Theodoret, *Historia religiosa* 12.4 (SC 234:466).

30. Theodoret, *Letter* 16 (SC 98:60).

31. Young, *Nicaea to Chalcedon*, 266.

32. E. Cavalcanti, "Theodoret of Cyrrhus," *EECh* 2:827.

33. Jones, *Later Roman Empire*, 2:1005.

34. Young, *Nicaea to Chalcedon*, 267.

35. Quasten, *Patrology*, 3:538.

36. M. M. Wagner, "A Chapter in Byzantine Epistolography," *DOP* 4 (1948), 119–81.

37. Price, "Introduction," xii.

38. Theodoret, *Letter* 113 (SC 111:66).

39. Theodoret notes that it is located three miles from Apamea, 75 from Antioch, and 120 from Cyr. Various scholars have identified this monastery as the one at Nicerte. Theodoret, *Letter* 119 (SC 111:80).

40. Alternate spellings found in the literature for Κύρρος are Cyr and Cyrrhus.

41. Theodoret, *Letter* 81 (SC 98:196).

42. Otto Bardenhewer, *Geschichte der Altkirchlichen Literatur* (Darmstadt: Wissenschaftliche Buchgesellschaft, 1962), 222.

43. Theodoret, *Letter* 42 (SC 98:110); he indicates elsewhere that the region was assessed at over sixty-two thousand acres, *Letter* 47 (SC 98:122).

44. Young, *Nicaea to Chalcedon*, 267.

45. Theodoret, *Letter* 113 (SC 111:62).

46. Bardy, "Theodoret," 15:299.

47. Theodoret, *Letter* 113 (SC 111:62).

48. It is significant to note that Arian bishops had held the seat at Antioch from 330–360, and despite the ruling of the Council of Constantinople in 381, Arianism was still present within the Syrian communities to which Theodoret ministered. Glenn F. Chesnut, *The First Christian Histories: Eusebius, Socrates, Sozomen, Theodoret and Evagrius* (Macon, Ga.: Mercer University Press, 1986), 210–11.

49. Theodoret, *Haereticarum fabularum compendium* 1, 20 (PG 83:372).

50. Theodoret, *Letter* 83 (SC:98:208).

51. Theodoret, *Letters* 79 (SC 98:186), 81 (SC 98:196).

52. Theodoret, *Letter* 115 (SC 111:68).

53. Theodoret, *Letters* 42–47 (SC 98:106–124).

54. Theodoret, *Letter* 81 (SC 98:196).

55. Bardy, "Theodoret," 15:300.

56. Theodoret, *Reprehensio duodecim capitum seu anathematismorum Cyrilli*. Condemned by the Fifth Ecumenical Council in 553, this document is not extant. Nevertheless, Theodoret's text seems to be preserved in Cyril's response, *Epistola ad Euoptium adversus impugnationem duodecim capitum a Theodoreto editam* (PG 76:385–452).

57. Bardy, "Theodoret," 15:300.

58. Ibid.; Bardenhewer, *Geschichte der Altkirchlichen Literatur*, 223; Quasten, *Patrology*, 3:537; Cavalcanti, "Theodoret of Cyrrhus," 827; J. N. D. Kelly, *Early Christian Doctrines* (rev. ed.; London: Adam & Charles Black, 1977), 330.

59. Theodoret, *Letter* 172 (PG 83:1485).

60. Bardenhewer, *Geschichte der Altkirchlichen Literatur*, 223.

61. Chesnut, *The First Christian Histories*, 211; Cavalcanti, "Theodoret of Cyrrhus," 827.

62. Theodoret discusses this apologetic strategy in *Letter* 21 (SC 98:76) and *Letter* 104 (SC 111:26).

63. Kelly, *Early Christian Doctrine*, 330.

64. Theodoret, *Letter* 83 (SC 98:204–218). This letter was also preserved in the *Acta Conciliorum* and was instrumental in the later discussions of Theodoret's orthodoxy.

65. Bardy, "Theodoret," 15:301.

66. Theodoret, *Letter* 119 (SC 111:78).

67. Kelly, *Early Christian Doctrine*, 334.

68. He wrote his *Ecclesiastical History* during this period. Bardy, "Theodoret," 15:302.

69. Theodoret, *Letters* 138–140 (SC 111:138–150) illustrate this activity.

70. Bardy, "Theodoret," 15:302.

71. Kelly, *Early Christian Doctrine*, 340–41.

72. Marcellinus Comes (d. 534) states in his *Chronicle* that Theodoret wrote *contra* Eutyches and Dioscorus regarding the incarnation in 466. Honigmann notes a second edition of the

Eranistes was directed at these two figures, and it is not impossible that Theodoret himself could have been responsible. Ernst Honigmann, "Theodoret of Cyrrhus and Basil of Seleucia. The Time of their Death," *PST* 173 (1953): 175–80.

73. Cavalcanti, "Theodoret of Cyrrhus," 827.

74. Honigmann, "Time of Their Death," 175.

75. Theodoret, *Letter* 145 (SC 111:176).

76. For a detailed treatment of his writings see Bardenhewer, *Geschichte der Altkirchlichen Literatur*, 219–47; Quasten, *Patrology*, 3:538–554.

77. Theodoret, *Interpretatio in quatuordecim epistolas S. Pauli* (PG 82:35–878).

78. Theodoret, *Interpretatio in Canticum Canticorum* (PG 81:27–214).

79. Theodoret, *Interpretatio in Danielem* (PG 81:1255–1546).

80. Theodoret, *Interpretatio in Ezechielem* (PG 81:807–1256).

81. Theodoret, *Interpretatio in duodecim Prophetas Minores* (PG 81:1545–1988).

82. Theodoret's *Interpretatio in Isaiam* was known only in fragments until a full manuscript was discovered at the end of the nineteenth century. For the most recent critical edition, see August Möhle, *Theodoret von Kyros, Kommentar zu Jesaia* (MSU; Berlin: Weidmann, 1932).

83. Theodoret, *Interpretatio in Jeremiam* (PG 81:495–806).

84. Theodoret, *Interpretation in Psalmos* (PG 80:857–1998; PG 84:19–32).

85. Theodoret, *Quaestiones in Octateuchum* (PG 80:75–528).

86. Theodoret, *Quaestiones in libros Regnorum et Paralipomenon* (PG 80:527–858).

87. For a detailed treatment of his apologies, see Joseph Schulte, *Theodoret von Cyrus als Apologet: Ein Beitrag zur Geschichte der Apologetik* (ThSt; Wien: Von Mayer, 1904).

88. Theodoret, *Ad quaesita magorum* (Schulte, *Apologet*, 2–6).

89. Quasten, *Patrology*, 3:545.

90. Theodoret, *De providential orations decem* (PG 83:555–774).

91. Theodoret, *Graecarum affectionum curatio* (PG 83:783–1152).

92. Price, "Introduction," ix; Quasten, *Patrology*, 3:543.

93. Cyril, *Epistola ad Euoptium adversus impugnationem duodecim capitum a Theodoreto editam* (PG 76:385–452).

94. For the only surviving Greek fragments see M. Richard, "Les citations de Théodoret conservées dans la chaîne de Nicétas sur l'Évangile selon Luc," *RB* 43 (1934): 88–96.

95. Albert Ehrhard, *Die Cyrill von Alexandrien zugeschriebene Schrift Περὶ τῆς τοῦ Κυρίου ἐναν-θρωπήσεως, ein Werk des Theodoret von Cyrus* (Tübingen: H. Laupp, Jr., 1888).

96. Cyril, *De sancta et vivifica Trinitate* (PG 75:1147–1190); *De incarnatione Domini* (PG 75:1419–1478).

97. Theodoret, *Eranistes seu Polymorphus* (PG 83:27–336).

98. This is preserved as part of *Letter* 151 (PG 83:1433–1441).

99. See J. C. T. Otto, ed., *Justini philosophi et martyris opera quae feruntur omnia* (CACSS 4; Jenae: Libraria Hermanni Dufft, 1880).

100. See Ibid. (CACSS 5; Jenae: Libraria Hermanni Dufft, 1881).

101. Theodoret, *Historia ecclesiastica* (PG 82:882–1280).

102. Chesnut, *The First Christian Histories*, 210.

103. Theodoret, *Historia religiosa seu ascetica vivendi ratio* (PG 82:1283–1496).

104. Theodoret, *Haereticarum fabularum compendium* (PG 83:335–556).

105. Quasten, *Patrology*, 3:551.

106. Ibid., 3:552.

107. Theodoret, *Letter* 83 (SC:98:208).

108. For the fragments see PG 84:53–64.

109. Quasten, *Patrology*, 3:552.

110. See footnote number 2 of this chapter for detailed information on the available editions of Theodoret's correspondence.

111. Bradley Nassif, "'Spiritual Exegesis' in the School of Antioch," in *New Perspectives on Historical Theology: Essays in Memory of John Meyendorff* (ed. Bradley Nassif; Grand Rapids, Mich.: Eerdmans, 1996), 343–77.

112. Metropolitan Demetrios Trakatellis, "Theodoret's Commentary on Isaiah: A Synthesis of Exegetical Traditions," in *New Perspectives on Historical Theology: Essays in Memory of John Meyendorff* (ed. Bradley Nassif; Grand Rapids, Mich.: Eerdmans, 1996), 313–42.

113. Christoph Schäublin, *Untersuchengen zu Methode und Herkunft der Antiochenischen Exegese* (Köln-Bonn: Peter Hanstein, 1974); Frances Young, *Biblical Exegesis and the Formation of Christian Culture* (Cambridge: Cambridge University Press, 1997); "The Rhetorical Schools and their Influence on Patristic Exegesis," in *The Making of Orthodoxy: Essays in Honour of Henry Chadwick* (ed. Rowan Williams; Cambridge: Cambridge University Press, 1989).

114. John O'Keefe, "'A Letter that Killeth': Toward a Reassessment of Antiochene Exegesis, or Diodore, Theodore, and Theodoret on the Psalms" JECS 8 (2000): 88. Young also ties the concern for methodology to the theological response to Origen; "The Fourth Century Reaction against Allegory " StPatr 30 (1997): 124.

115. The terms were used interchangeably by the Alexandrians. Heinrich Kihn, "Über θεωρία und ἀλλεγορία nach den verlorenen hermeneutischen Schriften der Antioch-ener," *TQ* 20 (1880): 531–82.

116. Alberto Vaccari, "La θεωρία nella scuola esegetica di Antiocha," *Bib* 1 (1920): 3–36.

117. Paul Ternant, "La θεωρία d'Antioche dans le cadre des sens de l'Eriture," *Bib* 34 (1953): 135–58; 354–83; 456–86.

118. Bertrand de Margerie, "θεωρία et tradition dans l'École d'Antioch," in *Introduction à l'histoire de L'exégèse* (vol. 1; Paris: Cerf, 1980): 191.

119. Ibid., 204.

120. John Breck, *The Power of the Word in the Worshiping Church* (Crestwood, NY: St. Vladimir's Seminary, 1986), 97.

121. Francisco Seisedos, "La θεωρία antioquena," *EstBib* 11 (1952): 60.

122. Nassif, "The School of Antioch," 373.

123. Theodoret, *Interpretatio in quatuordecim epistolas S. Pauli* (PG 82:35).

124. Ibid. (PG 82:37).

125. Quasten, *Patrology* 3:539; Price, "Introduction," x; Alberto Viciano, "Theodoret von Kyros als Interpret des Apostels Paulus," *TGl* 80 (1990), 279; Bardy, "Theodoret," 15:325.

126. Jean-Noël Guinot, "Theodoret of Cyrus: Bishop and Exegete," in *The Bible in Greek Christian Antiquity* (ed. Paul M. Blowers; South Bend, Ind.: University of Notre Dame Press, 1997): 164; see also O'Keefe, "A Reassessment of Antiochene Exegesis," 99.

127. For example, Theodoret attacks Theodore of Mopsuestia a number of times for advocating what Theodoret calls Jewish exegesis. See Theodoret, *Interpretatio in Canticum Canticorum* (PG 81:860).

128. See the chapter entitled "La Critique textuelle dans les Commentaires de Théodoret," pages 167–252 in Jean-Noël Guinot, *L'Exégèse de Théodoret de Cyr* (ThH 100; Paris: Beauchesne, 1995), which is the definitive work on Theodoret's exegetical method.

129. This is the text which was formerly held to be a Lucianic recension. Guinot states that "this text...bears the mark of a number of literary touch-ups, mainly in the form of atticisms, and depends essentially on the Origenian recension in the *Hexapla*...It is better to speak...of an 'Antiochene edition' of the Septuagint which was placed later on under Lucian's patronage." Guinot, "Bishop and Exegete," 185.

130. Ibid., 169–79.

131. Ibid., 170.

132. In his commentaries Theodoret divides the biblical text into something akin to chapters (τόμοι), for which he provides an introduction that discusses the theme of the section.

133. Ibid., 172–73.

134. Theodoret uses the phrase ἐκ μεταφορκᾶς or the adverb τροπικῶς to refer to this type of reading.

135. Guinot, "Bishop and Exegete," 175.

136. For a detailed analysis of Theodoret's use of θεωρία, see G. W. Ashby, *Theodoret of Cyrrhus as Exegete of the Old Testament* (Grahamstown: Rhodes University Press, 1972), 56–104.

137. Francis Rossiter, "Messianic Prophecy according to Theodoret of Cyrus" (Ph.D. diss., The Pontifical Gregorian University, 1949), 264.

138. Guinot, "Bishop and Exegete," 176.

139. Ibid., 179.

140. Quasten, *Patrology*, 3:539.

141. Theodoret, *Interpretation in Psalmos* (PG 80:860).

142. Young, *Nicaea to Chalcedon*, 286.

143. Ibid.

144. Trakatellis, "A Synthesis of Exegetical Traditions," 341.

145. O'Keefe, "A Reassessment of Antiochene Exegesis," 92–96.

146. Ibid., 96. Theodoret, however, is still too restrictive in the application of figural readings for O'Keefe, 99.

147. Ashby states, "The midway position between Theodore and Cyril is typical of Theodoret as exegete." Ashby, *Theodoret of Cyrrhus as Exegete*, 26. Likewise, Rossiter notes that "Theodoret as exegete manages a compromise position between the Scylla of allegorism and the Charybdis of historical-grammatical literalism." Rossiter, "Messianic Prophecy according to Theodoret of Cyrus," 38. Guinot concludes that "son exégèse ne realize pas seulement entre les tendances extrêmes d'Antioche et d'Alexandrie une heureuse synthèse: elle

dépasse en fait les querelles d'ècoles." Guinot, *L'Exégèse de Théodoret de Cyr*, 827. See also Gustave Bardy, who labels Theodoret's exegesis as "modéré" in "Interprétation chez les pères," *DBSup* 4: 582.

148. Young, *From Nicea to Chalcedon*, 285; Guinot, "Bishop and Exegete," 183.

149. Theodoret, *Interpretatio in quatuordecim epistolas S. Pauli* (PG 82:37).

150. Photius, *The Bibliotheca*, 164a–64b (trans. N. G. Wilson; London: Duckworth, 1994).

151. Guinot, "Bishop and Exegete," 163.

152. Price, "Introduction," x.

153. The Three Chapters controversy of this council centered over the anathamatization of the person and writings of Theodore of Mopsuestia, certain writings of Theodoret of Cyrus, and the letter of Ibas to Maris. These steps were taken in an effort to make peace with monophysites returning to the church.

154. Nestorius, *The Bazaar of Heracleides* (trans. G. R. Driver and Leonard Hodgson; Oxford: Clarendon, 1925); H. E. W. Turner, "Nestorius Reconsidered," StPatr 13 (1975): 306–321; M. V. Anastos, "Nestorius Was Orthodox," *DOP* 16 (1962): 119–140; Anthony Christian Daly, *Nestorius in the Bazaar of Heracleides: a Christology compatible with the third letter and anathemas of Cyril of Alexandria* (Ph.D. diss., University of California, Los Angeles, 1983); Richard Kyle, "Nestorius: The Partial Rehabilitation of a Heretic" *JETS* 32 (1989): 73–83; R. C. Chesnut, "The Two Prosopa in Nestorius' Bazaar of Heraclides" *JTS* 29 (1978): 392–409.

155. J. A. McGuckin maintains that Nestorius' fate was sealed before the Council of Ephesus because his initial actions as patriarch had managed to make enemies of the monks of Contantinople as well as the Byzantine aristocracy, particularly Augusta Pulcheria, the sister of the emperor. J. A. McGuckin, "Nestorius and the Political Factions of Fifth-century Byzantium: Factors in His Personal Downfall" *BJRL* 78 (1996): 7–21.

156. Young concludes that Theodoret's christological thought remained consistent throughout the controversy, although he allowed for some changes in emphasis and terminology. Young, *From Nicaea to Chalcedon*, 284.

157. Furthermore, the writings which were banned in 553 were condemned by Pope Vigilius *secundum subiectos intelligentiae sensus*, i.e., they had been interpreted in a manner different from that intended by the author, Theodoret. Berthold Altaner, *Patrology* (trans. Hilda C. Graef; New York: Herder & Herder, 1961), 397.

158. Price, "Introduction," x.

159. Ibid.

CHAPTER THREE

Translation of Commentary

This chapter will provide a translation of chapters 9–11 of Theodoret of Cyrus' Romans commentary. The purpose of this chapter is to set Theodoret's application of the Elijah *redivivus* tradition to Romans 11:26 within the broader context of his overall exegesis of Romans 9–11, which he treats as a distinct unit of the epistle.

The Greek Text

Since there is no modern critical edition of Theodoret's commentary on the letters of Paul (*Interpretatio in xiv epistulas sancti Pauli*), the following translation is from the text in J.-P. Migne's Patrologia Graeca 82.[1] Migne's text is a reprint of the edition published by J. L. Schulze in the eighteenth century,[2] and Schulze's text is an augmented version of the seventeenth century edition that Jacques Sirmond[3] compiled using two codices, Codex Augustanus and Codex Bavaricus. The New Testament text that Theodoret cites in his commentary is, according to R. C. Hill, "generally if not consistently" the Koine or Byzantine text.[4] The scope of this translation is limited to chapters 9–11 of Theodoret's Romans commentary.[5]

Translation

Part Four[6]

Ὅτι μὲν ἀναγκαία, καὶ τῶν ἀρρήτων πρόξενος ἀγαθῶν τοῖς πιστεύουσιν, ἡ τοῦ Θεοῦ καὶ Σωτῆρος ἡμῶν ἐνανθρώπησις, διαρρήδην ἀπέδειξεν ὁ θεῖος Ἀπόστολος. Ἰουδαίους γὰρ ἤλεγξεν ἐκ τῆς τοῦ νόμου θέσεως μείζοσι κατηγορίαις ὑπευθύνους γεγενημένους, καὶ τοὺς ἄλλους ἅπαντας τῆς φύσεως παραβαίνοντας τὸν νόμον· καὶ γυμνώσας τῆς τιμωρίας τὴν ἀπειλήν, τῆς εὐαγγελικῆς χάριτος τὰ δῶρα παρέθηκε, καὶ τὴν ἐκ τῆς πίστεως σωτηρίαν ὑπέδειξεν. Ἵνα δὲ μήτε Ἰουδαῖοι δυσχεραίνωσι, κατηγορεῖσθαι τὸν νόμον ὑπειληφότες, μήτε μὴν οἱ περὶ τὴν Παλαιὰν ἐπαχθεῖς Διαθήκην αἱρετικοὶ, πρόφασιν εἰς τὴν κατὰ τοῦ νόμου συκοφαντίαν λάβωσιν ἐκ τῆς γεγενημένης παρεξετάσεως, ἔδειξεν ἀναγκαίως τοῦ νόμου τὸ χρήσιμον, καὶ πολλαῖς αὐτὸν ἐταινίωσεν εὐφημίαις. Ἐπειδὴ δὲ πάλιν Ἰουδαῖοι, τὸν πατριάρχην Ἀβραὰμ προβαλλόμενοι, καὶ τὰς πρὸς αὐτὸν ὑπὸ τοῦ Θεοῦ γεγενημένας ἐπαγγελίας, ἐναντίον ταύταις ἐπειρῶντο δεικνύναι τῶν ἀποστόλων τὸ κήρυγμα, παρὰ τὴν θείαν ὑπόσχεσιν τοῖς ἔθνεσι προσφερόμενον, ἀναγκαίως καὶ τούτους εἰς μέσον προσφέρει τοὺς λόγους· καὶ σοφῶς ἄγαν διαλύει, καὶ Γραφικαῖς μαρτυρίαις, καὶ παραδείγμασι παλαιοῖς εἰς καιρὸν κεχρημένος, καὶ δεικνὺς ἐναργῶς τῶν θείων ὑποσχέσεων τὴν ἀλήθειαν. Μέλλων μέντοι τῆς Ἰουδαίων ἀπιστίας κατηγορεῖν, πρῶτον ἣν ἔχει περὶ αὐτοὺς φιλοστοργίαν γυμνοῖ, καί φησι·

It is necessary that the Divine Apostle demonstrate distinctly that the incarnation of our God and Savior is the provider of inexpressible good to those who believe. For Paul has censured both the Jews, who have become liable to greater charges due to the giving of the Law, and the Gentiles,[7] who transgress the law of nature. And after laying bare the threat of punishment,[8] he places beside it the gifts of evangelical grace and shows[9] that salvation comes from faith. But in order that the Jews might not be annoyed, supposing the law to be under attack, and in order that the ponderous heretics—regarding the Old Testament—might not be given an excuse[10] for their calumny against the law on the basis of the existing comparison, Paul points out, of necessity, the usefulness of the law and crowns it with many words of praise. But since the Jews again, by putting forward[11] the patriarch Abraham and the promises made by God to him, were trying to prove that the apostolic message—being offered to the Gentiles against the divine promise[12]—is contrary to these promises, Paul must focus on these matters out of necessity. He very wisely settles the matter by employing both scriptural witnesses and ancient examples at the appropriate time, clearly demonstrating the truth of the divine promises. Nevertheless, despite the fact that he is about to accuse the Jews of disbelief, Paul first lays bare the tender affection that he has for them; he says:

Romans 9:1[13]

α'. Ἀλήθειαν λέγω ἐν Χριστῷ, οὐ ψεύδομαι, συμμαρτυρούσης μοι τῆς συνειδήσεώς μου ἐν Πνεύματι ἁγίῳ. Καὶ ψεύδους ἐλεύθερον, καὶ ἀληθείᾳ κοσμούμενον τὸ ῥηθησόμενον ἔδειξε. Τοῦ γὰρ θείου Πνεύματος τὴν χάριν μετὰ τοῦ συνειδότος εἰς μαρτυρίαν ἐκάλεσε, πείθων δι' ἁπάντων μὴ ἀπιστῆσαι τῷ λόγῳ.

1. *I speak the truth in Christ, I am not lying, my conscience bears witness with me in the Holy Spirit.* He points out that what will be mentioned next is free of falsehood and adorned with truth. He called upon the help of the Divine

Spirit as a witness, along with his own conscience, trying by all of this to persuade the reader to believe the forthcoming statement.

Romans 9:2

[82.149]¹⁴ β'. Ὅτι λύπη μοι ἐστί μεγάλη, καὶ ἀδιάλειπτος ὀδύνη τῇ καρδίᾳ μου. Ἀτελὴς μὲν ἡ συνθήκη τοῦ λόγου. Ἔδει γὰρ προσκεῖσθαι, διὰ τὴν Ἰουδαίων ἢ ἀποβολὴν, ἢ ἀπιστίαν, τὴν ἀδιάλειπτον εἶναι λύπην. Φειδοῖ δὲ κεχρημένος, ταῦτα μὲν οὐ τέθεικε τὰ ῥήματα, τὴν δὲ τούτων διὰ τῶν ἑξῆς διδάσκει διάνοιαν. Λέγει δὲ οὕτως·

2. *That there is great sorrow and unceasing pain in my heart.* The composition of the sentence is incomplete, for he should have added that his sorrow was unceasing because of the rejection or unbelief of the Jews. Writing sparingly, Paul does not include these actual words, but he does indicate their sense through that which follows. He puts it this way:

Romans 9:3

γ'. *Ηὐχόμην γὰρ αὐτὸς ἐγὼ ἀνάθεμα εἶναι ἀπὸ τοῦ Χριστοῦ ὑπὲρ τῶν ἀδελφῶν μου, τῶν συγγενῶν μου τῶν κατὰ σάρκα.* Τὸ ἀνάθεμα διπλῆν ἔχει τὴν διάνοιαν. Καὶ γὰρ τὸ ἀφιερωμένον τῷ Θεῷ, ἀνάθημα ὀνομάζεται, καὶ τὸ τούτου ἀλλότριον τὴν αὐτὴν ἔχει προσηγορίαν. Καὶ τὸ μὲν δεύτερον ἐν τῇ πρὸς Κορινθίους ἡμᾶς ἐδίδαξεν ὁ θεῖος Ἀπόστολος· «Εἴ τις γὰρ οὐ φιλεῖ τὸν Κύριον ἡμῶν Ἰησοῦν Χριστὸν, ἤτω ἀνάθεμα.» Τὸ δέ γε πρότερον καὶ ἡ κοινὴ διδάσκει συνήθεια· ἀναθήματα γὰρ καλοῦμεν τὰ τῷ Θεῷ προσφερόμενα· καὶ αὐτὸς ὁ τῶν ὅλων Θεὸς, τὴν Ἱεριχὼ πόλιν ἀνάθεμα γενέσθαι κελεύσας. Ἐνταῦθα μέντοι ὁ μακάριος Παῦλος τὴν δευτέραν διάνοιαν τέθεικεν, ἣν ἔχει περὶ τοὺς ὁμοφύλους διδάσκων διάθεσιν. Καὶ οὐκ εἶπεν, Ἐβουλόμην, ἀλλ', *Ηὐχόμην* ἀλλότριος εἶναι τοῦ Χριστοῦ, ὥστε τοὺς κατὰ σάρκα μου συγγενεῖς, προσοικειωθέντας αὐτῷ, τὴν σωτηρίαν καρπώσασθαι. Σφόδρα δὲ ἁρμοδίως παρενέθηκε καὶ τὸ, *ἐγὼ αὐτός,* τῶν ἤδη περὶ τῆς ἀγάπης τῆς περὶ τὸν Χριστὸν εἰρημένων ἀναμιμνήσκων, καὶ μονονουχὶ λέγων, ὅτι Ἐγώ, ὃν οὔτε ζωὴ, οὔτε θάνατος, οὔτε τὰ ἐνεστῶτα, οὔτε τὰ μέλλοντα, οὔτε τις κτίσις ἑτέρα χωρίσαι δυνήσεται ἀπὸ τῆς ἀγάπης τοῦ Θεοῦ τῆς ἐν Χριστῷ Ἰησοῦ, ὑπὲρ τῆς Ἰουδαίων σωτηρίας ἥδιστα ἂν ἐχωρίσθην αὐτοῦ. Δῆλον δὲ ὅτι οὐ τούτους προτιμῶν τοῦ σεσωκότος, ἀλλὰ τὸν περὶ ἐκείνων ἔρωτά τε καὶ πόθον δηλῶν, ταῦτα εἴρηκε, πάντας ὑποκύπτοντας ἰδεῖν ποθῶν, καὶ ἀσπαστῶς δεχομένους τὸ σωτήριον κήρυγμα. Πιθανὸν δὲ τὸν λόγον κατασκευάζων, ἐπιδείκνυσιν αὐτῶν καὶ τὴν προτέραν εὐγένειαν, καὶ τῶν δωρεῶν τῶν θεοσδότων τὸν πλοῦτον, καί φησιν·

3. *For I would pray that I myself might be accursed, cut off from Christ for the sake of my brothers, my relatives according to the flesh.* The word anathema has two senses. For that which is consecrated to God is called anathema, and a sense

completely foreign to this has the same designation. The Divine Apostle taught us this second sense in the letter to the Corinthians, "For if anyone does not love our Lord Jesus Christ, let that one be anathema."[15] Now, the general use, at any rate, teaches the former sense, for we call anathema the things that are offered to God. Even the God of All himself commanded the city of Jericho to be anathema.[16] Here, the blessed Paul surely uses the second sense in order to show the disposition that he has toward his kin. And he did not say, "I would wish," but rather "I would pray" to be estranged from Christ so that my relatives according to the flesh, having been associated with Christ, might bear the fruit of salvation. And very fittingly Paul also inserted the words "I myself," recalling what has already been said about love in regard to Christ, and all but saying that I—whom neither life nor death, neither the things present nor those to come, nor any other creature will be able to separate from the love of God which is in Christ Jesus—I would most gladly be separated from him for the sake of the salvation of the Jews. It is clear that Paul has said these things not because he prefers the Jews over the one who saves, but rather he says them in order to show both the love and longing he has concerning them, yearning to see all bow down and receive with welcome the saving message.[17] And constructing a persuasive argument, he points out the superiority of their noble descent and the richness of their god-given gifts, and he says:

Romans 9:4

δ'. *Οἵτινές εἰσιν Ἰσραηλῖται.* Ἦν γὰρ καὶ τοῦτο τὸ ὄνομα πολυθρύλλητον, ἐπιτεθὲν μὲν παρὰ τοῦ Θεοῦ τῷ προπάτορι, καθάπερ δέ τις κλῆρος εἰς τοὺς ἐκγόνους παραπεμφθέν. *Ὧν ἡ υἱοθεσία.* Καὶ τοῦδε γὰρ μετέλαχον τοῦ ὀνόματος. «Υἱὸς γὰρ, φησὶ, πρωτότοκός μου Ἰσραήλ.» *Καὶ ἡ δόξα.* Περιφανεῖς γὰρ ἀπὸ τῶν θαυμάτων ἐγένοντο. *Καὶ αἱ διαθῆκαι.* Οὐ γὰρ μόνον τὴν παλαιὰν, ἀλλὰ καὶ τὴν καινὴν αὐτοῖς ὑπέσχετο δώσειν. «Θήσομαι γὰρ, φησὶ, τῷ οἴκῳ Ἰσραὴλ διαθήκην καινὴν, οὐ κατὰ τὴν διαθήκην ἣν διεθέμην τοῖς πατράσιν αὐτῶν, ἀλλὰ ταύτην αὐτοὶ λαβεῖν οὐκ ἠθέλησαν.» *Καὶ ἡ νομοθεσία.* Αὐτοῖς γὰρ τὸν Μωσαϊκὸν ἐδεδώκει νόμον. *Καὶ ἡ λατρεία.* Τῶν γὰρ ἄλλων αὐτοὺς [82.152] ἐθνῶν προτιμήσας, τὴν νομικὴν ἱερουργίαν ἐδίδαξε. *Καὶ αἱ ἐπαγγελίαι.* Ἴσως αἵ τε πρὸς τοὺς πατέρας παρὰ τοῦ Θεοῦ γεγενημέναι, καὶ αἱ διὰ τῶν προφητῶν προσενηνεγμέναι.

4. *Who are Israelites.* For this name was well-known, having been given by God to the forefather, and having been passed on like some allotment of land to the offspring. *Theirs is the adoption.* For they were given a share in the allotment of this name. "For, he says, Israel is my firstborn son."[18] *And the glory.* For they became illustrious[19] because of the wonders. *And the covenants.* For he

promised to give them not only the old but also the new. "For, he says, I will make a new covenant with the house of Israel, not according to the covenant which I made with their fathers; this covenant they did not desire to keep."[20] *And the law-giving.* For he had given them the Mosaic law. *And the worship.* For having preferred them over the other nations, he taught them the lawful religious service. *And the promises.* Perhaps both the things which have come to pass for the fathers from God, and the things which are brought forth through the prophets.

Romans 9:5

ε΄. *Ὧν οἱ πατέρες.* Οἱ ἀοίδιμοί τε καὶ πολυθρύλλητοι, ὧν Θεὸς ἐχρημάτισεν ὁ Θεός. Εἶτα τελευταῖον τέθεικε τὸ μέγιστον τῶν ἀγαθῶν. *Καὶ ἐξ ὧν ὁ Χριστὸς τὸ κατὰ σάρκα, ὁ ὢν ἐπὶ πάντων Θεὸς εὐλογητὸς εἰς τοὺς αἰῶνας. Ἀμήν.* Καὶ ἤρκει μὲν ἡ τοῦ κατὰ σάρκα προσθήκη, παραδηλῶσαι τοῦ Δεσπότου Χριστοῦ τὴν θεότητα. Ἀλλ' ὥσπερ ἐν τῷ προοιμίῳ, εἰρηκώς· «Τοῦ γενομένου ἐκ σπέρματος Δαβὶδ κατὰ σάρκα·» ἐπήγαγε· «Τοῦ ὁρισθέντος Υἱοῦ Θεοῦ ἐν δυνάμει·» οὕτως ἐνταῦθα εἰπὼν τὸ, *κατὰ σάρκα,* προστέθεικε τὸ, *Ὧν ἐπὶ πάντα Θεὸς εὐλογητὸς εἰς τοὺς αἰῶνας. Ἀμήν.* Καὶ τῶν φύσεων δεικνὺς τὴν διαφορὰν, καὶ τοῦ θρήνου διδάσκων τὸ εὔλογον, ὅτι ἐξ αὐτῶν μὲν κατὰ σάρκα ὁ ἐπὶ πάντων Θεὸς, αὐτοὶ δὲ τῆς εὐγενείας ἐξέπεσον, καὶ ἀλλότριοι τῆς συγγενείας ἐκείνης ἐγένοντο. Καὶ τὰς θρηνούσας ἐμιμήσατο γυναῖκας, αἳ τῶν τεθνεώτων καὶ θρηνουμένων, καὶ τὴν ὥραν τοῦ σώματος, καὶ τὴν ἀκμὴν τῆς ἡλικίας, καὶ τὴν τῶν προγόνων περιφάνειαν, καὶ τὴν περιουσίαν, καὶ τὴν δυναστείαν ἐνυφαίνουσι τοῖς θρήνοις. Οὕτω μέντοι γυμνώσας τὴν περὶ Ἰουδαίους φιλοστοργίαν, ἄρχεται λοιπὸν τοῦ προκειμένου νοήματος.

5. *Theirs are the fathers.* Those both famous and infamous, whose god was called God. And then, last of all, Paul has put the greatest of the good things. *And from them comes the Christ, according to the flesh, who is God over all, blessed forever.*[21] *Amen.* The addition of "according to the flesh" is sufficient to intimate the divinity of the Lord Christ. But just as in the opening of Romans where Paul added the phrase "who was appointed[22] Son of God in power" after the words "who came from the seed of David according to the flesh," in the same way here, having said "according to the flesh", Paul has added the phrase "who is God over all, blessed forever. Amen." He shows the reasonableness of the lament by pointing out the distinction of the natures. For, on the one hand, the God who is over all came from them according to the flesh, but, on the other hand, they have fallen from their noble descent, and foreigners have become related to it. And so he imitates the women who sing funeral dirges; they weave together in the funeral songs the prime of the body and the flower of age, the notoriety of the ancestors, and the abundance and

power of those who are dead and being lamented. Nevertheless, having thus exposed his affection for the Jews, he takes up the thought which lies at hand.

Romans 9:6

ϛ'. Οὐχ οἷον δὲ ὅτι ἐκπέπτωκεν ὁ λόγος τοῦ Θεοῦ. Ἐγὼ μὲν, φησὶ, οὐκ ἐβουλόμην μόνον, ἀλλὰ καὶ ηὐχόμην ἀλλότριος εἶναι τοῦ Χριστοῦ, εἴπερ οἷόν τε ἦν διὰ τῆς ἐμῆς ἀλλοτριώσεως Ἰουδαίους τῶν ἐπηγγελμένων τυχεῖν ἀγαθῶν. Ἀλλ' ὅμως, καὶ τούτων ἀντιλεγόντων, καὶ σωτηρίαν οὐ βουλομένων καρπώσασθαι, ἔχουσι τἀληθὲς αἱ πρὸς τοὺς πατέρας ἐπαγγελίαι. Πῶς ἔχουσιν; Οὐ γὰρ πάντες οἱ ἐξ Ἰσραὴλ, οὗτοι Ἰσραήλ. Οὐ γὰρ τῆς φύσεως ὁ Θεὸς, ἀλλὰ τῆς ἀρετῆς ἐπιζητεῖ συγγένειαν. Εἶτα διδάσκει τοῦτο σαφέστερον.

6. *For it is not as though the word of God has failed.* For I, he says, would not only wish but I would even pray to be estranged from Christ, if indeed it were possible through my estrangement for the Jews to obtain the good things which have been promised to them. But while they oppose[23] and fail to bear salvation as fruit, the promises made to the patriarchs are still true. How can this be? *For not all who are of* [24] *Israel are Israel.* For God does not seek after the one who is related by nature but rather by virtue. Paul then goes on to teach this more clearly.

Romans 9:7

ζ'. Οὐδὲ ὅτι εἰσὶ σπέρμα Ἀβραάμ, πάντες τέκνα· τουτέστι Θεοῦ. Τοῦτο γὰρ μετὰ βραχέα διδάσκει. Ἀλλ' ἐν Ἰσαὰκ κληθήσεταί σοι σπέρμα. Καὶ τεθεικὼς τοῦ Θεοῦ τὴν ὑπόσχεσιν, ἀναπτύσσει ταύτην, καὶ τῇ ἑρμηνείᾳ σαφῆ τὸν λόγον ποιεῖ.

7. *Nor, because they are descendants of Abraham, are all children,* that is, of God, for he teaches this with brevity. *But through Isaac shall your descendants be recognized.*[25] Having included the promise of God, Paul unfolds this and makes the statement clear by interpretation.

Romans 9:8

η'. Τουτέστιν, οὐ τὰ τέκνα τῆς σαρκὸς, ταῦτα τέκνα τοῦ Θεοῦ, ἀλλὰ τὰ τέκνα τῆς ἐπαγγελίας, λογίζεται εἰς σπέρμα. Καλεῖ δὲ σαρκὸς μὲν τέκνα, τὰ κατὰ τὴν τῆς φύσεως ἀκολουθίαν γεγεν[ν]ημένα· ἐπαγγελίας δὲ, τὰ κατὰ χάριν παρεσχημένα.

8. *That is, the children of the flesh are not the children of God, but rather the children of the promise are regarded as descendants.* On the one hand, he calls those who have been born according to the sequence of nature children of the flesh,

and on the other, he calls those who have been produced according to grace children of the promise.

Romans 9:9

θ'. Ἐπαγγελίας γὰρ ὁ λόγος οὗτος. Κατὰ τὸν καιρὸν τοῦτον ἐλεύσομαι, καὶ ἔσται τῇ Σάρρᾳ [82.153] υἱός. Τῆς γὰρ φύσεως ἀπειρηκυίας, κατὰ θείαν φιλοτιμίαν ἀπεφάνθη πατήρ. Λέγει δὲ τοῦτο, ὅτι καὶ Ἰσμαὴλ τοῦ Ἀβραὰμ ἦν υἱὸς, καὶ πρωτότοκος υἱός. Διὰ τί τοίνυν μέγα φρονεῖς, ὦ Ἰουδαῖε, ὡς μόνος σπέρμα τοῦ Ἀβραὰμ προσαγορευόμενος; Εἰ δὲ νομίζεις ἐκεῖνον, ὡς ἡμίδουλον, ἐκβεβλῆσθαι τῆς συγγενείας, οὐκ εἰκότως νομίζεις. Ἐκ πατέρων γὰρ, ἀλλ' οὐκ ἐκ μητέρων, ἔθος γενεαλογεῖν τῇ θείᾳ Γραφῇ. Καὶ ἠδύνατο μὲν ὁ θεῖος Ἀπόστολος, καὶ τοὺς ἐκ τῆς Χεττούρας γεγεννημένους εἰς μέσον παραγαγεῖν, καὶ δεῖξαι τούτους ἐξ ἐλευθέρας μὲν γεγεννημένους, σπέρμα δὲ τοῦ Ἀβραὰμ οὐ καλουμένους. Ῥάδιον ἦν αὐτῷ καὶ τοὺς δύο καὶ δέκα παῖδας τοῦ Ἰακὼβ ἐκ διαφόρων δεῖξαι μητέρων, καὶ τοὺς τέτταρας ἡμιδούλους, καὶ ὅλους Ἰσραὴλ χρηματίζοντας, καὶ οὐδὲν ἐκ τῆς τῶν μητέρων παραβλαβέντας δουλείας. Ἀλλὰ μετὰ φειδοῦς τοὺς ἐλέγχους προσφέρων, τοῦτο μὲν παραλέλοιπεν, ἐκ πολλοῦ δὲ τοῦ περιόντος ἐνίκησε. Τεθεικὼς γὰρ τὸ ὑπὸ τοῦ Θεοῦ πρὸς τὸν Ἀβραὰμ εἰρημένον, ὅτι Ἐν Ἰσαὰκ κληθήσεταί σοι σπέρμα, δείκνυσιν οὐδὲ τὸ τούτου γένος ἅπαν τῆσδε τῆς εὐλογίας μετειληφός. Τῶν γὰρ τούτου παίδων ὁ μὲν τὴν εὐλογίαν εἴληφεν, ὁ δὲ ταύτης διήμαρτε. Τοῦτο γὰρ ἐπήγαγεν·

9. *For this is the word of promise: "At the appointed time I will come, and Sarah will have a son.* For though forbidden by nature, Abraham became a father[26] by means of divine benefaction.[27] And Paul says that Ishmael was also a son of Abraham, even a firstborn son. Therefore, why are you so high-minded, O Jew, as if you alone are called a descendant of Abraham? For if you consider Ishmael, as a half-slave, to have been cast out of the family, then you are not thinking reasonably. It is customary in the divine Scripture to trace a person's genealogy from the fathers, not from the mothers. The divine apostle could have brought up those children born from Keturah and pointed out that they were born from a free woman, yet they are not called descendants of Abraham. It would have also been easy for him to point out that the twelve sons of Jacob came from different mothers, and four were half-slaves,[28] yet all of them bore the name Israel, and none of them were hindered by the slavery of their mothers. But putting forward the evidence with economy, he leaves all of this unsaid; nevertheless, he still prevails by means of the great deal of proof that remains at hand. For having included that which was said by God to Abraham, "Through Isaac shall your descendants be recognized," he proves that not all of this race[29] shares the blessing. For one of these sons has received the blessing, while one failed to obtain this blessing. So he brings this up:

Romans 9:10–13

ι'–ιγ'. *Οὐ μόνον δὲ, ἀλλὰ καὶ Ῥεβέκκα ἐξ ἑνὸς κοίτην ἔχουσα Ἰσαὰκ τοῦ πατρὸς ἡμῶν. Μήτε γὰρ γεννηθέντων, μηδὲ πραξάντων τι ἀγαθὸν, ἢ κακὸν (ἵνα ἡ κατ' ἐκλογὴν πρόθεσις τοῦ Θεοῦ μένῃ), οὐκ ἐξ ἔργων, ἀλλ' ἐκ τοῦ καλοῦντος, ἐρρέθη πρὸς αὐτήν, ὅτι Ὁ μείζων δουλεύσει τῷ ἐλάττονι.* Εἰ νομίζεις, φησί, διὰ τὴν Σάρραν προτιμηθῆναι τὸν Ἰσαὰκ τοῦ τε Ἰσμαὴλ καὶ τῶν ἀπὸ τῆς Χεττούρας γενομένων παίδων τῷ Ἀβραὰμ, τί ἂν εἴπῃς περὶ τῆς Ῥεβέκκας; Ἐνταῦθα γὰρ καὶ μία μήτηρ, καὶ εἷς πατὴρ, καὶ μία σύλληψις· δίδυμοι γὰρ οἱ παῖδες. Τοῦτο γὰρ εἶπεν· «*Ἐξ ἑνὸς κοίτην ἔχουσα*» ἀντὶ τοῦ, Κατὰ τὸν αὐτὸν καιρὸν ἀμφοτέρους συνέλαβεν. Ἀλλ' ὅμως ὁ μὲν θεοφιλής, ὁ δὲ τῆς θείας κηδεμονίας ἀνάξιος. Καὶ οὐκ ἀνέμεινεν ὁ Θεὸς τῶν πραγμάτων τὴν πεῖραν, ἀλλ' ἔτι κυϊσκομένων τὴν τούτων διαφορὰν προηγόρευσε. Προηγόρευ[σ]ε δὲ, τὴν τούτων πρόθεσιν προμαθών. Οὐ γὰρ ἄδικος ἡ ἐκλογὴ, ἀλλὰ τῇ προθέσει τῶν ἀνθρώπων συμβαίνουσα. Εἶτα καὶ προφητικὴν μαρτυρίαν προσφέρει. *Καθὼς γέγραπται· Τὸν Ἰακὼβ ἠγάπησα, τὸν δὲ Ἡσαῦ ἐμίσησα.* Οὐ τοίνυν τῇ φύσει προσέχει, ἀλλὰ ἀρετὴν μόνην ἐπιζητεῖ. Τοῦτο γὰρ διὰ πλειόνων κατασκευάζει.

10–13. *And not only that, but there is Rebecca also, who conceived twins*[30] *by one man, Isaac, our father. For they had neither been born nor had done anything good or bad—in order that God's purpose according to election might continue, not by works but by the one who calls—when it was said to her, "The older will serve the younger."* If you suppose, he says, that Isaac was preferred to Ishmael as well as to the children born to Abraham from Keturah on account of Sarah, then what would you say concerning Rebecca? For here there is one mother, one father, and one conception; for the children were twins. For this reason Paul says, "conceived by one," that is, she conceived both at the same time. But nevertheless, one is highly favored by God, and the other is deemed unworthy of divine care. And God did not wait for the proof of the matter, but while they were still in the womb, he foretold the difference between them. Since he knew their purpose beforehand, he foretold it. For election is not unjust, rather it corresponds to the plan[31] for humanity.[32] And then Paul cites a prophetic witness: *Just as it is written: Jacob I loved, but Esau I hated.* Accordingly, God is not concerned about one's natural origin,[33] but he seeks for virtue alone. Paul builds on this further.

Romans 9:14

ιδ'. *Τί οὖν ἐροῦμεν; μὴ ἀδικία παρὰ τῷ Θεῷ; Μὴ γένοιτο.* Οὐκ ἔχει, φησὶν, ἡ θεία ψῆφος τὸ ἄδικον, ἀλλὰ τῷ δικαίῳ κοσμεῖται. Καὶ τοῦτο δεῖξαι δυνάμενος, καὶ διδάξαι σαφῶς, ὡς οὐ τῇ φύσει προσέχειν ἔθος τῷ τῶν ὅλων Θεῷ, ἀλλ' ὅτι γνώμην ἀρίστην ἐπιζητεῖ· καὶ ἀναμνῆσαι αὐτούς, ὡς πολλοῖς πολλάκις παρεδόθησαν πολεμίοις, οὐδεμιᾶς διὰ τοὺς προγόνους φειδοῦς ἀπολαύσαντες, ἐπειδὴ τὴν ἐκείνων [82.156] οὐκ ἐζήλωσαν ἀρετήν· καὶ ὅτι Βαβυλωνίοις μὲν αὐτοὶ παρεδόθησαν ἅπαντες· Ἀβιμέλεχ δὲ, καὶ δοῦλος ὢν, καὶ Αἰθίοψ, σωτηρίας τετύχηκε διὰ τὴν εὐσέβειαν· τοῦτο μὲν οὐ ποιεῖ, πλῆξαι μὴ βουλόμενος· δείκνυσι δὲ τὰς θείας οἰκονομίας ὑπερβαινούσας τὸν ἀνθρώπινον λογισμὸν, καὶ πολλοὺς μὲν παρανομίας τολμῶντας, οὐ πάντας δὲ δίκας εἰσπραττομένους. Καὶ γὰρ ἐν τῇ ἐρήμῳ οἱ πλεῖστοι μὲν τοῦ μόσχου τὴν εἰκόνα προσεκύνησαν ὡς Θεὸν, ἀλλ' οὐχ ἅπαντες ἔδοσαν δίκας· ἀλλ' οἱ μὲν ἐκολάσθησαν, οἱ δὲ ταῖς ἐκείνων τιμωρίαις ἐσωφρονίσθησαν. Οὕτω τὸν Φαραὼ τιμωρούμενος, πολλοῖς ὠφέλειαν διὰ τούτου προσήνεγκε. Καὶ ταῦτα τέθεικεν ὁ θεῖος Ἀπόστολος. Λέγει δὲ οὕτως·

14. *What then shall we say? Is there injustice with God? By no means!* The divine decree, he says, does not possess injustice, but rather he rules with justice. And Paul is able to demonstrate this and to teach plainly how it is not customary by nature to give heed to the God of All, but that God seeks after the most virtuous mind. And Paul is able to remind them how they were frequently handed over to many enemies—not having the benefit of being spared on account of the forefathers, since they did not strive after[34] their virtue—and that they all were handed over to the Babylonians. But Abimelech, despite being a servant and Ethiopian, obtained salvation because of piety. Paul does not do this desiring to confound, but he shows that the divine plans surpass human reason, enduring many transgressions while not exacting all penalties. For even in the wilderness most of the people worshipped the image of the calf as God, but not all paid the penalty. Some were punished, and others were chastened by the punishment of those. In this manner, by visiting vengeance upon Pharaoh, God brought a benefit to many through this act. Now the Divine Apostle has assumed[35] these things, and he puts it this way:

Romans 9:15

ιε'. *Τῷ γὰρ Μωσῇ λέγει· Ἐλεήσω ὅν ἄν ἐλεῶ, καὶ οἰκτειρήσω ὅν ἄν οἰκτείρω.* Ταῦτα δὲ ἐπὶ τῆς μοσχοποιίας εἴρηκεν ὁ Θεός. Ἀναγκαίως δὲ καὶ τοῦ Μωσέως ἐμνημόνευσεν, ἵνα καὶ διὰ τοῦ εἰρηκότος, καὶ διὰ τοῦ ἀκηκοότος, δείξῃ τῶν εἰρημένων τὸ ἀξιόπιστον. Εἶτα ἐπισυλλογίζεται·

15. *For he says to Moses, "I will have mercy on whomever I have mercy, and I will have compassion on whomever I have compassion."*[36] God spoke these words about the calf-maker. But Moses is mentioned of necessity, in order that Paul might prove the trustworthiness of what was said, both through the one who spoke and the one who heard. Then Paul concludes:

Romans 9:16

ις'. Ἄρα οὖν οὐ τοῦ θέλοντος, οὐδὲ τοῦ τρέχοντος, ἀλλὰ τοῦ ἐλεοῦντος Θεοῦ. Καὶ τὴν λύσιν οὐκ ἐπάγει, ἀλλ' ἐπιτείνει τῇ τῶν ἐπιφερομένων προσθήκῃ τὴν ζήτησιν.

16. *So then it is not a matter of human will or effort but of God's giving mercy.* He does not propose a solution, but rather he increases the intensity of the inquiry by the addition of what comes next.

Romans 9:17

ιζ'. Λέγει γὰρ ἡ Γραφὴ τῷ Φαραώ, ὅτι Εἰς αὐτὸ τοῦτο ἐξήγειρά σε, ὅπως ἐνδείξωμαι ἐν σοὶ τὴν δύναμίν μου, καὶ ὅπως διαγγελῇ τὸ ὄνομά μου ἐν πάσῃ τῇ γῇ. Εἶτα πάλιν συλλογιστικῶς ἐπάγει·

17. *For the Scripture says to Pharaoh, "For this very purpose I have raised you up, that I might show my power through you and that my name might be proclaimed in all the earth."* Then he again continues logically.

Romans 9:18

ιη'. Ἄρα οὖν ὃν θέλει ἐλεεῖ, ὃν δὲ θέλει σκληρύνει. Σαφῆ, φησὶ, ταῦτα τὰ γράμματα. Οὐ γὰρ ἑτέρωθεν αὐτὰ συλλέξας προσφέρω· αὐτοῦ ἤκουσας τοῦ Θεοῦ εἰρηκότος· Ἐλεήσω ὃν ἂν ἐλεῶ, καὶ οἰκτειρήσω ὃν ἂν οἰκτείρω. Αὐτοῦ πάλιν ἐστὶ τὰ περὶ τοῦ Φαραὼ εἰρημένα. Αὐτὸς καταλιπὼν τὸν Ἰσμαὴλ καὶ τοὺς ἀπὸ τῆς Χεττούρας, τὸν Ἰσαὰκ ἐξελέξατο· αὐτὸς καὶ τὸν Ἰακὼβ τοῦ Ἠσαῦ προτετίμηκε, καίτοι ἐν μιᾷ γαστρὶ κατὰ ταυτὸν τὴν διάπλασιν αὐτῶν δεξαμένων. Τί τοίνυν θαυμάζεις, εἰ καὶ νῦν ταυτὸ τοῦτο πεποίηκε, καὶ τοὺς ἐξ ὑμῶν πεπιστευκότας ἐδέξατο, τοὺς δὲ τὴν ἀκτῖνα ταύτην μὴ δεξαμένους ἀπώσατο; Ἀλλὰ τοῦτο μὲν τέως οὐ λέγει, αὔξει δὲ τῶν ζητημάτων τὴν ἀπορίαν, καί φησι·

18. *So then he has mercy on whom he wills, and he hardens whom he wills.* These words are clear. I am not offering them because I have gathered them from some other place; you have heard God himself say, "I will have mercy on whomever I have mercy, and I will have compassion on whomever I have compassion." Again, this is that which was said by him concerning Pharaoh. Abandoning Ishmael and the children of Keturah, he chose Isaac. He also preferred Jacob rather than Esau, even though they received formation in one womb according to this passage. Why then do you wonder, since even now he has done the same thing, and he has received those of you who have believed, and he has rejected those who have not received this splendor? But while Paul

does not say this explicitly, he does increase the difficulty of the questions, and he says:

Romans 9:19

ιθ'. Ἐρεῖς οὖν μοι, τί ἔτι μέμφεται; τῷ γὰρ βουλήματι αὐτοῦ τίς ἀνθέστηκεν· Εἰ γὰρ ὃν θέλει ἐλεεῖ, καὶ ὃν θέλει σκληρύνει, τῆς αὐτοῦ βουλῆς ἐξήρτηται τῶν ἀνθρώπων ἡ γνώμη. Εἰ δὲ τοῦθ' οὕτως ἔχει, οὐκ ἐν δίκῃ τοῖς ἁμαρτάνουσιν ἐπιφέρει τὰς τιμωρίας. Ἀντιστῆναι γὰρ τοῖς αὐτῷ δοκοῦσιν οὐχ οἷόν τε. Οὕτω τὴν ἀπορίαν τῷ πλήθει τῶν ζητημάτων αὐξήσας, καὶ τὰς ἀντιθέσεις πάσας προστεθεικώς, ἐπήγαγε·

19. *You will say to me then, "Why does he still find fault? For who resists his will?"* For if he has mercy on whom he wishes and hardens whom he wishes, then the human mind is dependent upon his will. And if this is so, then he does not apply punishment to those who sin with justice, for to resist him—for those who presume to do so—is impossible. So, having increased the difficulty with a number of questions and having included all of the opposing responses, Paul continues on.

Romans 9:20

κ'. Μενοῦν γε, ὦ ἄνθρωπε, σὺ τίς εἶ ὁ ἀνταποκρινόμενος τῷ Θεῷ; Ἐπειδὴ εἶπας, φησί· Τῷ [157 1] βουλήματι αὐτοῦ τίς ἀνθέστηκεν; εἰπέ μοι, σὺ τίς εἶ; οὐκ ἄνθρωπος; Πῶς οὖν ἀνταποκρίνῃ, καὶ περιεργάζῃ τὰς θείας οἰκονομίας; Εἰ γὰρ οὐκ αὐτεξούσιος ἦσθα, οὐδὲ γνώμῃ τὸ πρακτέον ᾑροῦ, ἀλλὰ τῇ τοῦ θείου βουλήματος ἀνάγκῃ ἐδούλευες, παραπλησίως ἂν τοῖς ἀψύχοις ἐσίγησας, τὰ οἰκονομούμενα στέργων. Ἐπειδὴ δὲ λόγῳ τετίμησαι, καὶ τὰ δοκοῦντά σοι καὶ λέγεις καὶ πράττεις, καὶ οὐκ ἀγαπᾷς τὰ γινόμενα, ἀλλὰ τῶν θείων οἰκονομιῶν τὰς αἰτίας ἐπιζητεῖς, Μὴ ἐρεῖ τὸ πλάσμα τῷ πλάσαντι· Τί με ἐποίησας οὕτως;

20. *On the contrary, O human, who are you who answers back to God?* Because you spoke, Paul says, "Who has resisted his will?" Tell me, who are you? Are you not human? Then how can you dispute with God and meddle with the divine schemes? For if you were not autonomous, and if you did not choose with your own mind what you do, but rather served the divine will by necessity, then you would have been silent, resembling inanimate objects, acquiescing to the things being planned. But since you have been honored with reason, you both say and do what seems best to you. You do not like what is happening, so you search for the reasons[37] of the divine plans.

Romans 9:21

κα΄. Ἤ οὐκ ἔχει ἐξουσίαν ὁ κεραμεὺς τοῦ πηλοῦ, ἐκ τοῦ αὐτοῦ φυράματος ποιῆσαι, ὃ μὲν εἰς τιμὴν σκεῦος, ὃ δὲ εἰς ἀτιμίαν; Ἀπόβλεψον εἰς τὸν τοῦ κεραμέως πηλὸν, ὃς τῆς λογικῆς διακρίσεως ἄμοιρος ὢν, οὐκ ἀντιλέγει τῷ πλάττοντι· ἀλλὰ κἂν εἰς ἀτίμου σκεύους ἐργασίαν ἀφορισθῇ, σιγῇ τὸ γινόμενον δέχεται. Σὺ δὲ ἀντιτείνεις καὶ ἀντιλέγεις. Οὐ τοίνυν φυσικαῖς ἀνάγκαις προσδέδεσαι, οὐδὲ παρανομεῖς παρὰ γνώμην, ἀλλ' ἑκὼν ἀσπάζῃ τὴν πονηρίαν, καὶ αὐθαιρέτως καταδέχῃ τοὺς πόνους τῆς ἀρετῆς. Ὀρθὴ οὖν ἄρα καὶ δικαία τοῦ Θεοῦ τῶν ὅλων ἡ ψῆφος. Ἐνδίκως γὰρ κολάζει τοὺς ἁμαρτάνοντας, ὡς γνώμῃ τοῦτο ποιεῖν τολμῶντας· ἔχει δὲ καὶ ἡ φιλανθρωπία τὸ δίκαιον· πρόφασιν γὰρ παρ' ἡμῶν λαμβάνουσα, ὀρέγει τὸν ἔλεον. Τινὲς μέντοι τὸ, Μενοῦν γε, ὦ ἄνθρωπε, σὺ τίς εἶ ὁ ἀνταποκρινόμενος τῷ Θεῷ; κατ' ἐπιτίμησιν εἰρῆσθαί φασι. Πρότερον γὰρ ἐπιτιμήσας, φησὶ, τοῖς τὰ θεῖα πολυπραγμονοῦσι, καὶ τὴν εὐτέλειαν δείξας (πηλοῦ γὰρ οὐδὲν διενήνοχε τῶν ἀνθρώπων ἡ φύσις), οὕτω τὴν λύσιν ἐπήγαγεν. Ἡ δὲ λύσις ἐστὶν αὕτη·

21. *Or does not the potter have the right to make from the same lump of clay one vessel for honorable use and another for dishonorable*[38] *use?* Turn your attention to the potter's clay which, since it has no share in the logical process of decision, does not contradict the one who molds it. But even if it is set apart for work as a dishonorable vessel, it receives what happens with silence. But you counteract and contradict. Indeed, you have not been bound by physical constraint, nor do you break the law against your will, but you embrace wickedness willingly, and you accept voluntarily the labors[39] of virtue. Therefore, the decree of the God of All is correct and just; for he justly chastises those who sin, as they undertook to do this with intent. But benevolence is also a part of justice; for despite receiving an excuse from us, he extends mercy. Some commentators, in fact, say that the verse, "O human, who are you who answers back to God?" is written as censure. For after first rebuking those who meddle with the Divine things and showing their lowliness (for human nature is not at all different than mud), he then proposes the solution, and the solution is this:

Romans 9:22

κβ΄. Εἰ δέ. Ἐνταῦθα ὑποστίξαι δεῖ. Λέγει γάρ· Εἰ τοῦτο ποθεῖς μαθεῖν, τίνος ἕνεκα πλειόνων ἁμαρτανόντων τοὺς μὲν κολάζει, τοὺς δὲ δι' ἐκείνων εὐεργετεῖ· καὶ πολλῶν τὴν ἀρετὴν μετιόντων, τοὺς μὲν περιφανεῖς ἀποφαίνει, τοῖς δὲ διὰ τούτων ὑποφαίνει τὰς τῶν μελλόντων ἐλπίδας· ἄκουσον τῶν ἑξῆς· Θέλων ὁ Θεὸς ἐνδείξασθαι τὴν ὀργὴν καὶ γνωρίσαι τὸ δυνατὸν αὐτοῦ, ἤνεγκεν ἐν πολλῇ μακροθυμίᾳ σκεύη ὀργῆς κατηρτισμένα εἰς ἀπώλειαν.

22. *What if* is to be kept separate.[40] Since you are eager to learn this, he chastises some because of greater sinning, and he exercises beneficence

through those. Many abandon virtue, and on the one hand, God makes them conspicuous, but on the other hand, he brings to light through these the coming hope. Hear what comes next. *God, although willing to demonstrate his wrath and to make known his power, endured with much patience vessels of wrath prepared for destruction?*

Romans 9:23–24

κγ', κδ'. *Καὶ ἵνα γνωρίσῃ τὸν πλοῦτον τῆς δόξης αὐτοῦ ἐπὶ σκεύη ἐλέους, ἃ προητοίμασεν εἰς δόξαν. Οὓς καὶ ἐκάλεσεν ἡμᾶς, οὐ μόνον ἐξ Ἰουδαίων, ἀλλὰ καὶ ἐξ ἐθνῶν.* Οὐχ ὁ Θεὸς, φησὶ, δημιουργὸς τῆς τοῦ Φαραὼ πονηρίας· ἀλλ' αὐτὸς τῇ μακροθυμίᾳ συνήθως ἐχρήσατο· ἐκεῖνος δὲ ὑπέλαβε τὴν μακροθυμίαν ἀσθένειαν, καὶ διὰ ταύτης τὴν οἰκείαν ηὔξησεν ἀπείθειαν. Ἀλλ' ὅμως σοφὸς ὢν τῶν ὅλων ὁ Πρύτανις, καὶ τούτῳ δικαίως τὴν τιμωρίαν ἐπήγαγε, καὶ ἐκ τῆς τούτου πονηρίας τοῖς ἄλλοις ἀλεξίκακον κατεσκεύασε φάρμακον. Καὶ καθάπερ οἱ ἰατροὶ οὐκ αὐτοὶ τὰς ἐχίδνας [82.160] δημιουργοῦσιν, ἐκ δὲ τούτων ὠφέλιμον τοῖς ἀνθρώποις κατασκευάζουσι φάρμακον· οὕτως ὁ Θεὸς ἠβούλετο μὲν τὸν Φαραὼ τῆς τιμωρίας μὴ μεταλαχεῖν· ἐπειδὴ δὲ εἰς πολλὴν ἐκεῖνος θηριωδίαν ἐξώκειλε, παντοδαπὰς μὲν αὐτῷ τιμωρίας ἐπήγαγε, τὴν δὲ οἰκείαν πᾶσιν ἀνθρώποις ἐπέδειξε δύναμιν. Διό φησιν· «Εἰς αὐτὸ τοῦτο ἐξήγειρά σε, ὅπως ἐνδείξωμαι ἐν σοὶ τὴν δύναμίν μου, καὶ ὅπως διαγγελῇ τὸ ὄνομά μου ἐν πάσῃ τῇ γῇ.» Τὸ δὲ, *Ἐξήγειρά σε,* ἀντὶ τοῦ. Συνεχώρησά σοι τῆς βασιλείας τυχεῖν, καὶ κωλῦσαι δυνάμενος οὐκ ἐκώλυσα, τὴν ἐντεῦθεν τοῖς ἄλλοις γενησομένην προορῶν ὠφέλειαν. *Σκεύη δὲ ὀργῆς κατηρτισμένα εἰς ἀπώλειαν* καλεῖ τοὺς αὐθαιρέτῳ γνώμῃ τοῦτο γεγενημένους. Τοῦτο γὰρ καὶ Τιμοθέῳ γέγραφεν· «Ἐν οἰκίᾳ δὲ μεγάλῃ οὐκ ἔστι μόνα σκεύη χρυσᾶ καὶ ἀργυρᾶ, ἀλλὰ καὶ ξύλινα καὶ ὀστράκινα· καὶ τὰ μὲν εἰς τιμήν, τὰ δὲ εἰς ἀτιμίαν» Καὶ διδάσκων ὡς ἑκών τις τοῦτο γίνεται ἢ ἐκεῖνο, ἐπήγαγεν· «Ἐὰν οὖν τις ἑαυτὸν ἐκκαθάρῃ ἀπὸ τῶν τοιούτων, ἔσται σκεῦος εἰς τιμὴν ἡγιασμένον, καὶ εὔχρηστον τῷ Δεσπότῃ, εἰς πᾶν ἔργον ἡτοιμασμένον.» Καὶ Κορινθίοις οὕτω γράφει· «Εἰ δέ τις ἐποικοδομεῖ ἐπὶ τὸν θεμέλιον τοῦτον, χρυσὸν, ἄργυρον, λίθους τιμίους, ξύλα, χόρτον, καλάμην·» ἄντικρυς διδάσκων τῶν ἀνθρώπων τὸ αὐτεξούσιον. Οὕτω σκεύη ἐλέους ἐκάλεσε τοὺς τῆς θείας φιλανθρωπίας ἀξίους· τὸ δὲ, *Ἃ προητοίμασεν εἰς δόξαν,* τὴν πρόγνωσιν τὴν θείαν παραδηλοῖ. Τοῦτο γὰρ καὶ ἐν τοῖς πρόσθεν εἴρηκεν, ὅτι «Οὓς προέγνω, καὶ προώρισε συμμόρφους τῆς εἰκόνος τοῦ Υἱοῦ αὐτοῦ.» Σκοπὸς γὰρ τῷ Ἀποστόλῳ δεῖξαι, ὡς τοὺς ἀξίους σωτηρίας μόνος οἶδεν ὁ τῶν ὅλων Θεὸς, ἀνθρώπων δὲ οὐδὲ εἷς. Εἰρηκὼς δὲ, ὅτι *Ἐκάλεσεν ἡμᾶς, οὐ μόνον ἐξ Ἰουδαίων, ἀλλὰ καὶ ἐξ ἐθνῶν,* βεβαιοῖ τὸν λόγον τῇ Γραφικῇ μαρτυρίᾳ, καί φησιν·

23–24. *And what if he did this in order that he might make known the riches of his glory to vessels of mercy, which he prepared beforehand for glory, even us whom he called, not only from the Jews but also from the Gentiles?* For God is not the creator of Pharaoh's evil, but rather he behaved with patience, as usual. But Pharaoh assumed God's patience to be weakness, and through this he increased his own disobedience. And as a result, the Ruler of All, being wise, rightly brought punishment upon him. And God prepared for others, from Pharaoh's evil, a remedy to ward off evil, just as physicians do not create vipers, but from these vipers prepare a beneficial remedy for people. Thus, it was not God's wish that Pharaoh be allotted punishment, but because Pharaoh rushed headlong into much brutality, God brought all sorts of punishments upon him and displayed his own power to all humanity. Therefore, he says, "For this very purpose I have raised you up, that I might show my power through you and that my name might be proclaimed in all the earth."[41] The phrase "I have raised you up" is equivalent to the following: I allowed you to become king, and despite being able to prevent it, I did not, because I foresaw the benefit for others which would come from this. Now Paul calls those who have become like Pharaoh by means of free choice "vessels of wrath prepared for destruction." Paul also wrote about this to Timothy, "In a large house there are not only gold and silver vessels, but also vessels of wood and pottery; some are for special use and others are for ordinary use."[42] And teaching how someone willingly becomes one or the other, he adds, "Therefore, if someone cleanses himself from such things, he will be a vessel for special use, dedicated and useful to the Master, prepared for every work."[43] Paul puts it this way in writing to the Corinthians, "If anyone builds upon this foundation using gold, silver, precious stones, wood, hay, or straw,"[44] teaching outright the concept of human free will. Thus, he called those worthy of divine benevolence "vessels of mercy." Now the phrase "which he prepared beforehand for glory" indicates divine foreknowledge. For he also mentions this in an earlier verse, "whom he foreknew he also predestined to be conformed to the image of his Son."[45] The intent by the Apostle is to show how the God of All alone, and not one single human, knows those who are worthy of salvation. And having said, "He called us, not only from the Jews but also from the Gentiles," Paul confirms the statement with Scriptural testimony and says:

Romans 9:25–26

κε΄, κϛ΄. Ὡς καὶ ἐν τῷ Ὡσηὲ λέγει· Καλέσω τὸν οὐ λαόν μου, λαόν μου, καὶ τὴν οὐκ ἠγαπημένην, ἠγαπημένην. Καὶ ἔσται, ἐν τῷ τόπῳ, ᾧ ἐρρέθη αὐτοῖς· Οὐ λαός μου ὑμεῖς, ἐκεῖ κληθήσονται υἱοὶ Θεοῦ ζῶντος. Ταῦτα δὲ ὁ Θεὸς οὐ περὶ τῶν ἐθνῶν, ἀλλὰ περὶ αὐτῶν εἴρηκε τῶν Ἰουδαίων. Τῷ γὰρ Ὡσηὲ κελεύσας λαβεῖν γυναῖκα πόρνην, καὶ μέντοι καὶ μοιχαλίδα, οὕτω τὰ γεννηθέντα παιδία προσαγορευθῆναι ἐκέλευσε, τὸν μὲν Οὐ λαόν, τὴν δὲ Οὐκ ἠγαπημένην, τὰ συμβησόμενα Ἰουδαίοις προλέγων. Ἀλλ' ὅμως πάλιν ὑπέσχετο αὐτοῖς χρηστά, ὅτι Καὶ οὐ λαὸς κληθήσεται λαός, καὶ ἡ οὐκ ἠγαπημένη, ἠγαπημένη. Σκοπήσατε τοίνυν, φησίν, ὅτι καὶ ὑμεῖς οὐκ ἀεὶ τῶν αὐτῶν ἀπελαύσατε· ἀλλὰ ποτὲ μὲν λαός, ποτὲ δὲ οὐ λαός, καὶ πάλιν λαὸς ἐχρηματίσατε· καὶ ποτὲ μὲν ἠγαπημένη, εἶτα οὐκ ἠγαπημένη, καὶ πάλιν ἠγαπημένη. Οὐδὲν τοίνυν ἀπεικὸς οὐδὲ ἐπὶ τοῦ παρόντος γεγένηται. Συνήθως γὰρ ἀπεβλήθητε· ἀλλὰ κἂν πάλιν θελήσητε, λαὸς καὶ ἠγαπημένη κληθήσεσθε. Καὶ γὰρ τὰ ἔθνη οὐ λαὸς ὄντες νῦν λαὸς χρηματίζει. Προστέθεικε δὲ τῷ λόγῳ καὶ ἑτέραν μαρτυρίαν. [82.161]

25-26. *As he says also in Hosea, "I will call those who are not my people 'my people,' and I will call her who is not beloved 'beloved.' And it will happen in the place in which it was said to them, 'You are not my people.' There they will be called sons of the living God."*[46] Now God spoke these things not about the Gentiles but rather about the Jews themselves. For after commanding Hosea to take as his wife a prostitute and, of course, an adulterer, then he commanded the children who were born to be named "Not my people" and "Not beloved" as a means of warning[47] what would happen to the Jews. But still again God supplies them with good things, for "I will call those not my people 'my people' and those not beloved 'beloved.'" Consider then, Paul says,[48] that you have not always enjoyed the same status. But at one time you were called God's people, at another time you were not, and then you were called his people again. Likewise, you were at one time beloved, then not beloved, and beloved again. Therefore, nothing unusual at all has happened at the present time. For you were rejected as usual, but if you desire to be so again, you will be called God's people and beloved. For he now also calls the Gentiles, who were not his people, his people. Then Paul adds another witness to the discourse.

Romans 9:27-28

κζ', κη'. Ἡσαΐας δὲ κράζει ὑπὲρ τοῦ Ἰσραήλ· Ἐὰν ᾖ ὁ ἀριθμὸς τῶν υἱῶν Ἰσραήλ ὡς ἡ ἄμμος τῆς θαλάσσης, τὸ κατάλειμμα σωθήσεται. Λόγον γὰρ συντετμημένον ποιήσει Κύριος ἐπὶ τῆς γῆς. Εἰς καιρὸν δὲ μάλιστα ταύτην τέθεικε τὴν μαρτυρίαν, διδάσκων ὡς ἄνωθεν προεῖδεν ὁ τῶν ὅλων Θεός, καὶ τοὺς τῇ πίστει προσεληλυθότας, καὶ τοὺς ἀπιστίαν νενοσηκότας. Ἐπειδὴ γὰρ ἔλεγον οἱ Ἰουδαῖοι ὀλίγους ἐξ αὐτῶν δεδέχθαι τὸ κήρυγμα, τοὺς δὲ ἄλλους ἅπαντας ὡς ἐξαπάτην φυγεῖν, ἔδειξεν ἄνωθεν ταῦτα προειρημένα, καὶ ὅτι κἂν ὑπερβάλλωσι τῷ πλήθει τὸν ἀριθμόν, καὶ μιμῶνται τῆς θαλάσσης τὴν ψάμμον, οὐχ ἅπαντες τεύξονται τῆς σωτηρίας, ἀλλ' οἱ τῇ πίστει κοσμούμενοι. Τὸν γὰρ συντετμημένον λόγον τὴν πίστιν ἐκάλεσεν. Ἃ γὰρ διὰ πολλῶν ἐντολῶν ὁ νόμος ἐπαίδευσε, καὶ τελείαν παρασχεῖν τὴν σωτηρίαν οὐκ ἴσχυσεν, ἡ εἰς Χριστὸν ὁμολογία κατώρθωσε, καὶ τὴν πίστιν προὐξένησε. Σύντομος δὲ αὕτη, καὶ μακρῶν περιόδων οὐ δεομένη· διαθέσει δὲ ψυχῆς κρινομένη, καὶ διὰ γλώττης κηρυττομένη.

27-28. *And Isaiah cries out concerning Israel, "Though the number of the children of Israel be like the sand of the sea, the remnant will be saved. For the Lord will make his word trimmed-down upon the earth."*[49] And Paul includes this witness especially at the right time, teaching how the God of All saw beforehand, from the very beginning,[50] both those who have entered into faith and those who suffer from unbelief. Since the Jews were proclaiming the message, a few of them have received it, but all the others have taken refuge in[51] gross deceit. Paul demonstrates that these things have been spoken from the beginning, and that even if they exceed numbering in magnitude and imitate the sand of the sea, not all will attain salvation, but only those who adorn themselves with faith. Now Paul refers to faith here when he speaks of "the trimmed-down word." For what the law taught through many commandments—and it was not sufficient to produce complete salvation—the confessing of Christ[52] accomplished, putting faith into effect. It is judged by the disposition of the soul and proclaimed with the tongue.

Romans 9:29

κθ'. Καὶ καθὼς προείρηκεν Ἡσαΐας· Εἰ μὴ Κύριος Σαβαὼθ ἐγκατέλιπεν ἡμῖν σπέρμα, ὡς Σόδομα ἂν ἐγενήθημεν, καὶ ὡς Γόμορρα ἂν ὡμοιώθημεν. Οὓς ἄνω κατάλειμμα προσηγόρευσε, τούτους ὠνόμασε σπέρμα, δι' οὓς ὁ Προφήτης ἔφη τὰ Σοδόμων καὶ Γομόρρων μὴ παθεῖν Ἰουδαίους. Ἐκεῖνοι γὰρ πανωλεθρίαν ὑπέμειναν. Οὕτω διδάξας ὡς ὁ τῶν ὅλων Θεός, οὐκ εἰς τὴν κατὰ φύσιν ἀποβλέπει συγγένειαν, ἀλλὰ τῆς πίστεως τὴν κοινωνίαν ζητεῖ, διδάσκει σαφέστερον τίνος ἕνεκεν Ἰουδαῖοι μὲν τῆς προγονικῆς εὐγενείας ἐξέπεσον, τὰ δέ γε ἔθνη τῆς σωτηρίας μετέλαχον· καί φησι·

29. *And just as Isaiah foretold, "If the Lord Almighty had not left us a seed, we would have become like Sodom and have been made like Gomorrah."*[53] Here he applies the name "seed" to these whom he called a remnant above, on whose account the Prophet spoke in order that the Jews might not suffer the fate of Sodom and Gomorrah, for they were victims of utter destruction. Then after teaching how the God of All does not regard natural kinship but seeks the fellowship of faith, Paul teaches more clearly why the Jews fell from their ancestral nobility and the Gentiles received a share of salvation. He says:

Romans 9:30

λ'. Τί οὖν ἐροῦμεν; Κατ' ἐρώτησιν ἀναγνωστέον ὑποστίζοντας. Εἶτα κατ' ἀπόκρισιν τὰ ἑξῆς· Ὅτι ἔθνη τὰ μὴ διώκοντα δικαιοσύνην κατέλαβε δικαιοσύνην, δικαιοσύνην δὲ τὴν ἐκ πίστεως.

30. *What then shall we say?* This is to be read separately as a question, then that which follows as the answer. *That the Gentiles, who did not pursue righteousness, obtained righteousness, that is the righteousness that comes from faith.*

Romans 9:31

λα'. Ἰσραὴλ δὲ διώκων νόμον δικαιοσύνης, εἰς νόμον δικαιοσύνης οὐκ ἔφθασεν. Ἴσθι, φησὶν, ὡς ἡ πίστις αἰτία τοῖς ἔθνεσι τῶν ἀγαθῶν. Αὐτὴ γὰρ αὐτοὺς πάλαι πλανωμένους, καὶ τὴν δικαιοσύνην οὔτε ἔχοντας, οὔτε ζητῆσαι βουληθέντας, τῆς κατὰ χάριν δικαιοσύνης ἠξίωσεν· ὁ δέ γε Ἰσραὴλ, καίτοι τὸν νόμον κατέχων, καὶ τὴν δικαιοσύνην τὴν ἐκ τοῦ νόμου μεταδιώκων, διήμαρτε τοῦ σκοποῦ, καὶ τῆς δικαιοσύνης οὐκ ἔτυχεν. Εἶτα πάλιν κατ' ἐρώτησιν·

31. *But Israel, pursuing a law of righteousness, did not attain that law of righteousness.* Know, he says, that faith is the cause of the good which has happened to the Gentiles. For it made them, who were formerly in error, having neither righteousness nor the desire to seek it, worthy of the righteousness according to grace. But Israel, clinging further to the law and pursuing the righteousness that comes from it, strayed from the mark and did not obtain righteousness. Then Paul again presents a question.

Romans 9:32

λβ'. Διὰ τί, Τὴν αἰτίαν, φησί, τούτου θέλεις μαθεῖν; *Ὅτι οὐκ ἐκ πίστεως, ἀλλ' ὡς ἐξ ἔργων νόμου.* Ἐνόμισαν ἐξαρκεῖν αὐτοῖς τὴν κατὰ νόμον πολιτείαν εἰς κτῆσιν δικαιοσύνης, καὶ τῆς πίστεως κατεφρόνησαν. Οὗ δὴ χάριν, καὶ τῶν τῆς πίστεως οὐ μετέλαχον δωρεῶν, καὶ τὴν ἐξ ἐκείνης τῆς πολιτείας οὐκ ἔσχον δικαιοσύνην. Εἶτα διδάσκει διὰ ποίαν αἰτίαν τῶν τῆς πίστεως ἀγαθῶν οὐκ ἀπήλαυσαν. [82.164] *Προσέκοψαν γὰρ τῷ λίθῳ τοῦ προσκόμματος·*

32. *Why?* Do you want, Paul says, to know the reason for this? *Because they pursued it not on the basis of faith but as if it were on the basis of works of law.* They thought that the way of life according to the law was sufficient for them to acquire righteousness, and so they disregarded[54] faith. For this reason, they did not share in the gifts of faith nor have the righteousness that comes from that way of life. Then he teaches for what reason they did not enjoy the good things of faith. *For they stumbled over the stumbling stone;*

Romans 9:33

λγ'. καθὼς γέγραπται· *Ἰδοὺ τίθημι ἐν Σιὼν λίθον προσκόμματος, καὶ πέτραν σκανδάλου· καὶ πᾶς ὁ πιστεύων ἐπ' αὐτὸν οὐ καταισχυνθήσεται.* Προσπταίειν εἰώθασιν οἱ ἑτέρως τὴν διάνοιαν ἔχοντες, καὶ τὴν ὁδὸν προσκοπεῖν οὐκ ἐθέλοντες. Τοῦτο πεπόνθασιν Ἰουδαῖοι· περὶ γὰρ δὴ τὰ περιττὰ τοῦ νόμου κεχηνότες, τὸν ὑπὸ τῶν προφητῶν προαγορευθέντα λίθον ἰδεῖν οὐκ ἠθέλησαν, καίτοι σαφῶς ἐκείνων προθεσπισάντων ὡς ὁ τούτῳ πιστεύων, μεγίστων τεύξεται ἀγαθῶν. Τοῦτο γὰρ εἶπεν· *Οὐ καταισχυνθήσεται·* ὡς τῶν ἐλπιζόντων μὲν, διαμαρτανόντων δὲ τῆς ἐλπίδος, αἰσχυνομένων. Οὕτω μετρίως αὐτῶν καθαψάμενος, πάλιν ἣν ἔχει περὶ αὐτοὺς διάθεσιν δείκνυσιν, ἵνα μὴ δυσμενείας δόξαν οἱ ἔλεγχοι λάβωσι. Τὰς γὰρ μείζους κατηγορίας ἐσχάτας ἐφύλαξεν.

33. *Just as it is written, "Behold, I lay in Zion a stone of stumbling, a rock of offense, and everyone who believes in him will not be put to shame."*[55] Those who think otherwise are accustomed to stumbling, as they do not want to watch the path. The Jews suffer from this. For while busy gaping at the abundance[56] of the Law, they did not want to see the stone foretold by the prophets nor how, as those prophets clearly foretold, the one who believes in this stone will attain the greatest good. For the scripture says, "He will not be put to shame," since those who hope but abandon that hope are put to shame. Then, having upbraided them sufficiently, Paul shows once again the disposition that he has toward the Jews, in order that the dishonored may not receive a reputation for enmity, for he saves the greater accusations for later.

Romans 10:1[57]

α′. Ἀδελφοί, ἡ μὲν εὐδοκία τῆς ἐμῆς καρδίας, καὶ ἡ δέησις ἡ πρὸς τὸν Θεὸν ὑπὲρ τοῦ Ἰσραήλ ἐστιν εἰς σωτηρίαν. Εὐδοκίαν ἐνταῦθα τὴν ἐπιθυμίαν ἐκάλεσε. Καὶ γὰρ ἐπιθυμῶ, φησὶ, καὶ προσεύχομαι τῆς σωτηρίας αὐτοὺς τυχεῖν.

1. *Brothers, my heart's satisfaction and my prayer to God for Israel is for their salvation.* Here Paul uses the word "satisfaction"[58] for desire. For, he says, I desire and pray for them to obtain salvation.

Romans 10:2

β′. Μαρτυρῶ γὰρ αὐτοῖς, ὅτι ζῆλον Θεοῦ ἔχουσιν, ἀλλ' οὐ κατ' ἐπίγνωσιν. Ἐπαίνῳ τὸν ψόγον συνέζευξεν, οἷόν τινι δελέατι κατακρύπτων τὸ ἄγκιστρον, ἵνα τοῦ λόγου τὸ κέρδος δεκτικὸν αὐτοῖς γένηται.

2. *For I bear witness to them that they have zeal for God, but not according to knowledge.* He couples the censure together with praise, like a fishhook concealed in some bait, in order that they might derive some benefit from the word.

Romans 10:3

γ′. Ἀγνοοῦντες γὰρ τὴν τοῦ Θεοῦ δικαιοσύνην, καὶ τὴν ἰδίαν δικαιοσύνην ζητοῦντες στῆσαι, τῇ δικαιοσύνῃ τοῦ Θεοῦ οὐχ ὑπετάγησαν. Ἰδίαν δικαιοσύνην τὴν ἄκαιρον τοῦ νόμου προσηγόρευσε φυλακήν· πεπαυμένον γὰρ αὐτὸν φυλάττειν σπουδάζουσι· Θεοῦ δὲ δικαιοσύνην, τὴν κατὰ χάριν διὰ τῆς πίστεως γινομένην ὠνόμασε. Τοῦτο γὰρ ἐπήγαγε.

3. *For since they do not recognize the righteousness of God and they seek to establish their own righteousness, they have not submitted to the righteousness of God.* Paul calls the unreasonable keeping of the law "their own righteousness;" for they are zealous to keep that which has been brought to an end. On the other hand, he calls that which happens according to grace through faith "the righteousness of God." For this reason he adds:

Romans 10:4

δ'. *Τέλος γὰρ νόμου Χριστός, εἰς δικαιοσύνην παντὶ τῷ πιστεύοντι.* Οὐ γὰρ ἐναντία τῷ νόμῳ ἡ εἰς τὸν Κύριον πίστις, ἀλλὰ καὶ μάλα σύμφωνος. Ὁ γὰρ νόμος ἡμᾶς πρὸς τὸν Δεσπότην Χριστὸν ἐποδήγησε. Τὸν τοῦ νόμου τοίνυν πληροῖ σκοπὸν ὁ πιστεύων τῷ Δεσπότῃ Χριστῷ. Καλῶς δὲ πάλιν, *παντὶ τῷ πιστεύοντι,* τέθεικε. Συμπεριέλαβε γὰρ πᾶσαν τῶν ἀνθρώπων τὴν φύσιν. Κἂν γὰρ Ἕλλην ᾖ, κἂν βάρβαρος, πιστεύσῃ δὲ, τῆς σωτηρίας μετὰ λαγχάνει. Εἶτα διδάσκει πάλιν νόμου καὶ χάριτος τὴν διαφορὰν, καὶ ἀμφοτέρων εἰσάγει Μωϋσέα τὸν νομοθέτην διδάσκαλον, καί φησι·

4. *For Christ is the end[59] of the Law so that there may be righteousness for everyone who believes.* For faith in Christ is not contrary to the law but even more in harmony with it. For the law has led us to the Lord Christ. The one who believes in the Lord Christ fulfills, therefore, the aim[60] of the law. Again, he rightly places the phrase "for everyone who believes" here; for he includes every sort of human. Even if one be Greek or barbarian, if one believes, he or she has a share of salvation. Thus Paul teaches once again the difference between law and grace, and he introduces Moses the lawgiver as the teacher of both, saying:

Romans 10:5

ε'. *Μωσῆς γὰρ γράφει τὴν δικαιοσύνην τὴν ἐκ τοῦ νόμου, ὅτι ὁ ποιήσας αὐτὰ ἄνθρωπος ζήσεται ἐν αὐτοῖς.* Ὁ τὰ τῷ νόμῳ διηγορευμένα πάντα πεπληρωκώς, καρπὸν ἔχει τῆς φυλακῆς τὴν ζωήν· ἡ δὲ τυχοῦσα παράβασις τὴν τιμωρίαν ἐπάγει. [82.165]

5. *For Moses writes, concerning the righteousness which comes from the law, that the one who does these things will live by them.*[61] The one who has fulfilled everything spoken of in the law bears as fruit a life of observance. And when transgression happens, it brings on punishment.

Romans 10:6

ϛʹ. Ἡ δὲ ἐκ πίστεως δικαιοσύνη οὕτω λέγει. Ἀντὶ τοῦ, περὶ δὲ τῆς ἐκ πίστεως δικαιοσύνης, οὐ Μωσῆς ταῦτα λέγει, ἀλλὰ διὰ Μωσέως ὁ τῶν ὅλων Θεός. Μὴ εἴπῃς ἐν τῇ καρδίᾳ σου· Τίς ἀναβήσεται εἰς τὸν οὐρανόν; τουτέστι Χριστὸν καταγαγεῖν·

6. *But the righteousness that comes from faith speaks in this manner:* That is to say, Moses did not say these things concerning the righteousness that comes from faith, but rather the God of All spoke through Moses. *Do not say in your heart, "Who will ascend into heaven?"*[62] (That is, to bring Christ down.)

Romans 10:7–8

ζʹ, ηʹ. ἢ Τίς καταβήσεται εἰς τὴν ἄβυσσον; τουτέστι Χριστὸν ἐκ νεκρῶν ἀναγαγεῖν. Ἀλλὰ τί λέγει ἡ Γραφή; Ἐγγύς σου τὸ ῥῆμά ἐστιν ἐν τῷ στόματί σου, καὶ ἐν τῇ καρδίᾳ σου. Περὶ μὲν τοῦ νόμου ταῦτα εἴρηκεν ὁ τῶν ὅλων Θεός, διδάσκων Ἰουδαίους, ὡς δίχα πόνων τὴν τῶν πρακτέων διδασκαλίαν ἐδέξαντο, καὶ οὔτε τῆς εἰς οὐρανοὺς ἀναβάσεως, οὔτε τῆς εἰς τὸν ᾅδην καταβάσεως δέονται. Ἐγγύς σου γὰρ τὸ ῥῆμά ἐστι. Δέδοται γάρ σοι τῶν ποιητέων ἡ γνῶσις. Ὁ μέντοι θεῖος Ἀπόστολος εἰς τὸν περὶ τῆς πίστεως ταῦτα ἐξείληφε λόγον, διδάσκων ὡς οὐ δεῖ τὴν Δεσποτικὴν οἰκονομίαν περι ἐργάζεσθαι, ἢ ἀμφιβάλλειν ὡς ὁ μονογενὴς τοῦ Θεοῦ Υἱὸς ἐνηνθρώπησε, καὶ τὸ πάθος καταδεξάμενος ἐπραγματεύσατο τὴν ἀνάστασιν, ἀλλὰ πίστει καρποῦσθαι τὴν σωτηρίαν. Ἐγγύς σου γὰρ τὸ ῥῆμά ἐστιν ἐν τῷ στόματί σου, καὶ ἐν τῇ καρδίᾳ σου. Εἶτα ἐπάγει· Τουτέστι τὸ ῥῆμα τῆς πίστεως, ὃ κηρύσσομεν. Ὅπερ Μωϋσῆς περὶ τῶν νομικῶν εἴρηκεν ἐντολῶν, τοῦτο ἡμεῖς περὶ τῆς πίστεως λέγομεν.

7–8. *Or, "Who will descend into the abyss?"* (That is, to bring Christ up from the dead.) *But what does the scripture say? "The word is near you, in your mouth and in your heart."*[63] The God of All says these things concerning the law in order to teach the Jews that they received, apart from any labor on their part, the teaching of the things that must be done; thus, they have no need of going up into heaven nor of descending into Hades. "For the word is near you." For the knowledge of what must be done has been given to you. The Divine Apostle certainly understands these things in terms of the word[64] about faith, teaching that it is not necessary to trouble oneself with the Lord's plan or to doubt that the only begotten Son of God became incarnate, accepted the passion, and undertook the resurrection, but rather one must bear salvation as fruit by faith. "For the word is near you, in your mouth and in your heart." Then he adds: *The word of faith which we proclaim.* The very thing which Moses spoke concerning the legal commands, this we also say concerning faith.

Romans 10:9–10

θ′, ι′. Ὅτι ἐὰν ὁμολογήσῃς ἐν τῷ στόματί σου Κύριον Ἰησοῦν, καὶ πιστεύσῃς ἐν τῇ καρδίᾳ σου, ὅτι Θεὸς αὐτὸν ἤγειρεν ἐκ νεκρῶν, σωθήσῃ. Καρδίᾳ γὰρ πιστεύεται εἰς δικαιοσύνην, στόματι δὲ ὁμολογεῖται εἰς σωτηρίαν. Ἀμφοτέρων γὰρ χρεία, καὶ πίστεως ἀληθοῦς καὶ βεβαίας, καὶ ὁμολογίας σὺν παρρησίᾳ γινομένης· ἵνα καὶ ἡ καρδία κοσμῆται τῷ ἀναμφιβόλῳ τῆς πίστεως, καὶ ἡ γλῶττα λαμπρύνηται ἀδεῶς κηρύττουσα τὴν ἀλήθειαν. Εἶτα πάλιν ἀναμιμνήσκει τῆς Γραφικῆς μαρτυρίας.

9-10. *For if you confess with your mouth Jesus as Lord and believe in your heart that God raised him from the dead, you will be saved. For with the heart one believes, resulting in justification, and with the mouth one confesses, resulting in salvation.* For both things need to take place—a true and steadfast faith and a bold confession—so that the heart may be adorned with[65] the unambiguity of faith, and the tongue may be made brilliant[66] proclaiming the truth without fear. Next in turn he recalls the testimony of Scripture.

Romans 10:11

ια′. Λέγει γὰρ ἡ Γραφή· Πᾶς ὁ πιστεύων ἐπ' αὐτῷ οὐ καταισχυνθήσεται. Ἑρμηνεύει δὲ καὶ τὸ Πᾶς.

11. *For the scripture says, "Everyone who believes on him will not be put to shame."*[67] And Paul even provides an interpretation of the word "everyone."

Romans 10:12–13

ιβ′, ιγ′. Οὐ γάρ ἐστι διαστολὴ Ἰουδαίου τε καὶ Ἕλληνος. Ὁ γὰρ αὐτὸς Κύριος πάντων, πλουτῶν εἰς πάντας, καὶ ἐπὶ πάντας τοὺς ἐπικαλουμένους αὐτόν. Πᾶς γὰρ ὃς ἐὰν ἐπικαλέσηται τὸ ὄνομα Κυρίου, σωθήσεται. Πλοῦτον τοῦ Θεοῦ προσηγόρευσε τῶν ἀνθρώπων τὴν σωτηρίαν. Οἶδε γὰρ τὴν τοῦ Δεσπότου φιλανθρωπίαν. Ἁρμοδίως δὲ τῇ καρδίᾳ καὶ τῇ γλώττῃ τὰς μαρτυρίας προσήρμοσε· τῇ μὲν καρδίᾳ τὸ, Πᾶς ὁ πιστεύων ἐπ' αὐτῷ οὐ καταισχυνθήσεται· τῇ δὲ γλώττῃ· Πᾶς γὰρ ὃς ἐὰν ἐπικαλέσηται τὸ ὄνομα Κυρίου, σωθήσεται. Εἶτα διδάσκει ὡς ἑκόντες Ἰουδαῖοι τῆς σωτηρίας ἐστέρηνται, προσενεχθὲν τὸ κήρυγμα δέξασθαι μὴ θελήσαντες. Ἀλλ' ἐναργῶς οὐ προσφέρει τὸν ἔλεγχον, ἀλλ' ἑτέρως μεθοδεύει τὸν λόγον. [82.168]

12-13. *For there is no distinction between Jew and Greek; for the same Lord is Lord of all and is rich toward all, and to all who call upon him. For whoever calls upon the name of the Lord will be saved.* Paul calls the salvation of humanity the riches of God, for he knows the benevolence[68] of the Lord. Paul applies the testimonies to the heart and tongue in a well-fitting manner. The phrase "everyone who believes on him will not be put to shame" is applied to the heart, and the phrase "for whoever calls upon the name of the Lord will be saved" is applied to the tongue. He then teaches that the Jews have willingly been deprived of salvation since they did not desire to receive the message which was presented to them. However, Paul clearly does not propose censure of the Jews at this point, but rather he crafts the argument differently.

Romans 10:14–15

ιδ', ιε'. Πῶς οὖν ἐπικαλέσονται, εἰς ὃν οὐκ ἐπίστευσαν; Πῶς δὲ πιστεύσουσιν, οὗ οὐκ ἤκουσαν; Πῶς δὲ ἀκούσουσι χωρὶς κηρύσσοντος; Πῶς δὲ κηρύξουσιν, ἐὰν μὴ ἀποσταλῶσι; Προσήκει, φησί, πρότερον πιστεῦσαι, εἶτα ἐπικαλέσασθαι. Ἀδύνατον δὲ πιστεῦσαι τὸν διδασκαλίας οὐκ ἀπολαύσαντα· ταύτης δὲ τυχεῖν οὐχ οἷόν τε τῶν κηρυττόντων οὐκ ὄντων· καὶ τούτους πάλιν ἡ χειροτονία ποιεῖ. Οὕτω ταῦτα ὡς εἰς ἀπολογίαν τεθεικὼς Ἰουδαίων, δι' αὐτῶν αὔξει τὴν κατ' ἐκείνων κατηγορίαν· καὶ τελευταῖον πρῶτον τέθεικε, τὸ τῆς τῶν κηρύκων ἀποστολῆς, δεικνὺς ἄνωθεν ταῦτα προτεθεσπισμένα. Καὶ γὰρ ἀκόλουθον ἦν τοῦτο πρὸ τῶν ἄλλων ἐπι δεῖξαι. Δεῖ γὰρ πρῶτον χειροτονηθῆναι τοὺς κήρυκας, εἶτα κηρύξαι, ἔπειτα τῶν κηρυγμάτων ἀκοῦσαι, καὶ τηνικαῦτα πιστεῦσαι. Φέρει τοίνυν τοῦ Ἡσαΐου τὴν προφητείαν, καί φησιν· *Ὡς ὡραῖοι οἱ πόδες τῶν εὐαγγελιζομένων εἰρήνην, τῶν εὐαγγελιζομένων τὰ ἀγαθά!* Καὶ γὰρ τοῖς ἀποστόλοις ὁ Κύριος ἐνετείλατο εἰς οἰκίαν εἰσιοῦσι λέγειν· «Εἰρήνη τῷ οἴκῳ τούτῳ.» Κατεμήνυον γὰρ τὰς θείας καταλλαγάς, εὐηγγελίζοντο δὲ καὶ τῶν ἀγαθῶν τὴν ἀπόλαυσιν. Τούτων τοὺς πόδας ὡραίους ἀποκαλεῖ, ὡς τὸν καλὸν τρέχοντας δρόμον, ὡς ὑπὸ τῶν Δεσποτικῶν ἀπονιφθέντας χειρῶν. Οὕτω τὴν περὶ τῶν κηρύκων μαρτυρίαν παραγαγών, κατ' ἐρώτησιν λέγει·

14–15. How then can they call upon one in whom they have not believed? And how can they believe in one whom they have not heard? And how can they hear without people preaching. And how can these preach unless they have been sent? It is necessary, Paul says, to believe first, then to call upon the Lord. But it is impossible to believe without the benefit of instruction, and it is not possible to attain this instruction from false preachers. Again, these preachers are produced by election.[69] Thus, by including these things as a defense of the Jews, he actually uses them to increase the charge against the Jews. Paul places the first item last of all, the matter of the sending of the preachers, while demonstrating from the start that these things have been foretold. For it was in keeping with this priority to point it out before the others; for it is necessary for the preachers to be elected first and then to preach. Thereupon, one may hear the proclamations and then at that time believe. Paul goes on to cite the prophecy of Isaiah saying, *How beautiful are the feet of those who proclaim the good news of peace and of good things.*[70] For the Lord even commanded the apostles to say when they entered a house, "Peace to this household,"[71] for they were making known the divine reconciliation and proclaiming the good news of the fruition of good things. He calls beautiful the feet of those that run the good race, that have been washed by the Lord's hands. Having thus brought forward the testimony regarding the preachers, he asks a question.

Romans 10:16

ις΄. Ἀλλ' οὐ πάντες ὑπήκουσαν τῷ Εὐαγγελίῳ; Εἶτα κατὰ ἀπόκρισιν· Ἡσαΐας λέγει· Κύριε, τίς ἐπίστευσε τῇ ἀκοῇ ἡμῶν; Οὐδὲ τοῦτο, φησὶν, ἐσίγησεν ἡ θεία Γραφὴ, ἀλλὰ καὶ τοῦτο ἄνωθεν διὰ Ἡσαΐου προείρηκεν ὁ Θεός. Εἶτα συλλογιστικῶς·

16. *But not all have obeyed the good news, have they?* Then, by way of an answer, *Isaiah says, "Lord, who has believed our message?"*[72] The divine Scripture, Paul says, was not at all silent about this, but rather God spoke this word from the beginning through Isaiah. Then, concluding logically:

Romans 10:17

ιζ΄. Ἄρα ἡ πίστις ἐξ ἀκοῆς, ἡ δὲ ἀκοὴ διὰ ῥήματος Θεοῦ. Οὐκοῦν ὁ ἀπιστῶν, τοῖς θείοις λογίοις διαπιστεῖ· καὶ ὁ πιστεύων θεῖα δεχόμενος ῥήματα, καρπὸν προσφέρει τῆς ἀκοῆς, τὴν πίστιν.

17. *So then faith comes from hearing, and hearing through the word of God.* Accordingly, the one who does not believe distrusts the divine word, whereas the one who believes receives the divine word and bears the fruit of hearing, which is faith.

Romans 10:18

ιη΄. Ἀλλὰ λέγω, μὴ οὐκ ἤκουσαν; Καὶ τοῦτο πάλιν κατ' ἐρώτησιν ἀναγνωστέον. Εἶτα κατὰ ἀπόκρισιν· Μενοῦν γε εἰς πᾶσαν τὴν γῆν ἐξῆλθεν ὁ φθόγγος αὐτῶν, καὶ εἰς τὰ πέρατα τῆς οἰκουμένης τὰ ῥήματα αὐτῶν. Πῶς γὰρ οἷόν τε ἦν Ἰουδαίους μὴ ἀκοῦσαι τῶν κατὰ τὴν οἰκουμένην ἀκηκοότων ἐθνῶν; Πρώτοις γὰρ αὐτοῖς τῆς ἀληθείας οἱ κήρυκες προσήνεγκαν τὰ κηρύγματα. Καὶ γὰρ αὐτὸς ὁ Κύριος πρὸς αὐτοὺς ἔφη· «Πορεύεσθε μᾶλλον πρὸς τὰ πρόβατα τὰ ἀπολωλότα οἴκου Ἰσραήλ.» Καὶ ἐν ταῖς Πράξεσι τῶν ἀποστόλων· «Ὑμῖν ἦν ἀναγκαῖον πρῶτον λαληθῆναι τὸν λόγον τοῦ Θεοῦ.» Ὁ [82.169] δὲ θεῖος Ἀπόστολος ἐπέμεινε τῷ σχήματι, διὰ τῆς ἐρωτήσεως καὶ ἀποκρίσεως σαφέστερον ἀποφαίνων τὸν λόγον. Πάλιν γὰρ κατ' ἐρώτησιν ἀναγνωστέον·

18. *But I say, they have not heard, have they?* And this again, one must read as a question. Next is the answer, *On the contrary, they have. Their voice has gone*

out to all the earth, and their words to the ends of the inhabited world. For how could it be possible for the Jews not to hear what has been heard by the Gentiles throughout the inhabited world? For the preachers presented the message of truth to the Jews first. For even the Lord himself said, "Go rather to the lost sheep of the house of Israel."[73] And in Acts, it was said by the apostles, "It was necessary that the word of God be spoken first to you."[74] And the divine Apostle continues with this format, making the word known more clearly by means of question and answer. For once again, the next phrase must be read as a question.

Romans 10:19

ιθ'. Ἀλλὰ λέγω· Μὴ οὐκ ἔγνω Ἰσραήλ; Τὰ δὲ ἑξῆς κατὰ ἀπόκρισιν· Πρῶτος Μωσῆς λέγει· Ἐγὼ παραζηλώσω ὑμᾶς ἐπ' οὐκ ἔθνει, ἐπὶ ἔθνει ἀσυνέτῳ παροργιῶ ὑμᾶς. Ἀσυνέτους δὲ ἡμᾶς προσηγόρευσε, τὴν πρὸ τῆς πίστεως ἡμῶν ἀφροσύνην ἐπιδεικνύς. Τοῦτο γὰρ καὶ ὁ θεῖος Ἀπόστολος ἔφη· «Ἦμεν γὰρ καὶ ἡμεῖς ποτε ἀνόητοι, ἀπειθεῖς, πλανώμενοι, δουλεύοντες ἐπιθυμίαις καὶ ἡδοναῖς ποικίλαις, ἐν κακίᾳ καὶ φθόνῳ διάγοντες, στυγητοί, μισοῦντες ἀλλήλους.» Ταύτῃ διαφερόντως ἡνίασεν Ἰουδαίους ὁ Θεός. Οὐδὲ γὰρ αὐτοὺς οὕτως ἀλγύνει ἡ δουλεία, καὶ ἡ διασπορά, καὶ ἡ τοῦ ναοῦ ἐρημία, ὡς ἡ τῶν ἐθνῶν εὐσέβειά τε καὶ περιφάνεια.

19. *But I ask, did Israel not know?* The following things serve as an answer. First, Moses says, *"I will make you jealous of those who are not a nation, by a senseless nation I will make you angry."*[75] He calls us senseless, pointing out our folly before faith. For this reason the divine Apostle also said, "We also were once unwise, disobedient, being led astray, enslaved to various desires and sensual pleasures, spending our time in malice and envy, abominated, hating one another."[76] God grieved the Jews by this especially; for neither the bondage, nor the Diaspora, nor the desolation of the temple so distressed the Jews as does the godliness and notoriety of the Gentiles.[77]

Romans 10:20

κ'. Ἡσαΐας δὲ ἀποτολμᾷ, καὶ λέγει· Εὑρέθην τοῖς ἐμὲ μὴ ζητοῦσιν, ἐμφανὴς ἐγενόμην τοῖς ἐμὲ μὴ ἐπερωτῶσιν. Ἔδειξε κατὰ ταυτὸν καὶ τῆς τῶν ἐθνῶν θεογνωσίας τὴν πρόρρησιν, καὶ τὴν Ἰουδαίων μιαιφονίαν. Τὸ γάρ, ἀποτολμᾷ, τοῦτο δηλοῖ. Οὐκ ἔδεισε, φησί, φονῶντας Ἰουδαίους, καὶ μεμηνότας, ἀλλὰ σὺν παρρησίᾳ πολλῇ τὴν τῶν ἐθνῶν προεκήρυξε σωτηρίαν. Προεθέσπισε δὲ καὶ τῶν Ἰουδαίων τὴν ἀπιστίαν· τοῦτο γὰρ δηλοῖ τὰ ἑξῆς.

20. *Isaiah is very bold and says, "I was found by those who did not seek me; I became visible to those who did not ask for me."*[78] He demonstrates by this the proph-

ecy of the Gentile's knowledge of God and the blood guiltiness of the Jews. The use of the phrase "is very bold" shows this, in that he did not fear staining the Jews with blood and enraging them, but rather he proclaimed beforehand with great boldness the salvation of the Gentiles. He also foretold the unfaithfulness of the Jews, for this he reveals in the following verse.

Romans 10:21

κα΄. Πρὸς δὲ τὸν Ἰσραὴλ λέγει· Ὅλην τὴν ἡμέραν ἐξεπέτασα τὰς χεῖράς μου πρὸς λαὸν ἀπειθοῦντα καὶ ἀντιλέγοντα. Τὸ δὲ, ὅλην τὴν ἡμέραν, τὸ διηνεκὲς λέγει. Τοῦτο γὰρ καὶ ὁ Σύμμαχος καὶ ὁ Ἀκύλας, πᾶσαν ἡμέραν, ἡρμήνευσαν. Οὕτω δείξας τοὺς θαυμασίους προφήτας, καὶ Ἰουδαίων κατηγοροῦντας, καὶ τὴν τῶν ἐθνῶν προκηρύττοντας πίστιν, δοκεῖ μὲν αὐτοῖς διὰ τῶν ἑξῆς ψυχαγωγίαν προσφέρειν, αὔξει δὲ τὴν τῶν ἀπίστων κατηγορίαν. [82.172]

21. *But as for Israel he says, "All day long I have stretched out my hands to a disobedient and contrary people."* The phrase "all day long" indicates constancy. For this reason both Symmachus and Aquila employ the words "every day." Thus, having pointed out that the marvelous prophets both accuse the Jews and proclaim beforehand the faith of the Gentiles, it seems fitting to them to use persuasion by means of the following, increasing the accusation of unbelief.

Romans 11:1[79]

α΄. Λέγω οὖν· Μὴ ἀπώσατο ὁ Θεὸς τὸν λαὸν αὐτοῦ; Μὴ γένοιτο. Εἶτα τὴν τούτου ἀπόδειξιν ἐξ ἑτέρων πολλῶν δυνάμενος παρασχεῖν, καὶ ἀγαγεῖν εἰς μέσον τούς τε ἐν Ἱεροσολύμοις πεπιστευκότας τρισχιλίους, καὶ τὰς πολλὰς μυριάδας, περὶ ὧν ὁ μέγας Ἰάκωβος ἔφη, καὶ τοὺς κατὰ τὴν οἰκουμένην ἐξ Ἰουδαίων δεξαμένους τὸ κήρυγμα, ἀντὶ τούτων πάντων ἑαυτὸν ἐπιδείκνυσι, καὶ φησι· Καὶ γὰρ ἐγὼ Ἰσραηλίτης εἰμί, ἐκ σπέρματος Ἀβραάμ, φυλῆς Βενιαμίν.

1. *I ask then, has God rejected his people? By no means!* Then, although able to furnish the proof of this from many other examples by mentioning the three thousand who believed in Jerusalem, and the many thousands about whom the great James spoke,[80] not to mention those Jews throughout the inhabited world who have received the message, Paul instead uses himself as an example, saying, *"For I myself am an Israelite, from the seed of Abraham, of the tribe of Benjamin."*

Romans 11:2

β΄. Οὐκ ἀπώσατο ὁ Θεὸς τὸν λαὸν αὐτοῦ, ὃν προέγνω. Εἰ γὰρ ἀπώσατο, εἷς ἂν ἦν τῶν κατηγορουμένων κἀγώ. Ἐξ ἐκείνης γὰρ κἀγὼ τῆς ῥίζης ἐβλάστησα, καὶ τὸν Ἀβραὰμ αὐχῶ πρόγονον, καὶ τὸν Βενιαμὶν φύλαρχον, καὶ τῇ τοῦ Ἰσραὴλ προσηγορίᾳ σεμνύνομαι. Καλῶς δὲ καὶ, *ὃν προέγνω*, προστέθεικε, τουτέστι τοὺς τῆς θεογνωσίας ἀξίους, τοὺς τῆς πίστεως δεξαμένους τὴν αἴγλην. Τοῦτο γὰρ μετὰ ταῦτα διδάσκει. *Ἢ οὐκ οἴδατε ἐν Ἠλίᾳ τί λέγει ἡ Γραφή, ὡς ἐντυγχάνει τῷ Θεῷ κατὰ τοῦ Ἰσραήλ;*

2. *God did not reject his people whom he foreknew.* For if God had rejected his people, then even I myself would be one of those making an accusation against him. For I also came forth from that root; I also boast Abraham as an ancestor and Benjamin as a tribal chief, and I am proud of the name Israel. And rightly he also added the phrase "whom he foreknew," that is, those who are worthy of the knowledge of God, those who have received the sunlight of faith. For he teaches this in what follows. *Or do you not know what the Scripture says in the passage about Elijah, how he pleads with God against Israel?*

Romans 11:3–4

γ', δ'. *Κύριε, τοὺς προφήτας σου ἀπέκτειναν, καὶ τὰ θυσιαστήριά σου κατέσκαψαν. Κἀγὼ ὑπελείφθην μόνος, καὶ ζητοῦσι τὴν ψυχήν μου. Ἀλλὰ τί λέγει αὐτῷ ὁ χρηματισμός; Κατέλιπον ἐμαυτῷ ἑπτακισχιλίους ἄνδρας, οἵτινες οὐκ ἔκαμψαν γόνυ τῇ Βάαλ.* Καὶ κατ' ἐκεῖνον, φησὶ, τὸν καιρὸν πολλαὶ μυριάδες ἦσαν τοῦ Ἰσραὴλ, καὶ πάντες Ἰσραὴλ ὠνομάζοντο· ἀλλ' ὁ τῶν ὅλων Θεὸς τῶν ἑπτακισχιλίων ἑαυτὸν Θεὸν προσηγόρευσε, τοὺς δὲ ἄλλους ἀπεδοκίμασεν ἅπαντας. *Κατέλιπον γὰρ ἐμαυτῷ, ἔφη, ἑπτακισχιλίους ἄνδρας, οἵτινες οὐκ ἔκαμψαν γόνυ τῇ Βάαλ.* Ὁ μέντοι Προφήτης καὶ τοῦτο ἠγνόει, καὶ ἐν αὐτῷ μόνῳ τὰ λείψανα σεσῶσθαι τῆς εὐσεβείας ἐνόμιζεν. Οὐδὲν οὖν καινὸν, ἢ παράδοξον, εἰ καὶ ὑμεῖς ἀγνοεῖτε τοὺς ἐξ ὑμῶν τῷ Σωτῆρι πεπιστευκότας, οὓς λαὸν ὁ τῶν ὅλων προσαγορεύει Θεός. Εἰς καιρὸν δὲ τὸν μέγαν Ἠλίαν εἰς μέσον ἤγαγε, τὴν κατ' ἐκείνων πεποιημένον γραφὴν, ὡς οὐ μόνον τοὺς προφήτας ἀνελόντων, ἀλλὰ καὶ τὰ θυσιαστήρια ἐκ βάθρων ἀνασπασάντων. Δῶμεν γὰρ ὅτι δυσμενῶς περὶ τοὺς προφήτας διέκειντο, ὡς τὰ σκυθρωπὰ προθεσπίζοντας· τί τοῖς θείοις εἶχον ἐγκαλεῖν θυσιαστηρίοις; ἀλλ' ἐδήλωσαν δι' ὧν ἐτόλμησαν, ὡς τὸν τούτων ἐμίσουν Θεόν. Ὁ μέντοι θεῖος Ἀπόστολος ἐκ τῆς Γραφικῆς μαρτυρίας ἐπὶ τὸν οἰκεῖον μεταβαίνει λόγον, καί φησιν·

3–4. *"Lord, they have killed your prophets and they have torn down your altars. I alone am left, and they are seeking my life." But what is the divine reply to him? "I have left for myself seven thousand men who have not bent the knee to Baal."* And at that time there were countless thousands in Israel, and all were called Israelites. But the God of All called himself the God of the seven thousand, and he rejected all the others. "For I have left for myself," he said, "seven thousand men who have not bent the knee to Baal." The prophet, however, did not know this, and he presumed to save the remnants of godliness[81] by himself alone. Therefore, it is nothing new or incredible if you also do not know those among you who have believed in the Savior, those whom the God of All calls his people. At the right time, Paul brings up the great Elijah who made the statement[82] against those Israelites who not only killed the prophets but also tore down the altars from their pedestals. For if we grant that they were disposed in a hostile manner towards the prophets because of their gloomy forecasts, then why did they find fault with the divine altars? But they demonstrated through what they undertook that they hated the God of these altars. Then, of course, the divine Apostle turns from the scriptural testimony to his own word, and says:

Romans 11:5-6

ε′, ς′. Οὕτως οὖν καὶ ἐν τῷ νῦν καιρῷ λεῖμμα κατ᾽ ἐκλογὴν χάριτος γέγονεν. Εἰ δὲ χάριτι, οὐκ ἔτι ἐξ ἔργων· ἐπεὶ ἡ χάρις οὐκέτι ἐστὶ χάρις. Εἰ δὲ ἐξ ἔργων, οὐκέτι ἐστὶ χάρις, ἐπεὶ τὸ ἔργον οὐκέτι ἐστὶν ἔργον. Καθάπερ τότε, φησὶν, ἀπὸ [82.173] μυριάδων ἀπείρων ἑπτακισχίλιοι κατελείφθησαν μόνον τῆς ἀσεβείας ἐλεύθεροι· οὕτω καὶ νῦν πλείους μὲν οἱ ἀπιστήσαντες, ἐλάττους δὲ οἱ πιστεύσαντες, καὶ τῆς θείας χάριτος ἀπολαύσαντες. Οὐ γὰρ ἡ κατὰ νόμον αὐτοὺς ἐδικαίωσε πολιτεία (τοῦτο γὰρ λέγει, ἐξ ἔργων), ἀλλ᾽ ἡ τοῦ Θεοῦ διέσωσε χάρις. Διὰ τοῦτο καὶ χάρις ἡ σωτηρία καλεῖται, ἐπειδὴ κατὰ θείαν φιλοτιμίαν γεγένηται. Τοῦτο καὶ ἐν τοῖς κατὰ τὸν πατριάρχην Ἀβραὰμ φησί· «Τῷ δὲ ἐργαζομένῳ ὁ μισθὸς οὐ λογίζεται κατὰ χάριν, ἀλλὰ κατὰ ὀφείλημα.»

5-6. *In the same way then, there has come to be a remnant at the present time according to the election of grace. And if it is by grace, then it is no longer by works; otherwise, grace would no longer be grace. And if it is by works, then it is no longer grace; otherwise, works would no longer be works.* Just as he says then, from countless thousands, only seven thousand were left free of ungodliness.[83] Thus even now, those who have not believed are the majority, and those who have believed and enjoyed the divine grace are the minority. For the way of life according to the law (Paul calls this "by works") did not justify them, but rather the grace of God preserved them. For this reason salvation is also called grace, since it happens according to divine benefaction. In the earlier passage about Abraham Paul says, "Now to the one who works, the wage is reckoned not as a gift but as that which is owed."[84]

Romans 11:7

ζ′. Τί οὖν; Ἐνταῦθα ὑποστικτέον· κατ᾽ ἐρώτησιν γὰρ κεῖται, ἀντὶ τοῦ· Τί τοίνυν ἔστιν εἰπεῖν; Εἶτα κατὰ ἀπόκρισιν τὰ λοιπά· Ὃ ἐπιζητεῖ Ἰσραήλ, τούτου οὐκ ἐπέτυχεν· ἡ δὲ ἐκλογὴ ἐπέτυχεν· οἱ δὲ λοιποὶ ἐπωρώθησαν.—Ἐκλογὴν τοὺς ἐξ αὐτῶν πεπιστευκότας καλεῖ. Λέγει δὲ τοῦτο· Ὁ Ἰσραὴλ τῷ νόμῳ προστετηκὼς διήμαρτε τοῦ σκοποῦ· παρανόμως γὰρ νῦν φυλάττει τὸν νόμον, καὶ δικαιοσύνην οὐδεμίαν καρποῦται. Οἱ δὲ ἐξ αὐτῶν πεπιστευκότες ἐπέτυχον· *οἱ δὲ λοιποὶ ἐπωρώθησαν* ἀντὶ τοῦ, σκληροτέραν ἡ ἀπιστία τὴν καρδίαν αὐτῶν ἀπειργάσατο. Δείκνυσι δὲ καὶ τοῦτο ἄνωθεν προηγορευμένον.

7. *What then?* This part here is to be kept separate; for it occurs as a question, that is, what then is there to say? Then the rest serves as an answer. *What Israel is seeking it has not obtained. But the elect have obtained it, and the rest were hardened.* – He calls those of them[85] who have believed the "elect." And he says this: although Israel adhered to the law, they fell short of the mark. For now Israel keeps the law in a lawless manner and does not bear any righteousness as fruit. But those among them who have believed obtained it. "And the rest were hardened," that is to say, unbelief made their hearts harder. And this also shows what has been foretold from the beginning.

Romans 11:8

η'. *Καθὼς γέγραπται· Ἔδωκεν αὐτοῖς ὁ Θεὸς πνεῦμα κατανύξεως, ὀφθαλμοὺς τοῦ μὴ βλέπειν, καὶ ὦτα τοῦ μὴ ἀκούειν, ἕως τῆς σήμερον ἡμέρας. Τὸ ἔδωκεν, ὡς τὸ παρέδωκεν, ἀντὶ τοῦ συνεχώρησεν·* οὐ γὰρ ὁ Θεὸς αὐτοὺς παρεσκεύασεν ἀπιστῆσαι· πῶς γὰρ οἷόν τε καὶ αὐτὸν αὐτοῖς ἐνθεῖναι τὴν ἀπιστίαν, καὶ αὐτὸν δίκας ὑπὲρ ταύτης εἰσπρᾶξαι; Τοῦτο καὶ ὁ Προφήτης σαφέστερον ἐδίδαξεν· «Ἐπαχύνθη γὰρ ἡ καρδία τοῦ λαοῦ τούτου, καὶ τοῖς ὠσὶ βαρέως ἤκουσαν, καὶ τοὺς ὀφθαλμοὺς αὐτῶν ἐκάμμυσαν.» Οὐκ ἄλλος τοίνυν αὐτοὺς ἐτύφλωσεν, ἀλλ' αὐτοὶ τοὺς ὀφθαλμοὺς ἔμυσαν, καὶ τὸ φῶς ἰδεῖν οὐκ ἠθέλησαν. Πνεῦμα δὲ κατανύξεως τὴν ἀμετάβλητον ἐκάλεσε γνώμην. Ὥσπερ γὰρ ὁ τὴν ἐπαινουμένην ἔχων κατάνυξιν, τὴν ἐπὶ τὸ χεῖρον τροπὴν οὐκ εἰσδέχεται· οὕτως ὁ παντελῶς ἑαυτὸν ἐκδοὺς τῇ πονηρίᾳ, τὴν ἐπὶ τὸ κρεῖττον οὐχ αἱρεῖται μεταβολήν.

8. *Just as it is written, "God gave them a spirit of stupor, eyes that would not see and ears that would not hear, until the present day."*[86] The verb "give," like "hand over," is equivalent to "allow." For God did not cause them to disbelieve. For how is it even possible for him to inspire unbelief in them and then exact punishment for this? The prophet taught this even more clearly, "For the hearts of this people were thickened; they listened in disgust with their ears, and they shut their eyes."[87] Therefore, they were not blinded by another, but they closed their eyes and did not want to see the light. He called the unchangeable mind a spirit of stupor. For even as one holds the state of stupor as commendable, one does not admit the turn for the worse. Thus the one who has utterly surrendered himself to evil does not choose the change for the better.

Romans 11:9–10

θ′, ι′. Καὶ Δαβὶδ λέγει· Γενηθήτω ἡ τράπεζα αὐτῶν ἐνώπιον αὐτῶν εἰς παγίδα, καὶ εἰς θήραν, καὶ εἰς σκάνδαλον, καὶ εἰς ἀνταπόδομα αὐτοῖς. Σκοτισθήτωσαν οἱ ὀφθαλμοὶ αὐτῶν τοῦ μὴ βλέπειν, καὶ τὸν νῶτον αὐτῶν διὰ παντὸς σύγκαμψον. Τράπεζαν δὲ τὴν τρυφὴν προσηγόρευσεν, ἣν εἰς τοὐναντίον μεταβληθήσεσθαι προεθέσπισε.

9–10. *And David says, "Let their table become a trap and a snare before them, and a stumbling block and retribution to them. Let their eyes be darkened so that they cannot see, and bend their backs forever."*[88] He gives the name "table" to their luxuriousness, which he foretells will be turned into the opposite condition.

Romans 11:11

ια′. Λέγω οὖν· Μὴ ἔπταισαν ἵνα πέσωσι; Μὴ γένοιτο. Ἀλλὰ τῷ αὐτῶν παραπτώματι ἡ σωτηρία τοῖς ἔθνεσιν, εἰς τὸ παραζηλῶσαι αὐτούς. Τούτοις γὰρ πρώτοις οἱ ἐξ αὐτῶν πεπιστευκότες [82.176] προσήνεγκαν τὸ σωτήριον κήρυγμα· ἀντειπόντων δὲ τούτων, καὶ τὴν διδασκαλίαν οὐ δεξαμένων, τοῖς ἔθνεσι τὸ θεῖον προσήνεγκαν Εὐαγγέλιον· οἱ δὲ πιστεύσαντες, τῆς σωτηρίας ἀπήλαυσαν. Ἱκανὸν δὲ τοῦτο παρακνίσαι τῶν. Ἰουδαίων τοὺς ἀντιλέγοντας, καὶ εἰς ζῆλον ἐρεθίσαι, καὶ προξενῆσαι τῆς σωτηρίας τὴν μετουσίαν. Ὁρῶσι γὰρ τοὺς ἐσχάτους πρώτους γεγενημένους.

11. *Therefore I ask, did they stumble so as to fall? By no means! But by their transgression, salvation has come to the Gentiles in order to make them jealous.* For those from the Jews who have believed presented the saving gospel to these first; but when they spoke against the teaching and did not receive it, the believers offered the divine gospel to the Gentiles. And those who believed have enjoyed salvation. This is sufficient to irritate those Jews who speak against the gospel and to provoke them to jealousy and to effect their participation in salvation. For they see that the last have become first.

Romans 11:12

ιβ′. Εἰ δὲ τὸ παράπτωμα αὐτῶν πλοῦτος κόσμου, καὶ τὸ ἥττημα αὐτῶν πλοῦτος ἐθνῶν, πόσῳ μᾶλλον τὸ πλήρωμα αὐτῶν; Εἰ γὰρ τῶν πλειόνων ἀπιστησάντων, οἱ ἐξ αὐτῶν πεπιστευκότες τοῖς ἔθνεσι τῆς θεογνωσίας τὸν πλοῦτον προσήνεγκαν, δηλονότι πάντες πιστεύσαντες μειζόνων ἀγαθῶν πᾶσιν ἀνθρώποις ἐγένοντο ἂν πρόξενοι. Ῥᾷον γὰρ ἐπίστευον πάντες, οὐκέτι τούτων ἀντιλεγόντων, ἀλλὰ μεθ' ἡμῶν τὴν ἀλήθειαν κηρυττόντων. Ἐντεῦθεν τοῖς ἐξ ἐθνῶν πεπιστευκόσι προσφέρει παραίνεσιν, μετρίῳ κεχρῆσθαι συμβουλεύων φρονήματι· δύο κατὰ ταυτὸν μηχανώμενος· καὶ τούτων τὴν ὀφρὺν καταστέλλων, καὶ δεδοικέναι παρασκευάζων· καὶ Ἰουδαίους εἰς τὴν τῆς πατρῴας κληρονομίας κοινωνίαν τρέπων Ἄρχεται δὲ οὕτως·

12. *Now if their transgression means riches for the world, and their loss means riches for the Gentiles, how much more will their fullness*[89] *mean?* For if, when the majority of the Jews did not believe, those of them who did believe offered the riches of the knowledge of God to the Gentiles, then quite clearly all those who believed became patrons of the greater good to all humanity.[90] For all of those believed more readily; they no longer spoke against us but rather proclaimed the truth with us. Henceforth Paul offers exhortation to those Gentiles who believe, advising them to employ a moderate mindset. Paul is contriving to do two things at once—to check the Gentiles' pride and cause them to fear, while also turning the Jews toward sharing the inheritance of a homeland. And he begins in this way:

Romans 11:13-14

ιγ΄, ιδ΄. Ὑμῖν γὰρ λέγω τοῖς ἔθνεσιν· Ἐφ᾽ ὅσον μέν εἰμι ἐγὼ ἐθνῶν ἀπόστολος, τὴν δια κονίαν μου δοξάζω. Εἴ πως παραζηλώσω μου τὴν σάρκα, καὶ σώσω τινὰς ἐξ αὐτῶν. Ἐπειδή με τῶν ἐθνῶν ὁ Θεὸς προὐβάλετο κήρυκα, ἀναγκαίως τὴν σωτηρίαν τῶν ἐθνῶν πραγματεύομαι, καὶ τοὺς ὑπὲρ τούτων ποιοῦμαι λόγους, καὶ τοὺς θείους προφήτας ἄνωθεν ταῦτα δείκνυμι προθεσπίσαντας· ἵνα ταύτῃ γοῦν Ἰουδαίους εἰς ζῆλον ἐρεθίσω, καί τινας ἐξ αὐτῶν μεταλαχεῖν παρασκευάσω τῆς σωτηρίας. *Σάρκα* γὰρ *αὐτοῦ* τοὺς Ἰουδαίους λέγει ὡς κατὰ μὲν τὸ φρόνημα ἀλλοτρίους ὄντας, μόνης δὲ αὐτῷ κοινωνοῦντας τῆς συγγενείας.

13-14. *For I am speaking to you Gentiles. Inasmuch as I am an apostle to the Gentiles, I glorify my ministry, if somehow I may make my own people jealous and save some of them.* Since God has put me forward as a preacher to the Gentiles, of necessity I am engaged in the business of the salvation of the Gentiles, and I provide instruction[91] for them, and I explain the divine prophets, who have foretold these things from the beginning, in order that at least by this I might provoke the Jews to jealousy and cause some of them to have a share in salvation. Here Paul calls the Jews "his flesh" since they are foreigners according to their mindset and share only a familial relationship with him.

Romans 11:15

ιε΄. Εἰ γὰρ ἡ ἀποβολὴ αὐτῶν καταλλαγὴ κόσμου, τίς ἡ πρόσληψις, εἰ μὴ ζωὴ ἐκ νεκρῶν; Εἰ γὰρ τούτων ἀπιστησάντων, φησὶ, προσελήφθη τὰ ἔθνη, καὶ τῆς προτέρας ἀγνοίας ἠλευθερώθη, δῆλον ὡς εἰ πάντες οὗτοι πιστεῦσαι θελήσαιεν, οὐδὲν ἕτερον ὑπολείπεται, ἢ τὸ γενέσθαι τῶν νεκρῶν τὴν ἀνάστασιν. Τοῦτο δὲ καὶ ὁ Κύριος ἔφη· «Κηρυχθήσεται τὸ Εὐαγγέλιον τοῦτο τῆς βασιλείας εἰς πάντα τὰ ἔθνη εἰς μαρτύριον αὐτοῖς, καὶ τότε ἥξει τὸ τέλος.» Εἰδέναι μέντοι χρή, ὡς ταῦτα ὁ θεῖος Ἀπόστολος εἴρηκεν, οἰκονομικῶς κατασκευάζων τὸν

λόγον· καὶ τούς τε ἐξ ἐθνῶν πεπιστευκότας μετριοφρονεῖν ἐκπαιδεύων, καὶ τοῖς
ἀπιστοῦσι τῶν Ἰουδαίων χεῖρα ὀρέγων, καὶ τὴν ἐκ τῆς μεταμελείας ὑποδεικνὺς
σωτηρίαν. Καὶ τοῦτο τὰ ἑξῆς διδάσκει σαφέστερον.

15. *For if their rejection means the reconciliation of the world, what will their acceptance mean if not life from the dead?* For if when they did not believe, Paul
says, the Gentiles were added and freed from their former ignorance, then it is
clear that if all of these[92] should desire to believe, nothing else would be left
except for the resurrection of the dead to take place. Now even the Lord said
this, "This good news of the kingdom will be proclaimed to all the nations as a
witness to them, and then the end will come."[93] Nevertheless, it is necessary to
know that the divine Apostle has spoken these things, phrasing the argument
diplomatically as he educates those Gentiles who have believed to think mod-
estly while also extending a hand to those Jews who do not believe, providing a
glimpse of the salvation that comes from repentance. He teaches this more
clearly in the following verses.

Romans 11:16–18

ιϛ′–ιη′. *Εἰ δὲ ἡ ἀπαρχὴ ἁγία, καὶ τὸ φύραμα·* [82.177] *καὶ εἰ ἡ ῥίζα ἁγία, καὶ οἱ
κλάδοι. Εἰ δέ τινες τῶν κλάδων ἐξεκλάσθησαν, σὺ δὲ ἀγριέλαιος ὢν
ἐνεκεντρίσθης ἐν αὐτοῖς, καὶ συγκοινωνὸς τῆς ῥίζης καὶ τῆς πιότητος τῆς ἐλαίας
ἐγένου· μὴ κατακαυχῶ τῶν κλάδων.*—Ἀπαρχὴν καλεῖ τὸν Δεσπότην Χριστὸν
κατὰ τὴν ἀνθρωπείαν φύσιν· *ῥίζαν* δὲ, τὸν πατριάρχην Ἀβραάμ· *κλάδους* δὲ
ἐλαίας, τὸν τῶν Ἰουδαίων λαόν, ὡς ἐκεῖθεν βλαστήσαντα· πιότητα δὲ ἐλαίας,
τὴν τῆς εὐσεβείας διδασκαλίαν. Παρακελεύεται τοίνυν τοῖς ἐξ ἐθνῶν
πεπιστευκόσι, τῶν ἀπιστησάντων Ἰουδαίων μὴ κατεπαίρεσθαι· τούτους γὰρ
ὀνομάζει *κλάδους ἀποκλασθέντας.* Σκοπήσατε δὲ, φησὶν, ὅτι ὑμεῖς ἐξ ἐτέρας
συγγενείας ὁρμώμενοι εἰς ταύτην ἐνεκεντρίσθητε, καὶ τῆς εὐσεβοῦς ῥίζης
ἐδέξασθε τὴν πιότητα. *Εἰ δὲ κατακαυχᾶσαι, οὐ σὺ τὴν ῥίζαν βαστάζεις, ἀλλ᾽ ἡ
ῥίζα σέ.* Λογίζου δὲ καὶ τοῦτο, ὅτι σὲ ἡ ῥίζα φέρει, οὐ σὺ τὴν ῥίζαν· καὶ σὺ
ἐκείνης δέῃ, οὐκ ἐκείνη σοῦ.

16–18. *If the part of the dough offered as first fruits is holy, then the whole batch
is holy also; and if the root is holy, then the branches are also holy. But if some of the
branches were broken off, and you, though being a wild olive, were grafted in among
them and became a sharer of the root and of the richness of the olive tree, then do not
boast over the branches.* He calls the Lord Christ "first fruits" according to his
human nature. The patriarch Abraham is the "root," and the Jewish people
are the "branches of the olive tree" that have grown from it. The phrase "the
richness of the olive tree" refers to the teaching of godliness. Therefore, he ad-
vises those Gentiles who believe not to be arrogant towards the unbelieving
Jews, for he designates them as "broken off branches." Now consider, he says,

that you, although coming from another family tree, were grafted into this one, and you received the richness of the hallowed root. *But if you do boast, remember that you do not support the root, but the root supports you.* And consider this also, since the root bears you, you do not bear the root, so you need the root but it does not need you.

Romans 11:19–20

ιθ′, κ′. *Ἐρεῖς οὖν· Ἐξεκλάσθησαν οἱ κλάδοι, ἵνα ἐγὼ ἐγκεντρισθῶ. Καλῶς· τῇ ἀπιστίᾳ ἐξεκλάσθησαν, σὺ δὲ τῇ πίστει ἔστηκας. Μὴ ὑψηλὰ φρόνει, ἀλλὰ φοβοῦ.* Κἀκείνους ἡ ἀπιστία τῆς ῥίζης ἀλλοτρίους ἀπέφηνε, καὶ σὲ ἡ πίστις συνῆψε τῇ ῥίζῃ, καὶ τῆς ταύτης πιότητος μεταλαχεῖν παρεσκεύασε. Προσήκει σε τοίνυν μὴ μέγα φρονεῖν, ἀλλὰ δεδιέναι καὶ τρέμειν. Διὰ τί;

19–20. *You will say then, "The branches were broken off in order that I might be grafted in." Well said; they were broken off because of unbelief, but you stand by faith. So do not be proud but stand in awe.* Unbelief rendered even the Jews as foreigners of the root, and faith united you with the root and caused you to have a share in its richness. Therefore, it behooves you not to be arrogant but rather to fear and tremble. Why?

Romans 11:21

κα′. *Εἰ γὰρ ὁ Θεὸς τῶν κατὰ φύσιν κλάδων οὐκ ἐφείσατο, μήπως οὐδὲ σοῦ φείσεται.* Εἰ γὰρ ἐκεί νους οὐδὲν ὤνησεν ἡ τῆς φύσεως οἰκειότης, ἐπειδὴ τὴν αὐτὴν οὐκ ἔσχον προαίρεσιν· πολλῷ μᾶλλον σὺ μὴ φυλάξας τὴν χάριν, γενήσῃ τῆς ῥίζης ἀλλότριος.

21. *For if God did not spare the natural branches, perhaps he will not spare you either.* For if natural kinship did not help them at all, although they did not have the same purpose,[94] then it is much more likely that you may become a foreigner of the root if you do not cling to grace.

Romans 11:22

κβ′. *Ἴδε οὖν χρηστότητα καὶ ἀποτομίαν Θεοῦ· ἐπὶ μὲν τοὺς πεσόντας, ἀποτομίαν, ἐπὶ δὲ σὲ χρηστότητα, ἐὰν ἐπιμείνῃς τῇ χρηστότητι· ἐπεὶ καὶ σὺ ἐκκοπήσῃ.* Ὅρα νῦν ὅπως μὲν ἐκείνους ἀπέτεμεν ὁ Θεός, τὴν τῶν προγόνων οὐ ζηλώσαντας πίστιν· ὅπως δὲ σὲ φιλανθρωπίας ἠξίωσε, καὶ ῥίζης ἀλλοτρίας ἀπέφηνε κοινωνόν, ἧς ἀλλότριος ᾖ πάντως τὴν δοθεῖσαν οὐ φυλάξας δωρεάν.

22. *Behold then the kindness and severity of God; severity toward those who have fallen, but kindness toward you, if you remain in his kindness. Otherwise, you also will*

be cut off. See then how God cut them off because they did not strive after the faith of the forefathers. See how he deemed you worthy of his benevolence and made you a sharer of another's root, which might be completely foreign, since it did not keep the gift which was given.

Romans 11:23

κγ′. *Καὶ ἐκεῖνοι δέ, ἐὰν μὴ ἐπιμείνωσι τῇ ἀπιστίᾳ ἐγκεντρισθήσονται.* Πρέπει γὰρ τῇ τοῦ Θεοῦ δικαιοσύνῃ, καὶ σὲ παρ' ἐλπίδα τῆς ἐκείνων ῥίζης ἀξιωθέντα, εἶτα τὴν δοθεῖσαν μὴ φυλάξαντα χάριν, χωρίσαι πάλιν τῆς ῥίζης· καὶ τούτους τῆς ἀπιστίας ἀπαλλαγέντας, αὖθις ἐκείνῃ συνάψαι. Καλῶς δὲ καὶ ἐπὶ τούτων τὸ, *ἐγκεντρισθήσονται,* τέθεικεν, ὡς τῆς ἀπιστίας αὐτοὺς παντελῶς χωρισάσης, καὶ τῆς πίστεως παραπλησίως τοῖς ἔθνεσι συναπτούσης τῇ ῥίζῃ. *Δυνατὸς γάρ ἐστιν ὁ Θεὸς πάλιν ἐγκεντρίσαι αὐτούς.* Τῇ τοῦ Θεοῦ δυνάμει τὴν τοῦ πράγματος εὐ- [82.180] κολίαν ἐπέδειξε, καὶ τίθησι παράδειγμα, οὔτε ἀλλότριον, οὔτε παλαιὸν, ἀλλ' οἰκεῖον καὶ νέον. Αὐτοὺς γὰρ εἰς μαρτυρίαν τούτου καλεῖ, καί φησι·

23. *And they also, if they do not continue in their unbelief, will be grafted in.* For it is fitting with the righteousness of God to separate you also from the root, if, having first been deemed worthy of their root beyond hope, you then did not keep the grace which was given. And when the Jews have ceased their unbelief, they can be united with the root again. And rightly he applies the phrase "will be grafted in" to them, for unbelief separated them completely, and faith unites them with the root much like the Gentiles. *For God is able to graft them in again.* He demonstrates the ease of the matter with the power of God, and he includes an example, neither foreign nor old, but familiar and new. For he calls them as a witness to this, and he says:

Romans 11:24

κδ′. *Εἰ γὰρ σὺ ἐκ τῆς κατὰ φύσιν ἐξεκόπης ἀγριελαίου, καὶ παρὰ φύσιν ἐνεκεντρίσθης εἰς καλλιέλαιον, πόσῳ μᾶλλον οὗτοι οἱ κατὰ φύσιν, ἐγκεντρισθήσονται τῇ ἰδίᾳ ἐλαίᾳ;* Εἰ σὺ ἀγριέλαιος ὢν (οὐ γὰρ ἔσχες γεωργοῦντα τὸν νόμον, οὐδὲ τοὺς προφήτας ἄρδοντας, καὶ καθαίροντας, καὶ τὴν προσήκουσάν σου ἐπιμέλειαν ποιουμένους), τῶν μὲν δυσσεβῶν ἐχωρίσθης προγόνων τε καὶ συγγενῶν, τῆς δὲ τοῦ Ἀβραὰμ πίστεως κοινωνὸς ἀπεφάνθης, καὶ τοῦτον αὐχεῖς ῥίζαν, καὶ πατέρα, καὶ πρόγονον, οὐ κατὰ φύσιν νόμου, ἀλλὰ διὰ τὴν θείαν φιλοτιμίαν· πολλῷ δήπουθεν εὐλογώτερόν τε καὶ φυσικώτερον οὗτοι πιστεύσαντες τῇ οἰκείᾳ συναφθήσονται ῥίζῃ. Ταῦτα δὲ, ὡς ἔφην, λέγει, καὶ τοὺς ἐξ ἐθνῶν πεπιστευκότας μετριάζειν διδάσκων, καὶ τοὺς ἀπιστήσαντας τῶν Ἰουδαίων εἰς σωτηρίαν προτρέπων. Συμφωνεῖ δὲ τούτοις καὶ τὰ ἑξῆς.

24. *For if you were cut off of that which is by nature a wild olive tree, and contrary to nature were grafted into a cultivated olive tree, then how much more will these natural branches be grafted back into their own olive tree?* Since you, though being a wild olive tree—for you did not have the law to cultivate you, nor the prophets to refresh, purify, and take proper care of you—were separated from the impiety of your ancestors and relatives and made a sharer of the faith of Abraham, then you should boast in this, that you have a root, a father, and an ancestor, not according to the nature of the law but because of divine benevolence. It is, presumably, much more reasonable and natural that those who have believed will be united with their own root. Now these things, as I have noted, Paul says in order to teach the believing Gentiles to conduct themselves with moderation and to urge the unbelieving Jews toward salvation. These things are in harmony with that which follows.

Romans 11:25

κε'. Οὐ γὰρ θέλω ὑμᾶς ἀγνοεῖν, ἀδελφοί, τὸ μυστήριον τοῦτο, ἵνα μὴ ἦτε παρ' ἑαυτοῖς φρόνιμοι. Μυστήριόν ἐστι τὸ μὴ πᾶσι γνώριμον, ἀλλὰ μόνοις τοῖς θαῤῥουμένοις. Λέγει τοίνυν, ὅτι Βούλομαι ὑμᾶς μαθεῖν ὅπερ οἴδαμεν περὶ τῶν προκειμένων μυστήριον, ἵνα μὴ σφόδρα ἡγούμενοι ἑαυτοὺς συνετούς, ὑψηλὸν ἐντεῦθεν εἰσδέξησθε φρόνημα. Τί δὲ τὸ μυστήριον; *Ὅτι πώρωσις ἀπὸ μέρους τῷ Ἰσραὴλ γέγονεν, ἄχρις οὗ τὸ πλήρωμα τῶν ἐθνῶν εἰσέλθῃ, καὶ οὕτω πᾶς Ἰσραὴλ σωθήσεται.* Τὸ *ἀπὸ μέρους* τέθεικε, διδάσκων ὡς οὐ πάντες ἠπίστησαν· πολλοὶ γὰρ καὶ ἐξ ἐκείνων ἐπίστευσαν. Παρεγγυᾷ δὲ μὴ τῶν ἄλλων ἀπαγορεῦσαι τὴν σωτηρίαν· τῶν γὰρ ἐθνῶν δεξαμένων τὸ κήρυγμα, πιστεύσουσι κἀκεῖνοι, Ἠλία τοῦ πάνυ παραγενομένου, καὶ τῆς πίστεως αὐτοῖς τὴν διδασκαλίαν προσφέροντος. Τοῦτο γὰρ καὶ ὁ Κύριος ἐν τοῖς ἱεροῖς Εὐαγγελίοις ἔφη· «Ἠλίας ἔρχεται, καὶ ἀποκαταστήσει πάντα.» Τέθεικε δὲ καὶ τὴν προφητικὴν μαρτυρίαν.

25. *For I do not want you to be ignorant of this mystery, brothers and sisters, in order that you may not be wise in your own eyes.* This mystery is not well-known to all, but only to those who trust confidently.[95] Therefore Paul says, "I want you to learn that which we know about the mystery of the matters at hand so that you may not become arrogant from it by considering yourselves exceedingly wise. Now what is the mystery?" *That a hardening has happened partially to Israel, until the fullness of the Gentiles has come in, and so all Israel will be saved.*[96] Paul adds the word "partially" in order to teach that not all Jews have disbelieved; for many of them have believed. And he urges them not to despair of the salvation of the other Jews; for when the Gentiles have received the message, even they, the Jews, will believe, when the excellent Elijah comes, bringing to them the doctrine[97] of faith. For even the Lord said this in the sacred gospels:

"Elijah is coming, and he will restore all things."[98] Now Paul also adds the prophetic witness:

Romans 11:26-27

κϛ′, κζ′. *Καθὼς γέγραπται· Ἥξει ἐκ Σιὼν ὁ ῥυόμενος, καὶ ἀποστρέψει ἀσεβείας ἀπὸ Ἰακώβ. Καὶ αὕτη αὐτοῖς ἡ παρ' ἐμοῦ διαθήκη, ὅταν ἀφέλωμαι τὰς ἁμαρτίας αὐτῶν.* Εἰ ἡ κατὰ νόμον πολιτεία δωρεῖται τῶν ἁμαρτημάτων τὴν ἄφεσιν, αὐτὴν ὁ προφητικὸς προεθέσπισε λόγος. Εἰ δὲ κολάζει μὲν ὁ νόμος τοὺς παραβαίνοντας, ἀεὶ δὲ παρανομίαν ἐν ἐκλήθησαν Ἰουδαῖοι, εὔδηλον ὡς τὴν διὰ τοῦ βαπτίσματος χορηγουμένην ἄφεσιν ὁ λόγος δηλοῖ. Πάντα δὲ Ἰσραὴλ καλεῖ τοὺς πιστεύοντας, εἴτε ἐξ Ἰουδαίων εἶεν, τὴν φυσικὴν συγγένειαν πρὸς τὸν Ἰσραὴλ ἔχοντες, εἴτε ἐξ ἐθνῶν, κατὰ τὴν τῆς πίστεως συγγένειαν αὐτῷ συναπτόμενοι. [82.181]

26-27. Just as it is written, "The Deliverer will come from Zion, and he will banish ungodliness from Jacob. And this is my covenant with them, when I take away their sins."[99] If the way of life according to the law grants forgiveness of sins, the prophetic word would have foretold it. But if the law punishes those who transgress, and the Jews were always accused of transgressing the law, then it is quite clear that the text indicates forgiveness is supplied through baptism. Paul refers to those who believe as "all Israel," whether from the Jews, who have a physical relation to Israel, or from the Gentiles, who are united with Israel according to the kinship of faith.

Romans 11:28

κη′. *Κατὰ μὲν τὸ Εὐαγγέλιον, ἐχθροὶ δι' ὑμᾶς· κατὰ δὲ τὴν ἐκλογήν, ἀγαπητοὶ διὰ τοὺς πατέρας.* Ὅταν εἰς ὑμᾶς ἀποβλέψω, ὧν τὴν διδασκαλίαν ἐνεχειρίσθην, ἐχθροὺς ἐκείνους ὑπολαμβάνω καὶ δυσμενεῖς, πάντα εἰς ὑμετέραν βλάβην ἐργαζομένους. Ὅταν δέ γε εἰς τοὺς προγόνους ἀπίδω, καὶ λογίσωμαι ὡς ἐκείνους ἐξ ἁπάσης τῆς οἰκουμένης ὁ Θεὸς ἐξελέξατο, στέργω δι' ἐκείνους καὶ τούτους.

28. With regard to the gospel, they are enemies for your sake; but as regards election, they are beloved for the sake of the fathers. Whenever I consider you, for whom I was entrusted with the teaching, I take them to be hostile enemies who do everything for your harm. But whenever I look at the forefathers and consider that God chose them out of all the inhabited world, I also feel fondly for these contemporary Jews on account of the fathers.

Romans 11:29

κθ′. Ἀμεταμέλητα γὰρ τὰ χαρίσματα καὶ ἡ κλῆσις τοῦ Θεοῦ. Ταῦτα πάντα εἰς προτροπὴν λέγει τῶν Ἰουδαίων. Ὅτι γὰρ ἃ δίδωσι ὁ Θεὸς ἀγαθὰ, πάλιν λαμβάνει, ὅταν ἴδῃ τοὺς εἰληφότας ἀχαριστίαν νοσοῦντας, μάρτυς ὁ Σαοὺλ πνευματικῆς χάριτος ἀπολαύσας, εἶτα ταύτης ἔρημος μετὰ ταῦτα γεγενημένος. Καὶ ὁ Σολομὼν δὲ ὡσαύτως, εἰρήνης ἀπολαύσας διὰ τὴν θείαν φιλοτιμίαν, μετὰ τὴν παράβασιν ἐγυμνώθη τῆς χάριτος. Καὶ αὐτοὶ δὲ οἱ Ἰουδαῖοι, προφητικῆς ἐπιμελείας διηνεκῶς ἀπολαύσαντες, ἐπὶ τοῦ παρόντος τῆς κηδεμονίας ταύτης ἐστέρηνται. Τοῦτο καὶ τοῖς ἐξ ἐθνῶν πεπιστευκόσι πρὸ βραχέος ἠπείλησεν. Ἐὰν ἐπιμείνῃς γὰρ, φησὶ, τῇ χρηστότητι· ἐπεὶ καὶ σὺ ἐκκοπήσῃ.

29. *For the gifts and the call of God are irrevocable.* He says all these things in order to provide encouragement for the Jews. For since that which God gives is good, he takes it back again whenever he sees those who have received it being afflicted with ingratitude. Saul serves as a witness to this, for having had the benefit of a spiritual gift, he then became destitute of it after these things. And Solomon also serves as an example, for having enjoyed peace thanks to divine benevolence, he was stripped of favor after his transgression. And as for the Jews themselves, having enjoyed prophetic care from the beginning, they are deprived of this care at the present time. He had even made this threat a little before to those Gentiles who have believed. *If you remain in goodness; otherwise, even you will be cut off.*

Romans 11:30–31

λ′, λα′. Ὥσπερ γὰρ καὶ ὑμεῖς ποτὲ ἠπειθήσατε τῷ Θεῷ, νῦν δὲ ἠλεήθητε τῇ τούτων ἀπειθείᾳ· οὕτω καὶ οὗτοι νῦν ἠπείθησαν τῷ ὑμετέρῳ ἐλέει, ἵνα καὶ αὐτοὶ ἐλεηθῶσιν. Ἀναμνήσθητε δὲ, ὡς ἅπαντες ἐπὶ πλεῖστον ἠσεβήσατε χρόνον, καὶ οὐκ ἀπέβλεψεν ὁ φιλάνθρωπος Δεσπότης εἰς τὴν μακρὰν ἐκείνην καὶ χαλεπὴν ἀσέβειαν, ἀλλὰ τῆς ἀρρήτου φιλανθρωπίας τοὺς βουληθέντας ἠξίωσε, καὶ τούτων ἀπιστησάντων, ὑμᾶς ἀντὶ τούτων ἐκάλεσεν. Οὐδὲν τοίνυν ἀπεικὸς, καὶ τοὺς νῦν ἀντιλέγοντας δεχθῆναι παρὰ τοῦ Θεοῦ πιστεῦσαι θελήσαντας, καὶ τῆς αὐτῆς φιλανθρωπίας τυχεῖν. Τὸ δὲ *ἵνα* πάλιν κατὰ τὸ οἰκεῖον ἰδίωμα τέθεικεν. Οὐδὲ γὰρ διὰ τοῦτο ἠπείθησαν, ἵνα ἐλεηθῶσιν· ἀλλ᾽ ἠπείθησαν μὲν διὰ τὸ τῆς διανοίας ἀντίτυπον, ἐλεηθήσονται δὲ μεταμελείᾳ χρησάμενοι.

30-31. *For just as you were once disobedient to God but now have received mercy by their disobedience, so also they now have been disobedient so that, by the mercy shown to you, they may also receive mercy.* Now remember that all of you sinned against God for a long time, and the benevolence of the Lord did not regard this long and grievous impiety, but rather he deemed those who were willing as worthy of his inexpressible benevolence, and when they, the Jews, did not believe, he called you instead of them. Therefore, it is not unreasonable that those who now speak against us, when they desire to believe and be received by God, shall obtain the same benevolence. He adds the words "so that" again in his characteristic manner. For they were not disobedient for this reason—so that they might receive mercy; rather they were disobedient because of their obstinate attitude, and they will be given mercy when they have experienced repentance.[100]

Romans 11:32

λβ'. Συνέκλεισε γὰρ ὁ Θεὸς τοὺς πάντας εἰς ἀπείθειαν, ἵνα τοὺς πάντας ἐλεήσῃ. Τὸ, συνέκλεισεν, ἀντὶ τοῦ, ἤλεγξε, τέθεικεν. Ἤλεγξε δὲ καὶ τὰ ἔθνη, καὶ φυσικὴν εἰληφότα διάγνωσιν, καὶ τὴν κτίσιν ἐσχηκότα θεογνωσίας διδάσκαλον, καὶ μήτε ἐντεῦθεν, μήτε ἐκεῖθεν ὠφέλειαν εἰσδεξάμενα. Ἤλεγξε δὲ καὶ Ἰουδαίους πλείονος μὲν διδασκαλίας τετυχηκότας· πρὸς γὰρ τῇ φύσει, καὶ τῇ κτίσει, καὶ νόμον ἐδέξαντο, καὶ προφήτας τὸ δέον παιδεύοντας· καὶ μείζοσι τιμωρίαις ὑπευθύνους γεγενημένους· ἀλλ' ὅμως καὶ τούτους κἀκείνους πανωλεθρίας ὄντας ἀξίους, τῆς σωτηρίας ἠξίωσε, πιστεῦσαι μόνον θελήσαντας. Ταῦτα διεξελθὼν, καὶ θεασάμενος τῆς θείας φιλανθρωπίας τὴν ἄβυσσον, καὶ τὸ τῆς σοφίας ἀνέφικτον, ἐβόησεν·

32. *For God consigned all to disobedience so that he might show mercy to all.* Paul uses the word "consigned" as equivalent to "rebuke." He rebukes the Gentiles because, although having received natural discernment and having creation as a teacher of the knowledge of God, they have received benefit from neither one. He also rebukes the Jews since they have enjoyed more instruction; for in addition to nature and creation, they received the law and the prophets in order to educate them as to what is right, and thus they are accountable to greater punishments. But although both groups are deserving of utter destruction, he nevertheless deemed them worthy of salvation, but only those of them willing to believe. Having gone through these things in detail, and having looked at the depth of divine benevolence and God's unreachable wisdom, Paul cries out:

Romans 11:33

λγ'. Ὢ βάθος πλούτου καὶ σοφίας καὶ γνώσεως [82.184] Θεοῦ! Ἄνωθεν γὰρ καὶ ἐξ ἀρχῆς ταῦτα προέγνω, καὶ προγνοὺς σοφῶς ᾠκονόμησε, καὶ οἰκονομῶν τῆς φιλανθρωπίας τὸν πλοῦτον ὑπέδειξεν. Ὡς ἀνεξερεύνητα τὰ κρίματα αὐτοῦ, καὶ ἀνεξιχνίαστοι αἱ ὁδοὶ αὐτοῦ! Ὑπερβαίνει δὲ τὸν νοῦν τὸν ἀνθρώπινον τῶν θείων οἰκονομιῶν ὁ λόγος, οὐδὲ ταῖς ἀοράτοις δυνάμεσιν ἐφικτὴ τοῦ Θεοῦ τῶν ὅλων ἡ προμήθεια.

33. *O the depth of the riches and wisdom and knowledge of God!* For from of old, from the very beginning, he foreknew these things. Having foreknowledge, he governed wisely; and as he managed the affairs of the universe, he gave a glimpse of the riches of his benevolence. *How unfathomable are his judgments, and how inscrutable are his ways!* The unifying principle of the divine plans surpasses the human mind, and the providence of the God of All is not accessible to the unseen powers.

Romans 11:34–35

λδ', λε'. *Τίς γὰρ ἔγνω νοῦν Κυρίου; ἢ τίς σύμβουλος αὐτοῦ ἐγένετο; ἢ τίς προέδωκεν αὐτῷ, καὶ ἀνταποδοθήσεται αὐτῷ;* Τὰ τρία ταῦτα πρὸς τὰ τρία τέθεικε, τὸν πλοῦτον, καὶ τὴν σοφίαν, καὶ τὴν γνῶσιν· τὸ μὲν, *Τίς ἔγνω νοῦν Κυρίου*, πρὸς τὴν γνῶσιν· τὸ δὲ, *Τίς σύμβουλος αὐτοῦ ἐγένετο*, πρὸς τὴν σοφίαν· τὸ δὲ, *Τίς προέδωκεν αὐτῷ, καὶ ἀνταποδοθήσεται αὐτῷ*, πρὸς τὸν πλοῦτον. Οὕτω γὰρ ἀμέτρητος ὁ τῆς ἀγαθότητος πλοῦτος, ὅτι καὶ τοῖς μὴ οὖσι τὸ εἶναι δέδωκε, καὶ τοῖς γεγονόσι τὸ εὖ εἶναι χαρίζεται· καὶ οὐκ ἀντιδίδωσιν, ἀλλὰ δίδωσι τὰ ἀγαθά. Φιλάνθρωπος δὲ ὢν, ἀντίδοσιν τὴν δόσιν καλεῖ.

34–35. *For who has known the mind of the Lord? Or who has been his counselor? Or who has first given to him and will be repaid by him?* Paul has placed these three questions with the three preceding attributes—riches, wisdom, and knowledge. The question, "Who has known the mind of the Lord?" goes with knowledge. The question, "Who has been his counselor?" accompanies wisdom, and the question, "Who has first given to him and will be repaid by him?" is paired with riches. For the wealth of God's goodness is so immeasurable that he has brought into existence those who were not alive, and to those who are alive, he freely gives the good life. And God does not repay but simply gives good things. Since he is benevolent, God calls the gift an exchange.

Romans 11:36

λς'. *Ὅτι ἐξ αὐτοῦ καὶ δι' αὐτοῦ καὶ εἰς αὐτὸν τὰ πάντα. Αὐτῷ ἡ δόξα εἰς τοὺς αἰῶνας. Ἀμήν.* Αὐτὸς γὰρ τὰ πάντα πεποίηκεν, αὐτὸς τὰ γεγονότα διατελεῖ κυβερνῶν. Εἰς αὐτὸν ἀφορᾶν ἅπαντας προσήκει, ὑπὲρ μὲν τῶν ὑπαρξάντων χάριν ὁμολογοῦντας, αἰτοῦντας δὲ τὴν ἔπειτα προμήθειαν. Αὐτῷ δὲ χρὴ καὶ τὴν προσήκουσαν ἀναπέμπειν δοξολογίαν. Ἔδειξε δὲ διὰ τούτων ὁ θεῖος Ἀπόστολος, ὡς οὐκ οἶδε τῆς *ἐξ οὗ* καὶ τῆς *δι' οὗ* προθέσεως διαφορὰν, καὶ τὴν μὲν, ὡς μεῖζόν τι σημαίνουσαν, προσήκουσαν τῷ Πατρί· τὴν δὲ, ὡς ἔλαττόν τι διδάσκουσαν, ἁρμόττουσαν τῷ Υἱῷ. Ἀμφοτέρας γὰρ ἐφ' ἑνὸς προσώπου τέθεικεν. Ὅπερ εἴτε τοῦ Πατρὸς εἴποιεν εἶναι οἱ τὰ Ἀρείου φρονοῦντες καὶ Εὐνομίου, εὑρήσουσι τῇ *ἐξ οὗ* καὶ τὴν *δι' οὗ* συζευγνυμένην· εἴτε τῷ Υἱῷ προσαρμόσαιεν, ὄψονται τῇ *δι' οὗ* καὶ τὴν *ἐξ οὗ* συνημμένην. Εἰ δὲ ἡ μὲν *ἐξ οὗ* μεῖζόν τι σημαίνει, ἡ δὲ *δι' οὗ* τὸ ἔλαττον, ἀμφότεραι δὲ ἐφ' ἑνὸς κεῖνται προσώπου· ὁ αὐτὸς ἄρα ἑαυτοῦ μείζων μὲν διὰ τὴν *ἐξ οὗ*, ἐλάττων δὲ διὰ τῆς *δι' οὗ* εἰκότως ἂν νοηθῇ. Ἡμεῖς δὲ τούτους ἐπὶ τοῦ παρόντος καταλιπόντες, τὸν ἡμέτερον Δημιουργόν τε καὶ Σωτῆρα δοξάσωμεν· ᾧ πρέπει δόξα εἰς τοὺς αἰῶνας τῶν αἰώνων. Ἀμήν.

36. *For from him and through him and to him are all things. To him be the glory forever. Amen.* For he has made all things and he continues to govern that which is made. It behooves everyone to look to him, giving thanks on behalf of that which has come before and asking for future providence. It is fitting to send up to him the appropriate doxology. The divine Apostle demonstrates through these phrases that he does not know of a distinction between the prepositional phrases "from whom" and "through whom," as if the first signifies something greater, which is appropriate to the Father, and the second phrase teaches something lesser, which is fitting for the Son. For Paul uses both phrases to refer to one person. The very thing which those who hold the positions of Arius and Eunomius would want to claim to be true of the Father, this they will find in the pairing of the "through whom" with the "from whom." Or the very thing which they would like to attach to the Son, this they will see in the uniting of the "from whom" with the "through whom." Now if the phrase "from whom" signifies something greater, while the phrase "through whom" something lesser, and both rest upon one person, then reasonably it would mean that he is greater than himself because of the "from whom" and lesser than himself by means of the "through whom."[101] But having left these things behind at the present time, let us magnify both our Creator and Savior, to whom glory belongs forever and ever.

Notes

1. Patrologia graeca 82 (ed. J.-P. Migne; Paris, 1864).

2. Theodoret, *B. Theodoreti Opera Omnia* (ed. Johann Ludwig Schulze; Halae: Bibliopolii Orphanotrophei, 1769–74).

3. Theodoret, *Opera omnia in quatuor tomos distributa, quorum plurima, Graece, quaedam etiam Latine nunc primum prodeunt: Graeca cum manuscriptis exemplaribus...collata, Latinae versiones ad Graecorum normam exactae & recognitae* (ed. Jacques Sirmond; Paris: Sumptibus S. Cramoisy, 1642).

4. R. C. Hill, "Theodoret's Commentary on Paul," *Estudios Bíblicos* 58 (2000): 84.

5. Theodoret, *Interpretatio Epistolae ad Romanos* (PG 82 cols. 148–184).

6. ΤΟΜΟΣ ΤΕΤΑΡΤΟΣ in Greek. Theodoret divides his commentary on Romans into five sections, each containing a brief introduction. Part Four consists of chapters 9–11; this section begins at Migne 82.148.19.

7. Literally, "all the others."

8. Or "retribution."

9. Or "proves."

10. Or "pretext."

11. Or "citing in their defense."

12. So Paul's Jewish opponents argue.

13. Chapter 9 begins at Migne 82.148.48 under the heading ΚΕΦΑΛΑΙΟΝ Θ'. The text of Romans as cited by Theodoret will be italicized both in the Greek and English. Other biblical texts cited by Theodoret are enclosed within these marks (« ») in the Greek text and quotation marks in the English translation.

14. Column 149 of Migne 82 begins here; all other new columns will be so noted.

15. 1 Cor 16:22.

16. Josh 6:17.

17. Or "proclamation."

18. Exod 4:22

19. Or either "conspicuous" or "visible all round."

20. Jer 31:31–32.

21. Or "who is over all, God blessed forever." Either way, Theodoret sees the whole phrase as referring to Christ as his subsequent commentary demonstrates.

22. Or "designated."

23. The understood object of the verb "oppose" is likely "the gospel."

24. Or "from."

25. Or "named."

26. Literally "a father was produced."

27. Or "generosity."
28. That is, the child of a slave.
29. That is, Abraham's descendants.
30. Supplied by context.
31. Or "purpose."
32. Translated here as an objective genitive.
33. Or perhaps one's "natural endowment."
34. Or "emulate."
35. The use of τίθημι with regard to mental action.
36. Exodus 33:19.
37. Or "causes."
38. Or "ordinary."
39. Or "toils."
40. Or "it is necessary to place a comma here."
41. Rom 9:17.
42. 2 Tim 2:20.
43. 2 Tim 2:21.
44. 1 Cor 3:12.
45. Romans 8:29.
46. Hos 2:23 and Hos 1:10.
47. Or "foretelling."
48. Here Theodoret has Paul address the Jews directly, speaking to them using the second person plural.
49. Isa 10:22–23.
50. The word ἄνωθεν here could mean "from the very beginning" or "in an earlier passage."
51. Or "are charged with."
52. εἰς Χριστόν indicates that Christ is the object of confession here.
53. Isa 1:9.
54. Or "looked down upon."
55. Combination of Isa 28:16 and Isa 8:14.
56. Or "advantages."
57. Chapter 10 begins at Migne 82.164.18 under the heading ΚΕΦΑΛΑΙΟΝ Ι'.
58. εὐδοκία in Greek.
59. Or "goal."
60. Or "purpose."
61. Lev 18:5.
62. Deut 30:12.
63. Deut 30:14.
64. Perhaps "teaching" here.

65. Or "ruled by."

66. Or "the tongue may distinguish itself."

67. Isa 28:16.

68. Or "loving kindness."

69. Literally a "voting." The contexts suggests a use such as "calling."

70. Isa 52:7.

71. Luke 10:5.

72. Isa 53:1.

73. Matt 10:6.

74. Acts 13:46.

75. Deut 32:21.

76. Titus 3:3.

77. Theodoret must be referring to the present well-known piety of the Christian Gentiles, by way of contrast with their former (pre-conversion) notoriety for immorality.

78. Isa 65:1.

79. Chapter 11 begins at Migne 82.172.1 under the heading ΚΕΦΑΛΑΙΟΝ ΙΑ'.

80. This is a reference to Acts 21:20; Theodoret understands James to be the speaker on behalf of the Jerusalem Church.

81. Or "piety."

82. Literally "who made the scripture," that is, "wrote" it.

83. Or "impiety."

84. Rom 4:4.

85. The Jews.

86. Deut 29:4; Isa 26:10.

87. Isa 6:10.

88. Psalm 69:22–23.

89. Or "full inclusion."

90. This sentence is a second class (or contrary to fact) condition in Greek, using εἰ in the protasis plus ἄν in the apodosis with secondary tenses of the indicative mood. However, the statement in the protasis is not contrary to fact; Theodoret's commentary on the previous verse (Rom 11:11) indicates that he assumes the statement regarding Jewish disbelief and subsequent Gentile conversion to be true. Therefore, this sentence has been translated as a first class condition which assumes the reality of the statement in the apodosis, at least for the sake of argument. Porter states that "the perceived relation of any conditional to the real world is based on context, not on its grammatical structure." Stanley E. Porter, *Idioms of the Greek New Testament* (Sheffield: JSOT Press, 1994), 260.

91. Literally, "make the words."

92. Context suggests that the antecedent of "these" is Gentiles.

93. Matt 24:14.

94. Or "choosing."

95. Or possibly those who "are confidently trusted."

96. Rom 9:26a, "and so all Israel will be saved," is included with Rom 9:25 in Migne's text.

97. Or "teaching."

98. Matt 17:11; Mark 9:12.

99. Isa 59:20–21; 27:9; Jer 31:33–34.

100. Theodoret reads the ἵνα clause as consecutive, not final.

101. Theodoret is pointing out the futility of the heretics' argument.

CHAPTER FOUR

Jewish Elijah *Redivivus* Traditions

As stated in Chapter One, the predominant reading of the Elijah *redivivus* tradition in Christian history has been that John the Baptist, functioning as the forerunner of the Messiah, fulfilled the expectation of the return of Elijah. Such a reading seems to be confirmed by the dominical tradition, in which Jesus himself says of John, "if you are willing to accept it, he is Elijah who is to come" (Matt 11:14). However, the explicit denial that John the Baptist is the returning Elijah figure by the Fourth Gospel (John 1:21, 25) left the identity of this figure open. Furthermore, the pericope in the Apocalypse (Rev 11:3–13) which alludes to Elijah serving as an eschatological witness indicates that, for some early Christians, the return of Elijah was still to be expected in the future. After first examining the Elijah *redivivus* traditions in Middle Jewish texts in this chapter, Chapter Five will present the non-canonical early Christian texts that maintain a future role for Elijah.[1] The purpose of these chapters is to determine the uniqueness of Theodoret's reading and to present the broad trajectories of the Elijah *redivivus* traditions.

The Old Testament Tradition

Any discussion of the Elijah *redivivus* tradition must begin with the roots of such an expectation in the Jewish scriptures. According to J. Louis Martyn, the vitality of the speculations regarding Elijah in the early centuries B.C.E. and C.E. are the result of three primary factors: (1) Elijah's translation, (2) Elijah's miracles, and (3) Elijah's expected coming.[2] The last of these factors begins with the prophecy of Elijah's return that is found in the book of Malachi. This will be treated briefly before moving on to the subsequent expansions of the tradition.

Malachi 3:1; 3:23–24

In Malachi 3:1 Yahweh asserts, "See, I am sending my messenger to prepare the way before me, and the Lord whom you seek will suddenly come to his temple. The messenger of the covenant in whom you delight—indeed, he is coming, says the LORD of hosts."[3] Whereas this messenger of Yahweh (τὸν ἄγγελόν μου, מלאכי) is not initially named, Malachi 3:23–24 seems to identify the figure as Elijah: "Lo, I will send you the prophet Elijah before the great and terrible day of the LORD comes. He will turn the hearts of parents to their children and the hearts of children to their parents, so that I will not come and strike the land with a curse." The Septuagint and the Masoretic text read as follows:

ἰδοὺ ἐγὼ ἀποστέλλω ὑμῖν Ἠλίαν τὸν Θεσβίτην πρὶν ἐλθεῖν τὴν ἡμέραν κυρίου τὴν μεγάλην καὶ ἐπιφανῆ, ὃς ἀποκαταστήσει καρδίαν πατρὸς πρὸς υἱὸν, καὶ καρδίαν ἀνθρώπου πρὸς τὸν πλησίον αὐτοῦ, μὴ ἔλθων πατάξω τὴν γῆν ἄρδην.

הנה אנכי שלח לכם את אליה הנביא לפני בוא יום יהוה הגדול
והנורא׃ והשיב לב־אבות על־בנים ולב בנים על־אבותם פן־אבוא
והכיתי את־הארץ חרם׃

Mal 3:23–24 has generally been regarded as a later editorial addition to the book of Malachi.[4] These verses serve as an appendix, along with Malachi 3:22, which is an injunction to "remember the teaching of my servant Moses, the statutes and ordinances that I commanded him at Horeb for all Israel."[5] Some scholars even view Malachi 3:22 and Malachi 3:23–24 as two separate appendices.[6] A few recent commentators have, however, affirmed the integrity of this portion of Malachi.[7] While the majority of scholars view these verses as some sort of postscript or epilogue, the question is to what?

These concluding verses in Malachi have been variously read as an epilogue to the book of Malachi itself,[8] to the Book of the Twelve as a whole,[9] or to the entire corpus of the Latter Prophets (i.e., Joshua-Malachi).[10] David Petersen goes so far as to link this epilogue to the whole Hebrew canon. Identifying Hosea 14:10 [9] as an epilogue as well, he sees the two passages as forming an envelope which encloses the Book of the Twelve. Malachi 3:22–24 establishes a connection with the Torah and Former Prophets, while Hosea 14:10 links the Latter Prophets to the writings, thus providing canonical seams for the emerging tripartite division of scripture.[11] Expressing a view representative of most recent critics, Andrew Hill contends that Malachi 3:22–24 functions as a literary hinge that links the sections of the Hebrew Bible, commenting that "this appeal to the ideal figures of Moses and Elijah in the two appendixes of Malachi has significance for more than the book itself."[12]

A brief word must be said regarding the identity of the messenger in Malachi 3:1. The general consensus of modern scholars is that one of the ancillary, if not primary, purposes of the appendix (Mal 3:23–24) is the identification of the messenger figure.[13] Thus, Malachi 3:23 makes it clear that Yahweh's messenger is Elijah the prophet. Pieter Verhoef points out, however, that in the history of exegesis a number of interpreters have distinguished between the two figures of Malachi 3:1 and 3:23. He notes that the medieval Jewish exegetes Kimchi and Ibn Ezra identify the figure in Malachi 3:1 respectively as an angel and the Messiah ben Joseph. Furthermore, Verhoef mentions that Christian interpreters have made a similar distinction; John the Baptist, as forerunner of Christ's first coming, is the messenger of Malachi 3:1, whereas Elijah subsequently serves as the forerunner of Christ's second coming. Referring to this only as a Roman Catholic interpretation, Verhoef provides neither examples nor citations.[14] Such readings will be addressed later in this study.

The Function of Elijah in Malachi 3:23–24

In Malachi 3:1 the messenger or angel of the covenant is sent to fulfill an unspecified preparatory function in advance of Yahweh's coming to the temple. Given the identification of Elijah with this figure, Malachi 3:23 describes the nature of this preparation as follows: "He will turn the hearts of parents to their children and the hearts of children to their parents, so that I will not come and strike the land with a curse." The LXX renders this verse rather freely, substituting "the Tishbite" for "the prophet" and replacing the phrase "the hearts of children to their parents" with "the heart of a man to his neighbor." In addition, the LXX uses the verb ἀποκαθίστημι to render the Hebrew verb שׁוב instead of ἐπιστρέφω. Beth Glazier-McDonald suggests that "although 'to restore' is a recognized meaning of the hiphil of שׁוב, it is not the meaning which suits the context of Malachi 3:24 especially in view of Yahweh's demand in 3:7b, שׁובו אלי."[15] Malachi 3:7 reads in full: "Ever since the days of your ancestors you have turned aside from my statutes and have not kept them. Return to me, and I will return to you, says the Lord of hosts. But you say, 'How shall we return?'" Since the aim of the return or repentance is the restoration of the covenant relationship, the choice of ἀποκαθίστημι does not seem inappropriate.[16] Nevertheless, the word choice of the LXX is significant, for it opened the door for the further development in subsequent literature of Elijah's task upon his return.

There is disagreement as to the background of these verses in Malachi. What problem necessitates the return of Elijah in order to "turn the hearts of parents to their children and the hearts of children to their parents"? For those advocating an earlier date for these verses, the setting is the precarious economic situation in Judah during the Persian period. According to Glazier-McDonald, this caused young men to ally themselves with prosperous foreign families by means of intermarriage; furthermore, this often followed upon the divorce of a Judean wife. Thus, Malachi 3:23–24 is directed at the familial strife induced by such behavior.[17] For some who prefer a later dating of the epilogue, the background is to be found in the cultural conflict of the Hellenistic period. The parent-child discord is a result of the younger generation's assimilation to Hellenistic culture by adopting Greek attitudes, dress, and modes of behavior.[18] Other scholars prefer to speak of the background of Malachi 3:23–24 in more general terms. Understanding the word "fathers" as a reference to the ancient Israelites (the "ancestors" or "forefathers"), these commentators view Elijah's task as one of covenant renewal, i.e., reconnecting the Judean Yahwists with their pre-exilic roots.[19]

The book of Malachi, in its canonical form, presents Elijah as the forerunner, not of the messiah, but of Yahweh himself. His historical role as a prophet of covenant renewal coupled with his circumvention of death by means of being taken up into heaven serve to make him the ideal figure to fulfill the role of the coming prophet. Malachi 3:2 posits the question, "But who can endure the day of his [Yahweh's] coming, and who can stand when he appears?" Malachi 3:7 then adds the rhetorical question on behalf of Israel, "How shall we return?" The epilogues of Malachi provide the answers: one must keep the torah (Mal 3:22) and heed the message of the prophets (Mal 3:23–24).[20] Elijah will prepare the nation for the Day of the Lord by once again renewing covenant faithfulness.

The Middle Jewish Traditions

Gabriele Boccaccini proposes the term "middle Judaism" to refer to the period between the third century BCE and the second century CE. As a strictly chronological designation, it delimits a period in which many different ideological systems, including nascent Christianity, were competing with one another within the broad Jewish matrix.[21] Typically, the non-Christian Elijah *redivivus* traditions of this period have been grouped into two general classes: (1) Elijah as forerunner of the Day of the Lord and (2) Elijah as forerunner of the Messiah. This section of this chapter will classify the traditions of this period along these lines while also examining the validity of the second category.

Elijah as Forerunner of the Day of the Lord

Sirach

The book of Sirach, also known as Ecclesiasticus or the Wisdom of Ben Sira, is part of the group of texts within the LXX known as the Apocrypha, and thus it is canonical in the Catholic and Orthodox traditions. Written in Hebrew between 196 and 175 BCE, the work was translated into Greek by the author's grandson, Jesus ben Sira, during the last years of the reign of Ptolemy VII in Egypt; the Greek version was published shortly after Ptolemy's death in 117 BCE.[22]

In Sirach 44:1–50:24, a panegyric known as "Praise of the Ancestors," the author pays homage to the fidelity of a number of Jewish luminaries including Enoch, Noah, Abraham, Isaac, Jacob, David, Hezekiah, and Josiah. The prophet Elijah is included among them in Sirach 48:1–11. After noting the significant feats of Elijah's career, the author refers to the prophet's having been taken up into heaven and then says, "ὁ καταγραφεὶς ἐν ἐλεγμοῖς εἰς καιροὺς κοπάσαι ὀργὴν πρὸ θυμοῦ, ἐπιστρέψαι καρδίαν πατρὸς πρὸς υἱὸν καὶ καταστῆσαι φυλὰς Ιακωβ" (Sir 48:10). The NRSV renders it, "At the appointed time, it is written, you are destined[23] to calm the wrath of God before it breaks out in fury, to turn the hearts of parents to their children, and to restore the tribes of Jacob."

Sirach's depiction of Elijah's task evinces several changes with respect to Malachi. In speaking of the time of Elijah's return, Sirach employs the term "wrath" rather than "the Day of the Lord."[24] The task of stopping God's wrath parallels the forestalling of God's curse upon the land mentioned in Malachi 3:24. While retaining Malachi's phrase regarding the turning of the heart of the father to the son (note the use of the verb ἐπιστρέφω here in the Greek version), Sirach eliminates the following line which mentions the turning of the heart of the son to the father (or a person to his neighbor in the LXX). In its place, Sirach introduces a new element with the addition of καὶ καταστῆσαι φυλὰς Ιακωβ, "and to restore the tribes of Jacob."

The development of this task of tribal restoration may be attributed to one or more of the following three factors. First, the concept could have arisen from Malachi itself. It has been argued that the epilogue of Malachi 3:23–24 draws upon the Elijah tradition in an effort to bring about covenant renewal; therefore, Sirach 48:10 could simply have made the implicit notion of national restoration explicit.[25] Second, the task "to restore" the tribes may be due to the influence of the LXX's use of the word ἀποκαθίστημι.[26] Finally, some scholars have seen the influence of Isaiah 49:6 (στῆσαι τὰς φυλὰς) at work here.[27] If this is the case, then Elijah has taken on a role initially attributed to the Servant of Yahweh.

In conclusion, Elijah is given the task of reconciliation and national restoration in Sirach 48:10. As is the case in Malachi, Elijah functions as a forerunner of Yahweh himself, given that ὀργὴν πρὸ θυμοῦ is synonymous with the Day of the Lord. Since it is generally agreed that Sirach is a work devoid of messianic expectation, Elijah is not presented as a messianic forerunner here. One could argue, however, that Elijah himself is presented as a messianic figure in this text.

Sibylline Oracles

The first two books of the *Sibylline Oracles* consist of an original Jewish oracle that has been reworked by Christian redaction. Due to its composite nature, dating this material is particularly problematic. Johannes Geffcken argued for a late date, placing both the Jewish and Christian stages in the third century CE.[28] Alfons Kurfess, however, dates the initial Jewish portion at the turn of the era with the Christian interpolation coming no later than 150 CE;[29] John J. Collins concurs, dating the Jewish layer no later than the reign of Augustus.[30]

The Jewish oracle followed a typical Sibylline pattern by dividing history into ten generations. Beginning with *Sibylline Oracles* 2:15, the remainder of the second book presents the period of the tenth generation, featuring a number of eschatological events leading up to the final judgment. The coming of Elijah is mentioned in *Sibylline Oracles* 2:187–89:

> Then the Thesbite, driving a heavenly chariot at full stretch from
> heaven, will come on earth and then display three signs
> to the whole world, as life perishes.[31]

These lines are not from the portions of the text which have generally been recognized as Christian interpolations, and they do not appear to reflect a distinct Christian tradition.[32] Here Elijah appears prior to the destruction of the world by fire, which is followed in turn by the judgment and the resurrection of the dead. Collins states that "in view of the complicated redaction of the book, little can be said with confidence about the Jewish stage."[33] Given this word of caution, it appears that *Sibylline Oracles* 2:187–89 reflect a Middle Jewish tradition regarding the eschatological return of Elijah. As in the previous texts, Elijah arrives before the events associated with the Day of the Lord. Yet in this case, Elijah functions more as a herald who announces or confirms that the end is at hand. The task of restoration is not present in this text, nor is there any connection with a messianic figure.

4 Ezra

Chapters 3–14 of the book of 2 Esdras—as it is known in the Apocrypha in English—constitute a first century Jewish apocalypse known as *4 Ezra*.[34] Written a generation after the destruction of the temple, it was likely completed before 96 CE.[35] In the second of its seven visions, Ezra is given the signs of the end by an angelic mediator. The last of these signs refers to the appearance of Elijah in *4 Ezra* 6:26: "And they shall see the men who were taken up, who from their birth have not tasted death; and the heart of the earth's inhabitants shall be changed and converted to a different spirit."[36] So according to this tradition, it would seem that Elijah is accompanied by Enoch at his return.[37] Elijah's function here—repentance and the restoration of relationship—is reminiscent of Malachi 3:24, although the language is more universal ("the earth's inhabitants"). With regard to the forerunner role, there is no reference to a messiah in this vision.[38] Elijah, along with Enoch, is the last to appear before the end.

Pseudo-Philo

Pseudo-Philo, also known by the Latin title *Liber Antiquitatum Biblicarum*, is a retelling of the biblical story from Adam to David along the lines of Josephus' *Antiquities*. Although it was later attributed to Philo, the work's author is unknown. Daniel J. Harrington ascribes the work a Palestinian provenance and dates it around the turn of the era. Reflecting the general spirit of the Palestinian synagogues, Pseudo-Philo provides a glimpse of popular theology and legends.[39]

One such legend, the ascension of Phinehas, is pertinent to the subject at hand. Pseudo-Philo 48:1 reads:

And in that time Phinehas laid himself down to die, and the Lord said to him, "Behold you have passed the 120 years that have been established for every man. And now rise up and go from here and dwell in Danaben on the mountain and dwell there many years. And I will command my eagle, and he will nourish you there, and you will not come down to mankind until the time arrives and you be tested in that time; and you will shut up the heaven then, and by your mouth it will be opened up. And afterward you will be lifted up into the place where those who were before you were lifted up, and you will be there until I remember the world. Then I will make you all come, and you will taste what is death."[40]

After Phinehas is added to the number of those Old Testament heroes who were lifted up, the text then states that all of these figures will return when the Lord remembers the world. Is this last statement a reference to the end? It is not clear, but it seems likely. The role played by Phinehas here is new, in that he returns to taste death. One would naturally assume Elijah to be part of the company in view here. Yet it is interesting to note that Phinehas himself is described in terms reminiscent of Elijah, i.e., he is fed by birds and both shuts and opens the heavens by means of his word, not to mention his ascension. The concept of Elijah as a priestly figure is further developed in the rabbinic literature, which will be addressed briefly in the appendix.[41] The view of Elijah as one who returns to suffer will also see further development, particularly within the Christian apocalyptic tradition.

Lives of the Prophets

This first century Jewish writing survives in four Greek recensions. The earliest and best of these recensions is represented by Codex Marchalianus (Q), which lacks the obvious Christian interpolations of the others. Douglas Hare cites a number of factors that suggest an early first century date for the work, and like Pseudo-Philo, the *Lives of the Prophets* seems to be rooted in the folklore of Jewish Palestine.[42] Of particular interest for this study is the birth narrative of Elijah, which is present in all four recensions. The story reads as follows:

> Elijah, a Thesbite from the land of the Arabs, of Aaron's tribe, was living in Gilead, for Thesbe was given to the priests. When he was to be born, his father Sobacha saw that men of shining white appearance were greeting him and wrapping him in fire, and they gave him flames of fire to eat. And he went out and reported (this) in Jerusalem, and the oracle told him, "Do not be afraid, for his dwelling will be light and his word judgment, and he will judge Israel."[43]

Here Elijah is attributed with the function of judging Israel, although the text does not provide any specific temporal markers to indicate when this future judgment will take place. The birth narrative is followed subsequently by a description of the signs performed by the historical Elijah. Does the oracle refer to a role played by the historical Elijah or by the returning eschatological figure? Perhaps this question does not require an either/or answer. Hare concludes that this text "is one of the earliest witnesses to the belief that Elijah has been assigned a judging role in the eschatological drama."[44] Others, likewise, regard this text as an Elijah *redivivus* tradition,[45] and such a reading certainly seems in keeping with the folk religion of first century Palestine. Again, Elijah is presented as a principal eschatological actor without reference to another messianic figure. Note also that Elijah is once more given a priestly connection by being assigned to the tribe of Aaron.

Qumran

There are two texts from the Dead Sea Scrolls related to the expectation of a returning Elijah, 4Q558 and 4Q521. 4Q558 is a papyrus fragment from Cave 4 that Jean Starcky dated around 50–25 BCE. The fragment reads: "therefore I will send Elijah be[fore…]."[46] Unfortunately the context is unclear. Since the following line contains the word "lightning," Collins suggests that it may be a sign of the day of Lord.[47] Despite its fragmentary nature, this document provides evidence of a pre-Christian Elijah *redivivus* tradition. While his function remains unclear, his coming seems to be related to the end. Furthermore, his return is not mentioned in relation to any other figure.

The second of these texts, document 4Q521, speaks of a messiah whom heaven and earth will obey. This figure performs a catalog of works taken from Isaiah 61 to which has been added the raising of the dead, a feat for which the historical Elijah was known. Furthermore, there is allusion to the return of Elijah in frag. 2 iii, which reads:

> (1) and the precept of your mercy
> and I will liberate them . . .
> (2) for it is sure;
> "the fathers will return to the sons."[48]

The last line is a citation of Malachi 3:24 (cf. Sir 48:10). Collins takes God as the speaker in the preceding text; thus, the passage is about Elijah, who will be the agent of God's liberation. "Elijah is the 'messiah' whom heaven and earth obey, in whose time the sick are healed and the dead are raised."[49] For Collins, the Elianic messiah is to be understood as a prophetic messiah.[50] John Strugnell concurs, stating that "in all probability, the Mosaic eschatological prophet was, in the thought of Qumran (as probably also that of Mal. 3:23) identical with Elijah *redivivus*."[51]

John C. Poirier agrees with the identification of Elijah in 4Q521, but he thinks the characterization of Elijah as an eschatological prophet is a mistake. Pointing out the exegetical basis for the attribution of priesthood to Elijah, Poirier concludes that within the Qumran community, Elijah became the figure associated with the priestly messiah while Moses served as the paradigm for the eschatological prophet.[52] The rabbinic tradition attests that Elijah was known as a priestly figure outside of Qumran.[53] Regardless which of these two readings one favors, 4Q521 is evidence of further eschatological speculation regarding Elijah in Qumran. Moreover, a number of scholars, viewing the text through different exegetical lenses, have come to understand the allusion to Elijah here in messianic terms.

Elijah as Forerunner of the Messiah?

1 Enoch

1 Enoch (Ethiopic Apocalypse) is a composite work that was produced by numer- ous writers assembling different traditions and literary forms between the fourth century BCE and the turn of the era. Originally written in Aramaic, the text survives in its entirety only in an Ethiopic translation of an earlier Greek version.[54] The relevant portion with regard to the Elijah *redivivus* tradition is from the section known as the Dream Visions (*1 En.* 83–90), in which Enoch recounts two dreams to his son Methuselah. The second of these visions, known as the "Animal Apocalypse" (*1 En.* 85–90), employs the technique of *ex eventu* prophecy in order to recount biblical history beginning with Adam and culminating in the contemporary crisis of the Maccabean revolt. Thus, the date of this portion of *1 Enoch* is generally placed between the years 164–161 BCE.[55]

In the "Animal Apocalypse" human beings are presented as animals and angelic figures are given human form. In this zoomorphic history, the early pa- triarchs are presented as bulls, and Jacob and his descendants are portrayed as sheep that are continually preyed upon by the wild beasts which represent the Gentiles. While the name of Elijah is not mentioned in the text, commenta- tors have generally recognized two allusions to him in this section. The first reference is to the historical Elijah in *1 Enoch* 89:52; verses 51–52 read as fol- lows:

> Again I saw those sheep, how they went astray, going in diverse ways and abandoning that house of his. Then the Lord of the sheep called some from among the sheep and sent them to the sheep, but the sheep began to slay them. However, one of them was not killed but escaped alive and fled away; he cried aloud to the sheep, and they wanted to kill him, but the Lord of the sheep rescued him from the sheep and caused him to ascend to me and settle down.[56]

As a prophet, Elijah was one of the sheep sent to the sheep, and the refer- ence to ascension in verse 52 seems to confirm his identity here.[57] Elijah's jux- taposition with Enoch here is significant, for the two figures will become closely aligned in subsequent apocalyptic texts.

A second allusion to Elijah in the "Animal Apocalypse" has been detected by a number of commentators in *1 Enoch* 90:31. The text reads:

> And after this those three who were dressed in white and had taken hold of me by my hand, the ones who had brought me up at first—they, with the hand of that ram also holding me, took me up and put me down in the middle of those sheep before the judgement was held.[58]

Beginning with R. H. Charles, many have asserted that the ram holding Enoch is a reference to Elijah.[59] Charles includes but two words—"seemingly Elijah"—without explanation in a footnote.[60] This identification seems to have been accepted by most subsequent interpreters, yet such a reading of the text is not without difficulties. First, Elijah is initially identified in *1 Enoch* 89:52 as a sheep rather than a ram. Second, in the more immediate context of *1 Enoch* 90:31, the designation "that ram" is applied to the Jewish people's military leader, Judas Maccabaeus (cf. 90:13–14). Jozef Milik propounds that the ram in verse 31 is in indeed Judas Maccabaeus, who then accompanies Enoch to the new temple where judgment will take place.[61]

Responding to this claim, Matthew Black requires an explanation as to how Judas came to be with Enoch in the high tower from which these events are viewed; furthermore, he states that "in later traditions it was Elijah, not Judas, who was with Enoch to witness the last judgment."[62] It would seem that Black requires a consistency with respect to staging within the apocalypse that he does not require of the application of nomenclature. While he is correct that Enoch and Elijah are often paired as eschatological witnesses in later texts, particularly apocalyptic ones, one should not allow that to serve as the proof of Elijah's identity in this next. It is not the intention of this study, however, to exclude Elijah as a possibility for the identification of the ram in *1 Enoch* 90:31 but rather to demonstrate the cryptic nature of the allusion.

1 Enoch 90:31 has been cited frequently as a proof for the pre-New Testament existence of a Jewish expectation of Elijah as the forerunner of the messiah. The premise for such a statement is that the white bull of *1 Enoch* 90:37 is in fact an allusion to the Messiah. While this may very well be the case, most commentators have noted this with due caution.[63] While the ram appears temporally prior to the white bull, its function with respect to the bull is nebulous. After the ram guides Enoch to the scene of judgment, it then disappears from view; apparently its function is merely that of an inactive witness.[64] This character does not engage in any activity that could be defined as a preparatory role.[65] While the ram may be a reference to Elijah and the white bull may be a reference to the Messiah, the uncertain nature of these associations—not to mention the myriad problems with respect to manuscript tradition, dating, redaction, and Christian interpolation in the Enochic literature—makes any justification based upon this text of the Elijah as messianic forerunner claim tenuous at best. Nevertheless, given the Elijah identification, this text would provide further evidence of the expectation of Elijah's return in relation to the events of the end and, possibly, even in relation to a messianic figure. It is the contention of this study that *1 Enoch* 90:31 should not be cited in this regard without caveat.

4 Ezra 7:28

There is one other possible allusion to Elijah in *4 Ezra*. The third vision (6:35–9:25) does mention a messianic figure: "For my son the Messiah shall be revealed with those who are with him, and those who remain shall rejoice four hundred years."[66] John A. T. Robinson suggests that the phrase "with those who are with him" likely refers to the figures previously mention in *4 Ezra* 6:26.[67] Such a reading would then connect Elijah with the advent of the messiah, although the role would be of an attendant rather than a forerunner. Nevertheless, the identities of the messiah's companions are by no means clear, and at any rate, this text is not pre-Christian.

Mark 9:11 and Matthew 17:10

The New Testament itself provides evidence of another Middle Jewish Elijah *redivivus* tradition in the gospels. While the gospels are obviously Christian texts, the belief regarding Elijah's expected return reflected in Mark 9:11 and Matthew 17:10 is imputed to the scribes. On their way down from the mountain following the transfiguration, Peter, James, and John ask Jesus, "Why do the scribes say that Elijah must come first?" (see parallel in Matt 17:10). This text has been used to substantiate the claim that the concept of Elijah as a forerunner of the messiah was well known in Jesus' day. This traditional consensus has been buttressed by the work of such notables as Joachim Jeremias,[68] Sigmund Mowinckel,[69] Louis Ginzberg,[70] and George Foot Moore who put it simply, "It was the universal belief that shortly before the appearance of the Messiah Elijah should return."[71]

Morris Faierstein, on the other hand, has questioned this long held tenet of the study of Jewish backgrounds. Referring to Malachi 3:23–24, he asserts that the messianic forerunner concept "is not found in these verses if they are read without *a priori* assumptions."[72] Instead, he finds that Elijah stands in relation to the day of the Lord. With regard to the tradition contained in Mark 9:11 and Matthew 17:10, Faierstein would provide the same caution of superimposing a preconceived role for Elijah. Surveying the relevant texts, Faierstein finds no evidence that Elijah was widely viewed as a messianic forerunner in the first century. Furthermore, he suggests that possibility that "the concept of Elijah as a forerunner is a novum in the NT must be seriously considered."[73]

In a response to Faierstein, Dale Allison contends that the messianic figure is implied in Malachi 3:23–24. If one believed the Messiah to be associated with the Day of the Lord, then Elijah would logically be seen as a forerunner. Additionally, Allison asks why a Christian development would be attributed to the scribes. Maintaining that the New Testament is one of the best sources for first century Judaism, Allison believes that the tradition found in Mark 9:11 and Matthew 17:10 should be seen as a genuine reflection of the period.[74]

Joseph Fitzmyer responds, in turn, by suggesting that Allison is begging the question. In order for an implied messiah to be a logical reading of Malachi 3:23–24, one must first demonstrate that most first century Jews did in fact believe that a messiah would come on the Day of the Lord. The survey presented thus far in this study, however, has demonstrated diverse eschatological expectations involving manifold figures. So Fitzmyer is correct in concluding that the textual evidence does not support such a premise.[75] With regard to the scribal tradition of Mark 9:11 and Matthew 17:10, Fitzmyer asserts that it is not a matter of taking the material seriously as first century evidence but rather of reading it correctly. The disciples' question regarding the return of Elijah, Fitzmyer notes, arises in the context of a discussion regarding the resurrection of the dead (Mark 9:9–10; Matt 17:9). The scribal tradition cited merely states, "Elijah must come first." The question is: before what? Given the context of the narrative, Fitzmyer maintains that it must refer to Elijah's coming before the general resurrection of the dead or before the Son of Man's resurrection from the dead.[76] In appealing to the immediate context of the gospel narratives as proof, however, Fitzmyer has confused two separate levels of discussion. While Fitzmyer is correct in pointing out the ambiguity of the scribal tradition presented in Mark 9:11 and Matthew 17:10—which simply reflects a general expectation of Elijah's return at the end—his appeal to the narrative level of the gospels is problematic, for one could argue that the larger narrative context of each gospel does imply a forerunner role (Mark 1:7; Luke 3:16).

Justin Martyr

The Christian apologist Justin Martyr, writing in the middle of the second century CE, refers to an Elijah *redivivus* tradition that he identifies as being

Jewish. In the *Dialogue with Tyrpho*, Justin's adversary, Trypho the Jew, expresses his objections regarding the identification of Jesus as the Messiah. In *Dialogue* 8:4 Trypho says, "But the messiah, if indeed he has been born and exists somewhere, is unknown. He himself does not even know yet, nor does he have any power until Elijah comes to anoint him and to make him manifest to all."[77] The tradition is repeated once again in *Dialogue* 49:1: "For we all expect that the Messiah will be a person of human descent, and that Elijah, when he comes, will anoint him...And given that Elijah has not yet come, I [Trypho] conclude that this man is not [the Messiah]."[78]

The preliminary question at hand concerns the reliability of Justin in accurately representing contemporary Jewish beliefs. A. J. B. Higgins states that while Justin knew the Jewish messianic traditions well, his apologetic zeal often led him to attribute distinct Christian interpretations to his Jewish interlocutor.[79] Higgins concludes that the reliable elements of Jewish messianic belief presented here are the concepts of a human messiah and a hidden messiah.[80] Unfortunately, he makes no comment regarding the mention of Elijah at this juncture. Louis Ginzberg observes that "in the literature of the Midrash and Talmud there is no trace of the concept that the Messiah will be ceremoniously anointed."[81] He does point out, however, that the notion of Elijah's anointing the Messiah does appear in medieval texts and is attested to in Jewish folklore.[82] Faierstein contends that Justin employs this idea to justify Jesus' baptism by John the Baptist, whom Justin had previously identified as an Elijah figure.[83] Thus, it serves as an additional messianic proof for Justin.

Justin's citation of a Jewish Elijah *redivivus* tradition in which Elijah anoints the Messiah is a clear example of Elijah functioning as a messianic forerunner. Unfortunately, no contemporary Jewish texts indicate knowledge of such a tradition. Furthermore, given Jesus' baptism by John, the element of Elijah's anointing the Messiah seems to betray particular Christian concerns. Even if one were to concede that this was a valid Jewish tradition in Justin's time, the date would be late with respect to establishing first century expectation.

Conclusion

Consultation of the primary texts has yielded no certain evidence of the expectation of Elijah as a forerunner of the messiah prior to the Christian era.[84] Justin Martyr's tradition reflects such a role, but the date is mid-second century, and the accuracy is questionable. *4 Ezra* 7:28 is also post-Christian, and while it mentions the Messiah, Elijah's role is merely that of an attendant or witness. The scribal traditions of Mark 9:11 and Matthew 17:10, which make no explicit reference to a messiah figure at all, are ambiguous. The remaining proof-text, *1 Enoch* 90:31, could be read as a pre-Christian Elijah *redivivus* tradition in which Elijah precedes the advent of the Messiah. However, the uncertainty of dating this material—not to mention the uncertainty of the allusions themselves—and the ill-defined role played by "that ram" in the text combine to make *1 Enoch* 90:31 a weak peg on which to hang any broad generalization. While it is possible that some Jews in the early first century could have conceived of the returning Elijah figure as functioning in a preparatory role in relation to a messiah, to state that such a view was widespread or universal goes beyond the evidence at hand.

On the other hand, it would be entirely appropriate to state more generally that the return of Elijah was a feature of the eschatology of a number of Jews at the beginning of the Christian era. His role, initially rooted in the task of covenant restoration suggested by Malachi 3:23–24, was in a state of flux, as new developments presented him as a herald, a witness, a judge, and even a martyr. Given that the first clear presentation of Elijah as a preparer figure occurs in the Gospel's identification of John the Baptist as Elijah *redivivus*, one could argue that this understanding of his function is in fact a Christian innovation.[85] With respect to the incredible diversity of eschatological speculation during the Middle Jewish period, Robinson correctly suggests that

> it would probably be nearer the truth to see a considerable number of figures, in various strands of popular expectation, all of whom carried 'messianic' or eschatological overtones—the Coming One, Elijah, Jeremiah, the Prophet like Moses, the Son of David, the Elect One, the Son of Man, the Anointed One, and even the Anointed Ones. These might be variously combined...Or they might be assimilated to each other.[86]

In many of the texts surveyed in this chapter, the Elijah *redivivus* figure himself seems to carry just such messianic overtones.

Notes

1. The rabbinic materials demonstrate a considerable amount of speculation regarding the figure of Elijah. Although the dating of this material is particularly problematic (the written form of the texts is late), it certainly contains some earlier traditions that would have been contemporaneous with the development of the early Christian Elijah *redivivus* traditions. A detailed presentation of the diverse rabbinic references to the return of Elijah is beyond the scope of this study; nevertheless, a cursory description of the general functions of Elijah upon his return will be presented in an appendix.

2. J. Louis Martyn, "We Have Found Elijah," in *Jews, Greeks and Christians: Religious Cultures in Late Antiquity. Essays in Honor of William David Davies* (ed. Robert Hamerton-Kelly and Robin Scroggs. Leiden: E. J. Brill, 1976), 181-219.

3. Unless otherwise noted, the English translations of Malachi are from the NRSV.

4. Ralph L. Smith, *Micah-Malachi* (WBC; Waco, Texas: Word, 1984), 340.

5. This verse is 3:24 in the LXX.

6. Brevard Childs, "The Canonical Shape of the Prophetic Literature," *Int* 32 (1978): 46-55.

7. Beth Glazier-McDonald, *Malachi: The Divine Messenger* (SBLDS 98; Atlanta: Scholars, 1987), 244-45, 262-63; Peter A. Verhoef, *The Books of Haggai and Malachi* (Grand Rapids, Mich.: Eerdmans, 1987), 337-38.

8. Smith, *Micah-Malachi*, 340-41; Théophane Chary, *Aggée-Zacharie-Malachie* (SB; Paris: Gabalda, 1969), 276-77; Friedrich Horst, *Die zwölf kleinen Propheten: Nahum bis Maleachi* (HAT 1/14, 2; Tübingen: Mohr, 1954), 275.

9. Alfons Deissler, *Zwölf Propheten III: Zefanja. Haggai. Sacharja. Maleachi* (NEchtB 21; Wurzburg: Echter, 1988), 337-38; Paul L. Redditt, *Haggai, Zechariah, Malachi* (NCB; Grand Rapids, Mich.: Eerdmans, 1995), 243.

10. Wilhelm Rudolph, *Haggai, Sacharja 1-8, Sacharja 9-14, Maleachi* (KAT, Band 13, 4; Gütersloh: Mohn, 1976), 291-93; Otto Eissfeldt, *The Old Testament: An Introduction, including the Apocrypha and Pseudepigrapha, and also the works of similar type from Qumran: the history of the formation of the Old Testament* (trans. Peter Ackroyd; New York: Harper & Row, 1965), 442.

11. David L. Peterson, *Zechariah 9-14 and Malachi: A Commentary* (OTL; Louisville: Westminster John Knox, 1995), 233.

12. Andrew E. Hill, *Malachi: A New Translation with Introduction and Commentary* (AB 25D; New York: Doubleday, 1998), 365, 390.

13. Ibid., 390; Eissfeldt, *The Old Testament*, 442; Peterson, *Zechariah 9-14 and Malachi*, 230; Smith, *Micah-Malachi*, 342; Rex Mason, *The Books of Haggai, Zechariah and Malachi* (CBC; Cambridge: Cambridge University Press, 1977), 160; Sigmund Mowinckel, *He That Cometh* (trans. G. W. Anderson; New York: Abingdon Press, 1954), 299.

14. Verhoef, *Haggai and Malachi*, 340. Herbert Wolf concedes that perhaps John was Elijah in a limited way and that there may still be a future role for Elijah. Herbert Wolf, *Haggai and Malachi* (Chicago: Moody, 1976), 125.

15. Glazier-McDonald, *The Divine Messenger*, 268.

16. Lars Kruse-Blinkenberg calls the LXX's rendering of שׁוב incorrect. Lars Kruse-Blinkenberg, "The Book of Malachi according to Codex Syro-Hexaplaris Ambrosianus," *ST* 21 (1967): 72.

17. Glazier-McDonald, *The Divine Messenger*, 254-55.

18. Rudolph, *Maleachi*, 292-93; Mason, *Malachi*, 160-61.

19. Hill, *Malachi*, 387-88; Peterson, *Zechariah 9-14 and Malachi*, 231; Verhoef, while maintaining an early date for the epilogue, contends that the semantic domain of שׁוב here "is not so much the projected social order but the covenant relationship as such. When Elijah comes he will restore the covenant relationship. In this process he will turn about the hearts of the wicked posterity to the hearts of them with whom God has entered into a covenant at Horeb." Verhoef, Haggai and Malachi, 342.

20. The epilogues attempted to provide a balance between covenant theology and the developing apocalyptic theology. For a discussion of these competing outlooks see Paul D. Hanson, *The Dawn of Apocalyptic: The Historical and Sociological Roots of Jewish Apocalyptic Eschatology* (rev. ed.; Philadelphia: Fortress, 1979), 19-21; Joseph Blenkinsopp, *Prophecy and Canon: A Contribution to the Study of Jewish Origins* (Notre Dame: Notre Dame University Press, 1977), 121-123; Peter C. Craigie, *Twelve Prophets* (Philadelphia: Westminster, 1985), 248.

21. Boccaccini refers to these different ideological groups as "middle Judaisms" and labels them as different species of the genus Judaism. Boccaccini, *Middle Judaism*, 7-25.

22. Alexander A. Di Lella, "Wisdom of Ben-Sira," *ABD* 6:932. The Hebrew text, known only through a few rabbinic quotations, was unknown until the end of the nineteenth century. For the Hebrew version see Israel Levi, ed., *The Hebrew Text of the Book of Ecclesiasticus* (Leiden: E. J. Brill, 1969).

23. The Hebrew has "you are destined" in place of the Greek ἐν ἐλεγμοῖς, "by means of rebukes."

24. The Syriac version does, however, refer to "the Day of the Lord." Patrick W. Skehan and Alexander A. Di Lella, *The Wisdom of Ben Sira* (AB 39; New York: Doubleday, 1987), 531.

25. Danny P. Truitt, "The Function of Elijah in the Markan Messianic Drama" (Ph.D. diss., Baylor University, 1993), 61-62.

26. Glazier-McDonald, *The Divine Messenger*, 269.

27. Skehan and Di Lella, *Ben Sira*, 534.

28. Johannes Geffcken, *Komposition und Entstehungszeit der Oracula sibylline* (TUGAL 23, 1; Leipzig: J.C. Hinrichs, 1902), 49.

29. Alfons Kurfess, "Oracula Sibyllina," *ZNW* 40 (1941): 151-65.

30. John J. Collins, "The Sibylline Oracles," in *The Old Testament Pseudepigrapha* (vol. 1; ed. James H. Charlesworth; Garden City, NY: Doubleday, 1983), 331.

31. *Sib. Or.* 2:187-89 (Collins).

32. Didache 16:6 does mention three apocalyptic signs without reference to Elijah: the sign spread out in heaven, the trumpet sound, and the resurrection of the dead. Here as well, the date and source of the material in chapter 16 is uncertain. At any rate, Elijah's signs in the *Sibylline Oracles* are given prior to the general resurrection.

33. John J. Collins, "Sibylline Oracles," *ABD* 6:5.

34. Chapters 1–2 (also known as *5 Ezra*) and 15–16 (*6 Ezra*) are later Christian additions that were combined with *4 Ezra* to form 2 Esdras.

35. Michael E. Stone, "Second Book of Esdras," *ABD* 2:612.

36. *4 Ezra* 6:26 (Metzger).

37. Moses may have been understood to be one of these figures. Josephus relates an account of Moses being taken without death (*Antiquitates judaicae* 4:326); the *Assumption of Moses* may have known such a tradition as well.

38. A possible reference by *4 Ezra* to Elijah in relation to the messiah will be examined later in this chapter.

39. Daniel J. Harrington, "Pseudo–Philo," *ABD* 5:345.

40. *L.A.B.* 48:1 (Harrington).

41. Elijah continues to be identified with Phinehas as well as with other priestly figures, such as John Hyrcanus I.

42. Douglas R. A. Hare, "Lives of the Prophets," *ABD* 5:502.

43. *Liv. Pro.* 21:1–3 (Hare).

44. Douglas R. A. Hare, "Lives of the Prophets," *ABD* 5:503.

45. Markus Öhler, *Elia im Neuen Testament: Untersuchungen zur Bedeutung des alttestamentlichen Propheten im frühen Christentum* (BZNW 88; Berlin: Walter de Gruyter, 1997), 296.

46. Jean Starcky, "Les quatres étapes du messianique à Qumran," *RB* 70 (1963): 498.

47. John J. Collins, "The Works of the Messiah." *DSD* 1 (1994): 106.

48. Ibid., 102.

49. Ibid., 105.

50. Ibid., 110.

51. John Strugnell, "Moses-Pseudepigrapha at Qumran: 4Q375, 4Q376, and Similar Works," in *Archaeology and History in the Dead Sea Scrolls: The New York University Conference in Memory of Yigael Yadin* (ed. Lawrence H. Schiffman; JSPSup 8; Sheffield: JSOT Press, 1990), 234. For similar views see Johannes Zimmermann, *Messianische Texte aus Qumran: königliche, priesterliche und prophetische Messiasvorstellungen in den Schriftfunden von Qumran* (Tübingen: Mohr Siebeck, 1998), 332–42; Florentino García Martínez and Julio C. Trebolle Barrera, *The People of the Dead Sea Scrolls: Their Writings, Beliefs, and Practices* (trans. Wilfred G. E. Watson; Leiden: E. J. Brill, 1995), 163.

52. John C. Poirier, "The Endtime Return of Elijah and Moses at Qumran," *DSD* 10 (2003): 227–36.

53. See Appendix; Robert Hayward, "Phinehas—the same as Elijah: The Origins of a Rabbinic Tradition," *JJS* 29 (1978): 26–27; D. G. Clark, "Elijah as Eschatological High Priest: An Examination of the Elijah Tradition in Mal. 3:23–24" (Ph.D. diss., University of Notre Dame, 1975).

54. George W. E. Nickelsburg, "Enoch, First Book of," *ABD* 2:508.

55. Mitchell G. Reddish, ed., *Apocalyptic Literature: A Reader* (Peabody, Mass.: Hendrickson, 1995), 43; E. Isaac, "1 (Ethiopic Apocalypse of) Enoch: A New Translation and Introduction," in *The Old Testament Pseudepigrapha* (vol. 1; ed. James H. Charlesworth; Garden City, NY: Doubleday, 1983), 7; Nicklesburg, "Enoch," 2:511.

56. *1 En.* 89:51–52 (Isaac).

57. There is an additional reference to Elijah in *1 En.* 93:8, which is part of the "Apocalypse of Weeks" (91:11–17; 93:1–10), which states, "a (certain) man shall ascend." This, however, is simply another reference to the historical Elijah; it is not connected with any Elijah *redivivus* tradition.

58. *1 En.* 90:31 (Knibb).

59. R. H. Charles, *The Apocrypha and Pseudepigrapha of the Old Testament* (Oxford: Clarendon, 1913), 259; Joachim Jeremias, "'Ηλ(ε)ίας," *TDNT* 2:931; Geza Vermes, *Jesus the Jew* (London: SCM, 1973), 94–95; Matthew Black, *The Book of Enoch or 1 Enoch* (SVTP; Leiden: E. J. Brill, 1985), 279.

60. Ibid., fn. 31, 259.

61. Jozef Milik, "Problèmes de la littérature Hénochique à la lumière des fragments araméens de Qumrân," *HTR* 64 (1971): 359.

62. Black, *The Book of Enoch*, 279.

63. The white bull may represent a second Adam (cf. 85.3), which could be read messianicly or generally in terms of the restoration of human purity. Ibid., 279–80; Nicklesburg, "Enoch," 511; Reddish, *Apocalyptic Literature*, 43.

64. Donatus Haugg, *Die Zwei Zeugen: Eine exegetische Studie über Apok 11, 1–13* (NTAbh 17.1; Münster: Aschendorffschen, 1936), 91.

65. James C. VanderKam notes that 1 Enoch does not assign any function to Enoch or Elijah (whose identity he notes is uncertain) at the judgment. James C. VanderKam, "1 Enoch, Enochic Motifs, and Enoch in Early Christian Literature," in *The Jewish Apocalyptic Heritage in Early Christianity* (CRINT; ed. James C. VanderKam and William Adler; Minneapolis: Fortress, 1996), 97–100.

66. *4 Ezra* 7:28 (Metzger).

67. John A. T. Robinson, "Elijah, John and Jesus: An Essay in Detection," *NTS* 4 (1957–58): 269.

68. In fairness to Jeremias, he says that it was widespread, but he does not say when. Jeremias, "'Ηλ(ε)ίας," *TDNT* 2:931.

69. Sigmund Mowinckle, *He That Cometh* (trans. G. W. Anderson; New York: Abingdon Press, 1954), 299.

70. Louis Ginzberg, *An Unknown Jewish Sect* (New York: The Jewish Theological Seminary of America, 1970), 209–56.

71. George Foot Moore, *Judaism in the First Centuries of the Christian Era, the Age of the Tannaim* (3 vols.; Cambridge: Harvard University Press, 1927–1930), 2:357.

72. Morris Faierstein, "Why Do the Scribes Say that Elijah Must Come First?" *JBL* 100 (1981): 77.

73. Ibid., 86.

74. Dale C. Allison, Jr., "Elijah Must Come First," *JBL* 103 (1984): 256–58.

75. Joseph Fitzmyer, "More About Elijah Coming First," *JBL* 104 (1985): 296.

76. Ibid., 295.

77. Justin Martyr, *Dial.* 8:4 (PTS).

78. Ibid., 49:1.

79. A. J. B. Higgins, "Jewish Messianic Belief in Justin Martyr's Dialogue with Trypho," *NovT* 9 (1967): 299.

80. Ibid., 305.

81. Ginzberg, *Unknown Jewish Sect*, 245.

82. Ibid.

83. Faierstein, "Elijah Must Come First," 86.

84. Collins, "Works of the Messiah," 103; Robinson, "Elijah, John, and Jesus," 269; John A. Fitzmyer, "The Aramaic 'Elect of God' Text from Qumran Cave 4," in *Essays on the Semitic Background of the New Testament* (London: Chapman, 1971), 137.

85. This is the conclusion of Markus Öhler, *Elia im Neuen Testament*, 296. Collins concedes that the precursor role "may well have been a Christian development." Collins, "Works of the Messiah," 104.

86. Robinson, "Elijah, John, and Jesus," 269–70.

CHAPTER FIVE

Christian Elijah *Redivivus* Traditions

As has been previously noted, the Elijah *redivivus* tradition persisted in the early church despite the predominant understanding that John the Baptist had already fulfilled such expectation. The continued speculation regarding a future role for Elijah can be attributed to the Fourth Gospel's denial of a connection between John and Elijah (John 1:21, 25) as well as to an active apocalyptic tradition that continued to employ the motif of the return of those who had been taken up into heaven (Rev 11:3–13). The subsequent use of Elijah *redivivus* traditions in early Christianity can be grouped into two broad categories: (1) the return of Elijah as an eschatological witness, and (2) the return of Elijah as a forerunner or herald of the Parousia. The traditions in the first category, in which Elijah is usually presented in relation to an antichrist figure, seem to be dependent upon the pericope in Revelation 11:3–13.[1] Those in the second category, on the other hand, seem to be rooted in the prophecy of Malachi 3:23–24.

Elijah as Eschatological Witness

The Apocalypse

Any discussion of the Christian traditions featuring Elijah as an eschatological witness must begin with the canonical account in Revelation 11:3–13, which reads as follows:

> 3 "And I will grant my two witnesses authority to prophesy for one thousand two hundred sixty days, wearing sackcloth." 4 These are the two olive trees and the two lampstands that stand before the Lord of the earth. 5 And if anyone wants to harm them, fire pours from their mouth and consumes their foes; anyone who wants to harm them must be killed in this manner. 6 They have authority to shut the sky, so that no rain may fall during the days of their prophesying, and they have authority over the waters to turn them into blood, and to strike the earth with every kind of

plague, as often as they desire. 7 When they have finished their testimony, the beast that comes up from the bottomless pit will make war on them and conquer them and kill them, 8 and their dead bodies will lie in the street of the great city that is prophetically called Sodom and Egypt, where also their Lord was crucified. 9 For three and a half days members of the peoples and tribes and languages and nations will gaze at their dead bodies and refuse to let them be placed in a tomb; 10 and the inhabitants of the earth will gloat over them and celebrate and exchange presents, because these two prophets had been a torment to the inhabitants of the earth. 11 But after the three and a half days, the breath of life from God entered them, and they stood on their feet, and those who saw them were terrified. 12 Then they heard a loud voice from heaven saying to them, "Come up here!" And they went up to heaven in a cloud while their enemies watched them. 13 At that moment there was a great earthquake, and a tenth of the city fell; seven thousand people were killed in the earthquake, and the rest were terrified and gave glory to the God of heaven.[2]

Naturally, the identity of the two witnesses poses a key interpretive question. The presence of the definite article (τοῖς δυσὶν μάρτυσίν μου) suggests that the audience may have been expected to know their identity.[3] The text itself presents a complex set of allusions with regard to these figures. On the one hand, the reference in verse 4 to the two olive trees and the two lampstands connects the witnesses to Zechariah 4.[4] In Zechariah 4 the olive trees refer to "the two anointed ones of the Lord" (Zech 4:14): a kingly messiah (Zerubbabel) and a priestly messiah (the high priest Joshua). On the other hand, the powers exhibited by the two witnesses in Revelation 11:6 recall the deeds of Elijah ("to shut the sky, so that no rain may fall") and Moses ("the waters to turn them into blood, and to strike the earth with every kind of plague").

Modern interpreters have generally viewed the two figures symbolically; thus, they represent the prophetic testimony of the Christian church.[5] David Aune suggests that the author omitted the names of the figures intentionally in order to present them as Christian witnesses.[6] Most early Christian interpreters, however, identified the two witnesses as Elijah and Enoch, despite the Mosaic allusions in the text. As the two Old Testament figures who had been translated to heaven, they were naturally considered as figures who would return to fulfill an eschatological role, which, in some cases, resulted finally in their death. Several texts in the previous section have demonstrated the circulation of the traditions in which the two are paired (4 *Ezra* 6:26; 7:28; *1 En.* 89:52; 90:31).

In the present passage, the two witnesses, having completed their testimony, are killed by the beast from the bottomless pit. Then after a period of three and a half days, the witnesses are resurrected and taken up into heaven. Commenting on the roles of the returning figures, Richard Bauckham declares, "If early Christian writers took over from Judaism the expectation that

Enoch and Elijah would return to earth before the Judgment, it is not clear that they took over any specific functions that the two were to perform."[7] Here, the Elijah *redivivus* figure functions as an eschatological witness. Then, a new role—that of a martyr—appears. Given that there is no evidence of a pre-Christian Jewish tradition of the martyrdom of Enoch and Elijah, this appears to be a Christian innovation.[8] It is interesting to note that the antichrist figure does not appear on the scene until the completion of the witnesses' testimony. In other words, the testimony, at this point in the development of the tradition, does not appear to be related to the antichrist figure itself. The remainder of this section will examine the non-canonical Christian traditions that present the Elijah *redivivus* figure along similar lines, as an eschatological witness and martyr.

The Ethiopic Apocalypse of Peter

There are three works which bear the title *Apocalypse of Peter*.[9] The Ethiopic *Apocalypse of Peter*, which is the concern of this section, is best known for its presentation of the earliest Christian portraits of heaven and hell.[10] Dated *circa* 135,[11] references to and citations of the work by other Fathers at least confirm a second century date.[12] The work begins with Jesus on the Mount of Olives, where Peter and the disciples ask him about the signs of his return and the end. Warning them against the appearance of false christs, Jesus says:

> But this deceiver is not the Christ. And when they reject him, he shall slay them with the sword, and there shall be many martyrs. Then shall the twigs of the fig-tree, that is, the house of Israel, shoot forth: many shall become martyrs at his hand. Enoch and Elijah shall be sent to teach them that this is the deceiver who must come into the world and do signs and wonders in order to deceive. And therefore those who die by his hand shall be martyrs, and shall be reckoned among the good and righteous martyrs who have pleased God in their life.[13]

In this text both Elijah and Enoch appear together again in conjunction with an antichrist figure. Here, however, their testimony seems to be aimed specifically at the antichrist. Their function is to identify him to others so that the people will no longer be deceived. While there is no mention of Elijah and Enoch's death, one could argue that it is implied given the frequent reference to martyrs (four times). Such an implication would seem likely for a reader who knew of a tradition like that of Revelation 11:3–13 in which Elijah and Enoch are martyred by the antichrist.

Tertullian

A native of Carthage in North Africa, Tertullian produced a large body of writings in Latin between the years 195–220 CE. His work *On the Soul* (*De anima*), which is categorized as a controversial treatise, is dated *circa* 210–213.[14] In the fiftieth chapter of this work, Tertullian takes aim at the views of Epicurus and Menander on death. Mocking the claim that Menander's baptism ("this wondrous bath") yields immortality and incorruptibility, Tertullian declares:

> All nations have "to ascend to the mount of the Lord and to the house of the God of Jacob," who demands of his saints in martyrdom that death which he exacted even of his Christ...Such power was not accorded to the great Medea herself—over a human being at any rate, if allowed her over a silly sheep. Enoch no doubt was translated, and so was Elijah; nor did they experience death: it was postponed, (and only postponed) most certainly: they are reserved for the suffering of death, that by their blood they may extinguish Antichrist.[15]

So for Tertullian, the duo of Elijah and Enoch return to suffer martyrdom at the hand of the antichrist, and their deaths, in some way, serve to conquer the antichrist figure. Tertullian makes another general reference to this tradition in *The Resurrection of the Flesh*, while combatting the notion that the resurrection is past. He states, "No one has as yet fallen in with Elijah; no one has as yet escaped from Antichrist; no one has as yet had to bewail the downfall of Babylon."[16] Here, once again, Elijah is associated with the antichrist figure and the events of the end, although the brevity allows for no definition of his particular role.

Hippolytus

Hippolytus was a priest of the Roman church who died as a martyr in 235 CE, having served as the first anti-pope for several decades. Hellenistic in education and Eastern in theological outlook, Hippolytus was the last Roman Christian to write in the Greek language. His only dogmatic work to survive in its entirety is *The Antichrist* (*De antichristo*), which was written around the year 200 CE.[17] In this work Hippolytus merges the two main streams of the Elijah *redivivus* tradition. He first mentions the return of Enoch and Elijah with reference to Daniel 9:27, but they are merely given the task of preaching repentance.[18] After pointing out that there are two advents of the Lord, Hippolytus identifies John the Baptist as the forerunner for the first. When he begins to discuss the second glorious advent, Hippolytus then states, "It is a matter of course that His forerunners must appear first."[19] Then upon citing the promise of the return of Elijah the Tishbite (Mal 3:23–24), Hippolytus returns to the use of the plural as he discusses the manner in which "they" shall bring repentance.

From this point forward the remainder of the presentation of the Elijah tradition appears to be dependant on Revelation 11:3–11. Beginning at *De antichristo* 47 Hippolytus writes:

> For John says, "And I will give power to my two witnesses, and they shall prophesy a thousand two hundred and threescore days, clothed in sackcloth." That is the half of the week of which Daniel spoke. "These are the two olive trees and the two candlesticks standing before the Lord of the earth. And if any man will hurt them, fire will proceed out of their mouth, and devour their enemies; and if any man will hurt them, he must in this manner be killed. These have power to shut heaven, so that it does not rain in the days of their prophecy; and have power over waters, to turn them to blood, and to smite the earth with all plagues as often as they will. And when they shall have finished their course and their testimony," what does the prophet say? "the beast that ascends out of the bottomless pit shall make war against them, and shall overcome them, and kill them," because they will not give glory to Anichrist.[20]

Hippolytus adheres closely to the account of *The Apocalypse*, adding only comments that connect the tradition with the book of Daniel. So after presenting Elijah and Enoch as eschatological preachers of repentance, Hippolytus appends the tradition of their conflict with antichrist and subsequent martyrdom without further development. Elijah and Enoch are not named explicitly in this passage,[21] but they can be inferred as the two witnesses given that Hippolytus has earlier identified the pair in connection with Daniel 9:27, which is also referred to in this passage. Furthermore, Hippolytus does name the duo in his commentary on Daniel:

> For when the sixty-two weeks are fulfilled, and Christ is come, and the Gospel is preached in every place, the times being then accomplished, there will remain only one week, the last, in which Elijah will appear, and Enoch, and in the midst of it the abomination of desolation will be manifested, Antichrist, announcing desolation to the world.[22]

The collections of Hippolytus' writings include another work that contains the Elijah *redivivus* tradition, *De consummatione mundi*.[23] Since it is generally considered spurious,[24] this treatise is often cited with the name Pseudo-Hippolytus.

The Apocalypse of Elijah

References from a number of early Christian writers seem to indicate that more than one apocalypse circulated in the name of Elijah.[25] David Frankfurter comments that "if there ever was an original text disclosing the revelations of Elijah—and there is no evidence that there ever was—it is inextricable from the profusion of Elianic texts and, more importantly, Elianic lore that circulated in the Greco-Roman period."[26] There are two extant Elijah apocalypses: the Coptic *Apocalypse of Elijah* and the Hebrew *Apocalypse of Elijah*. The remainder of this section will deal with the Coptic version.[27]

The Coptic *Apocalypse of Elijah* is a composite work that is the result of a Christian reworking of earlier Jewish apocalyptic material around the middle of the third century.[28] While the subject matter is apocalyptic, the literary framework does not correspond formally to the genre of an apocalypse. Contrary to the suggestion of the title, Elijah is not the recipient of a heavenly message. Instead, he appears twice as an eschatological actor, and both times he is paired with Enoch. The duo appears first in chapter 4, where they are portrayed as martyrs at the hand of the antichrist figure.[29] In *Apocalypse of Elijah* (C) 4:7 they arrive from heaven after the "son of lawlessness" has killed the virgin Tabitha:

> Then when Elijah and Enoch hear that the shameless one has revealed himself in the holy place, they will come down and fight with him, saying,
>
> > Are you indeed not ashamed?
> > When you attach yourself to the saints,
> > because you are always estranged.
> > You have been hostile to those who belong to heaven.
> > You have acted against those belonging to the earth.
> > You have been hostile to the thrones.
> > You have acted against the angels.
> > You are always a stranger.
> > You have fallen from heaven like the morning stars.
> > You were changed, and your tribe became dark for you.
> > But you are not ashamed,
> > when you stand firmly against God.
> > You are a devil.
>
> The shameless one will hear and he will be angry, and he will fight with them in the market place of the great city. And he will spend seven days fighting with them. And they will spend three and one half days in the market place dead while all the people see them. But on the fourth day they will rise up and they will scold him saying, "O shameless one, O son of lawlessness. Are you indeed not ashamed of yourself since you are leading astray the people of God for whom you did not suffer? Do you not know that we live in the Lord? As the words were spoken, they prevailed over him,

saying, "Furthermore, we will lay down the flesh for the spirit, and we will kill you since you are unable to speak on that day because we are always strong in the Lord. But you are always hostile to God. The shameless one will hear, and he will be angry and fight with them. And the whole city will surround them. On that day they will shout up to heaven as they shine while all the people and all the world see them.[30]

In this first encounter, Elijah and Enoch arrive after the advent of the antichrist, and their initial function is to bear witness against him. This testimony leads to their death in a confrontation with "the shameless one," after which they lie dead for three and a half days. Upon their resurrection, they renew their testimony and foretell the death of the antichrist by their hands. Then, according to most commentators, they are taken back up into heaven while the world looks on. Although the text does not explicitly mention their ascension, *Apocalypse of Elijah* (C) 4:19 is reminiscent of Revelation 11:12, which reads, "Then they heard a loud voice from heaven saying to them, 'Come up here!' And they went up to heaven in a cloud while their enemies watched them." Their ascension is confirmed by their return from heaven at their second appearance.

In the last chapter of the Coptic *Apocalypse of Elijah*, both Elijah and Enoch return again, this time following the Lord's judgment of heaven and earth. Their second advent begins in *Apocalypse of Elijah* (C) 5:32:

> After these things, Elijah and Enoch will come down. They will lay down the flesh of the world, and they will receive their spiritual flesh. They will pursue the son of lawlessness and kill him since he is not able to speak. On that day he will dissolve in their presence like ice which was dissolved by a fire. He will perish like a serpent which has no breath in it. They will say to him, "Your time has passed by for you. Now therefore you and those who believe you will perish." They will be cast into the bottom of the abyss and it will be closed for them.[31]

In this passage, Elijah and Enoch are given the additional function, which is not present in Revelation 11:3–11, of killing the antichrist figure.

Victorinus

Victorinus was bishop of Pettau, which is now in modern Styria, at the end of the third century. He died as a martyr in 304 CE, likely during the persecutions of Diocletian.[32] His *Commentary on the Apocalypse*, which exhibits chiliastic tendencies, is the only surviving work of this first exegete to write in Latin. This commentary refers to Elijah as the forerunner of the antichrist:

> He speaks of Elijah the prophet, who is the precursor of the times of Antichrist, for the restoration and establishment of the churches from the great and intolerable persecution. We read that these things are predicted in the opening of the Old and

New Testament; for he says by Malachi: "Lo, I will send to you Elijah the Tishbite to turn the hearts of the fathers to the children, according to the time of calling, to recall the Jews to the faith of the people that succeed them."[33]

Here Elijah comes prior to antichrist, serving as an agent of restoration and establishment for the church. The most interesting feature of this passage is the unique citation of Malachi 3:22–23, to which Victorinus adds: "according to the time of calling, to recall the Jews to the faith of the people that succeed them."[34] Given that the phrase "the people that succeed them" refers to the Gentiles, this rendering of the Malachi prophecy seems to present Elijah's task as unifying Jews and Gentiles by facilitating Jewish conversion. In essence, they are "recalled" to covenant loyalty by turning to Christian faith. In this portion of the commentary, Victorinus presents a version of the Elijah *redivivus* tradition in which Elijah appears alone.

In the portion of the commentary dealing with Revelation 11, Victorinus addresses the identity of the second prophetic figure:

> Many think that there is Elisha or Moses with Elijah, but both of these died while the death of Elijah is not heard of. All our ancients have believed that it was Jeremiah [with Elijah]. For even the very word spoken to him testifies to him, saying, "Before I formed you in the belly I knew you; and before you came forth out of the womb I sanctified you, and I ordained you a prophet to the nations." But he was not a prophet to the nations, and thus the truthful word of God makes it necessary, which it has promised to set forth, that he should be a prophet to the nations.[35]

So Victorinus does demonstrate that some ancient Christians did in fact read the second witness as Moses, and he even demonstrates knowledge of a tradition regarding Elisha. Nevertheless, Victorinus identifies Elijah's partner as Jeremiah, who returns to complete an unfulfilled role as prophet to the nations.[36] Enoch, interestingly, is not even listed as an option.

In the remainder of the work, Elijah is given priority as Jeremiah is not mentioned again. The "two wings of the great eagle" given to the woman in Revelation 12:14 are interpreted as the two prophets, who are identified as "Elijah and the prophet who will be with him."[37] Then once again, at 12:7–9 (which follows 12:16 in the commentary) Elijah appears alone:

> This is the beginning of Antichrist; yet previously Elijah must prophesy, and there must be times of peace. And afterwards, when the three years and six months are completed in the preaching of Elijah, he also must be cast down from heaven, where up till that time he had had the power of ascending; and all the apostate angels, as well as Antichrist, must be roused from hell.

There is a focus on the preaching of Elijah in Victorinus. For when the catholic church is given the gift of the prophets, it is the preaching of Elijah that results in the belief of the 144,000.[38]

The Acts of Pilate

Also known as the *Gospel of Nicodemus*, the *Acts of Pilate* is a work in two parts: the "Acts of Pilate" proper and "Christ's Descent into Hell."[39] Justin Martyr mentions an *Acts of Pontius Pilate* (*Apologia i* 35, 48), but it is unlikely that he knows of this particular work.[40] Eusebius (*Hist. eccl.* 1:9:3, 9:5:1) refers to a spurious *Acts of Pilate* that was published officially under Emperor Daia Maximinus (*circa* 311–12 CE) for use against the Christians.[41] According to the prevailing view of scholarship, the Christian *Acts of Pilate* was first devised and published to counteract this particular pagan forgery.[42] The work was certainly circulating by the year 375, for Epiphanius cites specific details from it (*Panarion* 50:1). As to the present form of the text, the consensus is that it goes back to the fifth or sixth century.[43]

The relevant passage for this study is located in the second part of the work, "Christ's Descent into Hell" (*Descensus Christi ad Inferos*), which addresses what transpires between Jesus' death and resurrection. After having shattered the gates of Hades and loosed the chains, Christ takes Adam by the hand and leads him—along with the patriarchs, prophets, martyrs, and forefathers—out of the underworld. Then *Acts of Pilate* 25 reads:

> Thus he went into paradise holding our forefather Adam by the hand, and he handed him and all the righteous to Michael the archangel. And as they were entering the gate of paradise, two old men met them. The holy fathers asked them, "Who are you, who have not seen death nor gone down into Hades, but dwell in paradise with your bodies and souls?" One of them answered, "I am Enoch, who pleased God and was removed here by him. And this is Elijah the Tishbite. We are to live until the end of the world. But then we are to be sent by God to withstand Antichrist and to be killed by him. And after three days we shall rise again and be caught up in clouds to meet the Lord.[44]

The tradition here is a streamlined version of Revelation 11:3–13. Elijah and Enoch will both return to fulfill the role of martyr in relation to antichrist, after which they will be resurrected.

Commodian

The Christian poet Commodian has proved particularly difficult for scholars to date and locate. The majority of scholars prefer a date in the third century and a provenance of North Africa. Recent challenges, however, have called for a date as late as the mid fifth century.[45] Nevertheless, such a late date would, at least, still make Commodian a contemporary of Theodoret. In writing about the events of the end, Commodian presents a unique reading of the Elijah/antichrist tradition:

> Then, doubtless, the world will be finished when he will appear. He himself will divide the globe into three ruling powers, when, moreover, Nero will be raised up from hell, Elijah shall first come to seal the beloved ones; at which things the region of Africa and the northern nation, the whole earth on all sides, for seven years will tremble. But Elijah will occupy half of the time, and Nero will occupy half. Then the whore Babylon, being reduced to ashes, its embers shall then advance to Jerusalem; and the Latin conqueror will then say, I am the Christ, to whom you always pray; and, indeed, the original ones who were deceived combine to praise him. He does many wonders, since his is the false prophet. Especially that they may believe in him, his image will speak. The Almighty has given it power to appear so. The Jews, recapitulating Scriptures from him, exclaim at the same time to the Highest that they have been deceived.[46]

In this text Elijah performs the function of sealing the believers before the advent of the antichrist figure. In the parallel account in Commodian's *Carmen de Duobus Populis* (or *Carmen apoligeticum*), Elijah returns to prophesy against the antichrist.[47] There is, however, no mention of martyrdom. It should be noted that Commodian's tradition initially speaks of the return of Elijah alone (*Carm.* 833, 839, 850), but then later speaks of *prophetae* (*Carm.* 856–62).

Lactantius

At the end of the third century, Lactantius was brought to the eastern capital of Nicomedia in Bithynia by the Emperor Diocletian in order to teach Latin rhetoric. Having become a Christian, he was forced to resign his chair during the persecution of 303 CE. At this time he turned to writing, although he later became a tutor to Constantine's son Crispus *circa* 317. Called the Christian Cicero for his elegant style, Lactantius penned the first systematic presentation of Christian doctrine in Latin, the *Divine Institutes*, beginning in the year 304. Book Seven, which deals with the second coming, is dedicated to Constantine, thus presupposing the Edict of Milan in 313.[48]

Addressing the advent of the antichrist, Lactantius maintains that "a great prophet" will be sent first:

> I will explain more fully how this will come about. Now, when the end of these times is imminent, a great prophet will be sent by God to convert men to a recognition of God, and he will have the power of working miracles. Wherever men will not hear

him, he will close heaven and will hold back the rains; he will change water into blood and will torture them with thirst and hunger; and fire will proceed from his mouth and burn whoever will attempt to hurt him. By these prodigies and powers, he will convert many to the worship of God. When these works of his have been carried out, another king will rise from Syria, born of the evil spirit, the overthrower and destroyer of the human race, who will destroy the remains of that previous evil one together with itself.[49]

Bauckham observes that Lactantius, like Commodian, attempts to interpret Revelation 11 in the light of an alternate tradition of the return of Elijah alone.[50] It should be noted, however, that the prophetic figure is not named in the text. Since the reference to turning the water into blood is retained, one could argue for Moses. Yet the preponderance of related Elijah texts makes the Tishbite the more likely referent. Here the Elijah *redivivus* figure functions to engender repentance and restoration (of relationship to God), after which he encounters antichrist and suffers martyrdom.

Conclusion

In all of the texts presented in this section, Elijah's return is connected in some way to an antichrist figure. Moreover, in all but two authors (Commodian[51] and Lactantius), Elijah is accompanied by a second figure, usually Enoch. Munck argued that the Christian tradition, in evidence here, of the return of Elijah and Enoch is simply the result of mistaken exegesis on the part of writers like Hippolytus.[52] Bauckham, however, has argued persuasively that the pairing of Enoch and Elijah is probably pre-Christian, as is the destruction of the antichrist. Bauckham observes that "the elimination of the last great enemy of the people of God was a messianic function in both Jewish and Christian apocalyptic. A Christian author is unlikely to have originated a tradition in which Enoch and Elijah are permitted in this way to usurp the role of Christ."[53] The varied nature of messianic expectation during the Middle Jewish period would certainly allow for such a role to be given to the pair, as the messianic functions given to them individually attest. As for the development of the martyrdom of the two figures, Bauckham and Munck agree, against Jeremias, that it is secondary, likely arising under the influence of Revelation 11:3–13, which itself is derivative of the Christian innovation of the martyrdom of the Messiah.[54]

This section has presented texts in which Elijah functions as an eschatological witness who appears in relation to the antichrist figure. While elements of the tradition derive from the broader apocalyptic milieu of the Middle Jewish period, the preceding texts are, for the most part, heavily dependent upon the canonical pericope from *The Apocalypse*. Generally speaking, Elijah appears with Enoch and they suffer martyrdom at the hands of antichrist.[55] In relation to the antichrist, Elijah is presented as performing the following functions: witness, martyr, exposer of antichrist, vanquisher of antichrist, forerunner of antichrist, and sealer of believers before antichrist. Finally, several of the authors (Victorinus,[56] Tertullian, and Hippolytus) exhibit a blend of the two broad categories, also depicting Elijah as the forerunner of the Parousia and an agent of restoration, which will be addressed in the following section.

Elijah as Forerunner or Herald of the Parousia

Justin Martyr

In addition to reporting an allegedly Jewish Elijah *redivivus* tradition, Justin Martyr reveals a second century Christian understanding of the role of Elijah as well. Justin's dialogue with Trypho regarding Elijah's return goes as follows:

> Then I inquired of him, "Does not Scripture, in the book of Zechariah,[57] say that Elijah shall come before the great and terrible day of the Lord?
>
> And he [Trypho] answered, "Certainly."
>
> "If therefore Scripture compels you to admit that two advents of Christ were predicted to take place—one in which He would appear suffering, and dishonored, and without comeliness; but the other in which He would come glorious, and Judge of all, as has been made manifest in many of the fore-cited passages—shall we not suppose that the word of God has proclaimed that Elijah shall be the precursor of the great and terrible day, that is, of His second advent?"
>
> "Certainly," he answered.
>
> "And, accordingly, our Lord in His teaching," I continued, "proclaimed that this very thing would take place, saying that Elijah would also come. And we know that this shall take place when our Lord Jesus Christ shall come in glory from heaven; whose first manifestation the Spirit of God who was in Elijah preceded as herald in [the person of] John, a prophet among your nation...Wherefore also our Christ said, [when He was] on earth, to those who were affirming that Elijah must come before the Christ: 'Elijah shall come, and restore all things; but I say unto you, that Elijah has already come, and they knew him not, but have done to him whatsoever they chose.' And it is written, 'Then the disciples understood that he spoke to them about John the Baptist.'"
>
> And Trypho said, "This statement also seems to me paradoxical; namely, that the prophetic Spirit of God, who was in Elijah, was also in John."

To this I replied, "Do you not think that the same thing happened in the case of Joshua the son of Nave (Nun), who succeeded to the command of the people after Moses...God said to him, 'I will take of the spirit which is in you and put it on him?'"

And he said, "Certainly."

"...even so God was able to cause [the spirit] of Elijah to come upon John; in order that, as Christ at His first coming appeared inglorious, even so the first coming of the spirit, which remained always pure in Elijah like that of Christ, might be perceived to be inglorious."[58]

This strand of the tradition is rooted in Malachi's prophecy regarding the return of Elijah, which Justin quotes correctly but erroneously attributes to Zechariah. The conflict between the Synoptic tradition, which identified John as Elijah, and the still existent expectation of Elijah in relation to the Day of the Lord is neatly resolved. Justin states that there are two advents of the Messiah and thus two forerunners as well. John the Baptist served as the forerunner for the Incarnation, Christ's first advent in humility. Elijah, on the other hand, will serve as the forerunner of the Parousia, Christ's second advent in glory. Justin argues that just as God gave the same spirit to Joshua that he had given to Moses, so also John was given the same spirit as Elijah. Elijah will then return himself to fulfill the role of precursor or herald of Christ's glorious return from heaven. Beyond that, few details are given as to what Elijah will specifically do at that time. It should be noted that there is no reference to an encounter with an antichrist figure at all.

Hippolytus

It has already been observed that Hippolytus knows the tradition in which Elijah and Enoch suffer as martyrs at the hands of the antichrist figure. His presentation of that tradition in *De antichristo* 47 is essentially a reproduction of the account in Revelation 11:3–13, with the exception that he identifies the two witnesses, albeit in an earlier passage, as Elijah and Enoch. Yet in the majority of his treatment of the Elijah *redivivus* tradition (*Antichr.* 43–46), Hippolytus presents Elijah (and Enoch) as fulfilling a forerunner function in a manner reminiscent of Malachi 3:23–24:

Now Daniel will set forth this subject to us. For he says, "And one week will make a covenant with many, and it shall be that in the midst (half) of the week my sacrifice and oblation shall cease." By one week, therefore, he meant the last week which is to be at the end of the whole world; of which week the two prophets Enoch and Elias will take up the half. For they will preach 1,260 days clothed in sackcloth, proclaiming repentance to the people and to all the nations. (44) For as two advents of our Lord and Savior are indicated in the Scriptures, the one being His first advent in the flesh, which took place without honor...But his second advent is announced as glorious...Thus also two forerunners were indicated. The first was John the son of Zacharias, who appeared in all things a forerunner and herald of our Savior, preaching of the heavenly light that had appeared in the world. He first fulfilled the course of forerunner.[59]

Then having declared John the Baptist to be the forerunner of the first advent, Hippolytus turns to the second, when the risen Lord shall be manifested to judge the world:

> It is a matter of course that His forerunners must appear first, as He says by Malachi and the angel, "I will send to you Elijah the Tishbite before the day of the Lord, the great and notable day, comes; and he shall turn the hearts of the fathers to the children, and the disobedient to the wisdom of the just, lest I come and smite the earth utterly." These, then, shall come and proclaim the manifestation of Christ that is to be from heaven; and they shall also perform signs and wonders, in order that men may be put to shame and turned to repentance for their surpassing wickedness and impiety.[60]

Like Justin, Hippolytus understands the Malachi prophecy to refer to two forerunners. He names the first as John the Baptist, but when addressing the second forerunner, Hippolytus shifts to the plural, "These, then, shall come." "These" could refer to Elijah and John the Baptist, but the identification of Elijah and Enoch with the "one week" of Daniel makes the latter pair the most likely referents. So then for Hippolytus, the second forerunner is in fact a pair, Elijah and Enoch. In the two passages above, their function is to proclaim repentance or perform signs that lead to repentance. This is in keeping with the reading of Malachi 3:24 as a promise of the restoration of the covenant relationship. Thus, in these passages, Elijah and Enoch function as forerunners of the messiah—as opposed to the Day of the Lord in the Old Testament tradition—and their preparatory role is that of engendering repentance in the people of the world. Having presented this stream of the Elijah *redivivus* tradition, Hippolytus then abruptly attaches the martyriological account of the two witnesses from Revelation 11.

Tertullian

Tertullian also addresses the uncertainty regarding the identification of John the Baptist with the returning Elijah. Yet for Tertullian, the issue driving his discussion is the Pythagorean concept of the transmigration of souls. Vigorously opposing Carpocrates and his followers, Tertullian explains the relationship between Elijah and John:

The fact, however, is that their metempsychosis or transmigration theory signifies the recall of the soul, which had died long before, and its return to some other body. But Elijah is to come again, not after quitting life (in the way of dying), but after his translation (or removal without dying); not for the purpose of being restored to the body from which he had not departed, but for the purpose of revisiting the world from which he was translated; not by way of resuming a life which he had laid aside, but of fulfilling prophecy—really and truly the same man, both in respect of his name and designation, as well as of his unchanged humanity. How, therefore, could John be Elijah? You have your answer in the angel's announcement: "And he shall go before the people," he says, "in the spirit and power of Elijah"—not, observe, in his soul and his body. These substances are, in fact, the natural property of each individual, while "the spirit and power" are bestowed as external gifts by the grace of God, and so may be transferred to another person according to the purpose and will of the Almighty, as was formerly the case with respect to the spirit of Moses.[61]

In his refutation of the transmigration of souls, Tertullian displays knowledge of the two forerunners tradition, in which John appears only in the spirit and power of Elijah, while Elijah himself is still expected to fulfill the prophecy of Malachi 3:23. In this particular instance, no reference is made to the presence of Enoch or an antichrist, nor is there any depiction of Elijah's function.

Origen

Origen (185–253) likewise addresses the confusion caused by the conflicting accounts of the Synoptics and the Fourth Gospel. In his *Commentary on John* he asks, "Who of those who hear Jesus say of John, 'If you wish to receive it, he is Elijah who is to come,' would not inquire how John says to those who ask, 'Are you Elijah?', 'I am not'?"[62] Like Tertullian, Origen proceeds here at length to refute the doctrine of the transmigration of souls, and once again the key interpretive text is Luke 1:17, in which the angel says to Zechariah, "With the spirit and power of Elijah he will go before him, to turn the hearts of parents to their children, and the disobedient to the wisdom of the righteous, to make ready a people prepared for the Lord." In a homily on this passage, Origen asserts, "Luke does not say, 'in the soul of Elijah,' but, 'in the spirit and power of Elijah'."[63] By answering the question "Are you Elijah" (John 1:21) in the negative, the Baptist is simply affirming, according to Origen, that he is not the Elijah who is expected to reappear without being born, for that one, having been taken up, had still not returned.[64]

Thus, using Luke 1:17 to distinguish between John the Baptist and the expected Elijah, Origen advances the two forerunner doctrine as well. John, in the spirit and power of Elijah, is the forerunner of the first advent, while Elijah precedes Christ's arrival in glory. Depicting Elijah's task in general terms, Origen states that he will prepare people for the glory of the restoration.[65]

Jerome

Jerome (331–420), in his *Commentary on Malachi*, interprets the angel of Malachi 3:1 as John the Baptist, but then he concedes that John appeared in the "spirit and power" of Elijah.[66]Further on he demonstrates awareness of Elijah's role as the precursor of the Day of Judgment:

> Therefore before the day of judgment should come and the Lord should strike the earth with a curse, either entirely, or suddenly,...the Lord sends with Elijah—which translates, my God, he is from the town of Tisbia, the one who sounds the turning and repentance—the whole chorus of the prophets, and Isaac and Jacob, and of all the patriarchs, so that the descendents of them may believe in the Lord Savior, in whom those also have believed: *For Abraham has seen the day of the Lord and was glad.* If the heart of the father [is turned] to the son, it is the heart of God to all, who have received the spirit of adoption. And the heart of the sons to their fathers, as both Jews and Christians, who now disagree among themselves, equally in religion they agree on Christ. Whence it is spoken to the apostles, who have produced a breeding ground of the gospel in the whole world: *On behalf of your fathers your sons are born.* For if Elijah has not converted the heart of the fathers above all to the sons, and the heart of the sons to the heart of the fathers, when the great and horrible day of the Lord has come—great to holy ones, horrible to sinners—the true and just judge will strike; not the heavens, nor those whom are transformed in the heavens, but the earth with a curse, those who do earthly works.[67]

In this text Elijah returns to bring unity, in Christ, to both Jews and Christians. The unique feature of this text is Elijah's return with the prophets and patriarchs, who help lead their descendants to faith in Christ.

Augustine

Jerome's contemporary Augustine (354–430) also demonstrates knowledge of the two-fold fulfillment of the prophecy in Malachi. Augustine asserts that there is no contradiction with respect to the statement of Jesus (Matt 11:14) and the denial by the Baptist (John 1:21). Augustine also employs the standard phrase, referring to John as being "in the spirit of Elijah." As there are two advents for the one Judge, there are necessarily two heralds. Therefore, he concludes, "Elijah will be in the second advent what John was in the first."[68]

Augustine also knows the Elijah *redivivus* tradition in which Elijah returns in order to lead the Jews to salvation through Jesus Christ. It is found in chapter 29 of *The City of God:*

It is a familiar theme in the conversation and heart of the faithful, that in the last days before the judgment the Jews will believe in the true Christ, that is, our Christ, by means of this great and admirable prophet Elijah who will expound the law to them. For not without reason do we hope that before the coming of our Judge and Savior, Elijah will come, because we have good reason to believe that he is now alive; for, as Scripture most distinctly informs us, he was taken up from this life in a chariot of fire. When, therefore, he comes, he will give a spiritual explanation of the law which the Jews at present understand carnally, and will thus "turn the heart of the father to the son,"...And the meaning is, that the sons, that is, the Jews, shall understand the law as the fathers, that is, the prophets, and among them Moses himself, understood it.[69]

Here, Elijah returns, alone, as a forerunner of Christ. As such, his task is the exposition of the law to the Jews. Augustine puts forth a tradition which reads the phrase from Malachi 3:24—"to turn the heart of the father to the son"—along the general lines of restoring covenant faithfulness. Elijah will teach the Jews to understand the law as their ancestors did. Yet, as Augustine explains, this ancient understanding was christological, and so Elijah must turn the mind of the Jews away from earthly things, teaching the true spiritual understanding of the scriptures—that Jesus is the Christ.

Augustine himself, however, favors a different reading of Malachi 3:24. He writes:

Another and a preferable sense can be found in the words of the Septuagint translators, who have translated Scripture with an eye to prophecy...that Elijah will turn the heart of God the Father to the Son...meaning that he should make it known, and that the Jews also, who had previously hated [him], should then love the Son who is our Christ.[70]

Taking his cue from the LXX's use of the singular of "son" (it is plural in the MT), Augustine argues that the first phrase of Malachi 3:24 (ἀπο-καταστήσει καρδίαν πατρὸς πρὸς υἱόν, 3:23 LXX) refers to God's demonstration of his love for Jesus, while the second phrase refers to Jewish recognition of Jesus as the Christ.[71] Nevertheless, Elijah's role is still that of leading the Jews to salvation by means of a proper understanding of the scriptures. Augustine does make other general references to the eschatological salvation of the Jews without specifically mentioning Elijah.[72]

Diodore of Tarsus

One of the foremost teachers and scholars of the Antiochene School, Diodore of Tarsus was hailed as a defender of Nicene orthodoxy during his lifetime. He was in the vanguard of the Christian reaction to Julian the Apostate (361–363 CE), and he also served as a principal figure in the Second Ecumenical Council at Constantinople (381). Made bishop of Tarsus in Cilicia in 378, Diodore proved an influential teacher, training such notables as John Chrysostom and Theodore of Mopsuestia. Although a prolific writer, Diodore's literary bequest is mostly non-extant due to his posthumous condemnation in 499 for allegedly being the father of Nestorianism.

Karl Staab found fragments of a commentary on Romans in Codex Vaticanus Graecus 762, which he published as part of a commentary on Paul by the Greek fathers.[73] A vague Elijah *redivivus* tradition is preserved in Diodore's comments on Romans 12:25–26, which, to our knowledge, have not been previously translated into English:

> What does "And thus all Israel will be saved" mean? Just as we say that all the world and all the Gentiles will be saved in order that there may be some from all ends of the earth and from every nation who approach in faith, so also the phrase "all Israel will be saved" does not indicate all the people as a whole, but surely those from the dispersion throughout the whole world who will approach in faith in the future or those who are gathered by Elijah.[74]

To begin with, the language itself is uncertain. The use of the verb καταλαμβάνω to describe Elijah's action is unusual in that it does not appear to correspond to the traditional semantic domains of the term. Karl Schelkle renders it as *Aufgenommenen* in German, and it seems that "gathered" fits the context most closely in English. Nothing, however, is said about when this gathering takes place nor about how it transpires. It seems safest to merely state that Diodore knows of a tradition in which Elijah plays a role in Jewish salvation. This role will be more defined in Diodore's Antiochene successors.

John Chrysostom

A student of Diodore, John Chrysostom (c. 350–407) became a priest in Antioch in the year 386. Assigned the post of preacher in Antioch's principal church by Bishop Flavian, Chrysostom established a reputation as a preeminent orator during the period from 386 until 397, when he reluctantly became Bishop of Constantinople. Among these sermons are 90 homilies on Matthew, delivered *circa* 390, which constitute the oldest complete commentary on that gospel.[75]

In *Homiliae in Mattheum* 37 Chrysostom addresses Jesus' identification of John the Baptist with Elijah in Matthew 11:14:

> And he said this requiring a thoughtful mind, showing that John is Elijah, and Elijah is John. For both received one ministry, and both have become forerunners. Therefore, he did not say simply, "This one is Elijah," but rather, "If you are willing to receive it, this one is [Elijah]," that is, if you pay attention to what is happening with a

thoughtful mind. And he did not stop here, but he added to the phrase, "This is Elijah who is to come," the additional words, "The one who has ears to hear, let him hear," demonstrating that sagacity is needed.[76]

Maintaining a distinction between Elijah and John, who was not a Tishbite, Chrysostom declares that John, fulfilling the ministry of Elijah, was the forerunner of the first advent, as Elijah will be for the second.[77] Thus, the tradition of the two forerunners is present in the Antiochene stream of interpretation as well.

Speaking of the coming of the Tishbite in *Homiliae in Mattheum* 55, Chrysostom proclaims:

> And he teaches the reason of his coming in the same place [Malachi]. And what is the reason? That when he comes he may persuade the Jews to believe in Christ, and that they all may not be completely destroyed when he comes. Therefore, bringing that recollection to them, he says, "And he will restore all things," that is, he will correct the unbelief of the Jews who are found at that time."[78]

Chrysostom then goes on to point out that the scripture does not say that Elijah will restore "the heart of the son to the father," but rather it says he will restore "the father to the son."[79] Identifying the Jews as the fathers of the apostles, Chrysostom says that the mind of the Jewish people will be restored to the doctrines of their sons, the apostles.[80] So in Chrysostom, Elijah is identified as the forerunner of the Parousia with the expressed function of correcting Jewish unbelief regarding Jesus Christ.

Theodore of Mopsuestia

Born in Antioch, Theodore of Mopsuestia (c. 350–428) was a fellow student of John Chrysostom under both Diodore and the sophist Libanius. After being consecrated bishop of Mopsuestia in Cilicia in 392, Theodore made a name for himself as a scholar, and his orthodoxy was unquestioned. Nevertheless, he suffered the same fate as his teacher Diodore, being condemned as a heretic over a century after his death at the Fifth Ecumenical Council at Constantiople in 553.[81] As a result, most of his works have not survived.

Although he wrote commentaries on nearly every biblical book, only one such treatise is fully extant in Greek, his *Commentary on the Twelve Minor Prophets*. In his treatment of Malachi 3:1, Theodore maintains that the prophecy regarding the coming angel or messenger is a disclosure about the period of the Maccabees. He concedes that it is not surprising that the gospel writers cite this verse in relation to John the Baptist, who did, in fact, fulfill a forerunner role (Matt 11:10; Mark 1:2; Luke 7:27). Nevertheless, the type of coming exhibited in Malachi 3:2—"who can endure the day of his coming, and who can stand when he appears?"—is, according to Theodore, not in keeping with the "lamb of God who takes away the sin of the world."[82] Theodore certainly makes no connection between John the Baptist and Elijah.

Elijah is mentioned, of course, at the end of the commentary. Speaking directly to the Jews, who are the addressees of the prophecy, Theodore states:

> But since even at that revealing you will demonstrate your usual lack of sense, the blessed Elijah will be sent to you before the second coming of Christ the Lord from heaven, so as to unite those who have been divided because of religion (εὐσέβεια) and, through the knowledge (ἐπιγνώσις) of religion, to bring fathers—who were formerly divided on the grounds of religion—into unity of mind with their children. In short, to set all people upon the same footing, so that those formerly in the grip of impiety (ἀσέβεια) may, by receiving the knowledge of truth from him [Elijah], have fellowship with the godly (τοὺς εὐσεβεῖς).[83]

Another Antiochene interpreter demonstrates knowledge of Elijah's return at the second advent of Christ. As with Chrysostom, Elijah appears to address the problem of Jewish unbelief. The language here, however, is more subtle and less explicitly christological. Elijah does not persuade them to believe in Christ, rather he engenders a knowledge or recognition (ἐπιγνώσις) of religion (εὐσέβεια), which could also be rendered as godliness or piety.[84] He does not expound upon the phrasing of Malachi 3:24 with the detail of Chrysostom, but his reading appears to be along similar lines, for it is the fathers who are brought into agreement with the children. The key function, for Theodore, is Elijah's establishment of unity.

Theodoret of Cyrus

An additional reference to the Elijah *redivivus* tradition can be found in Theodoret's *Commentary on Malachi*. He reads the messenger in Malachi 3:1 as a reference to John the Baptist, while Malachi 3:2 is seen as foretelling the second coming of Christ.[85] Elijah, however, is not mentioned at all in relation to the Baptist at this juncture. In his treatment of Malachi 3:23–24, Theodoret provides an expanded treatment of the tradition which he mentions in passing in his *Commentary on Romans*:

> Then—although he clearly knows that they will neither be persuaded by the law nor will they receive him when he is near, but rather they will hand him over to the cross—employing an ineffable philanthropy, he promises to send to them again the herald Elijah. He says, "Behold, I send you Elijah the Thesbite." And signifying the time, he added, "before the great and manifest day of the Lord comes." He spoke of the day of the second epiphany, and he teaches what the great Elijah will do when he comes. "He will restore the heart of the father to the son and the heart of a man to

his neighbor." And demonstrating the reason why Elijah is coming first, he added, "Lest I strike the earth with a curse when I come." Lest, that is, when I find you all faithless, I send you all into everlasting chastisement. Elijah will come first, and he will teach you about my coming. He will persuade you, O Jews, both to be in union with the people from the nations who have believed in me without doubt and to manifest my church as one. Indeed, he calls the Jews "fathers" because they were called first, but the "sons" are the nations that are saved after them. Since, therefore, on the one hand we are even now turning Jews toward godliness (εὐσέβεια), but on the other hand they continue to be faithless because they are jealous of our salvation, he said appropriately that Elijah will restore the heart of the father to the son. Indeed, he will persuade them to receive fellowship (κοινωνία) with us.[86]

Theodoret is specific as to Elijah's function: he will teach about the second coming of Christ and establish unity between Jews and Gentiles by persuading the Jews to believe in Christ. Here once again, the Jews are presented as "the fathers" and the Christians are presented as "the sons" of Malachi 3:24.

Cyril of Alexandria

Theodoret's nemesis Cyril of Alexandria (d. 444) provides additional evidence of the Elijah *redivivus* tradition beyond the Antiochene stream of interpretation. In his *Commentary on Malachi*, Cyril, like Theodoret, makes a distinction between the figures of Malachi 3:1 and Malachi 3:23. The messenger of 3:1 is identified as John the Baptist, whereas Malachi 3:23 presents Elijah as the forerunner of the second coming:

> [It is] a manifestation of God's gentleness and patience that Elijah the Thesbite shines out to us at the appropriate time, proclaiming, then, in advance when the judge will be present to everyone in the inhabited world. For the son will come down as a judge...But since we are involved in the greatest sins, the divine prophet usefully goes before us leading the people on earth to concord, in order that everyone who has been brought to unity in faith and who has been impeded from eagerly seeking wickedness might choose to do good and thus be saved when the judge descends. Anticipating this then, the blessed John the Baptist came forth "in the spirit and power of Elijah." However, just as he proclaimed, "prepare the way of the Lord, make straight his paths," so the divine Elijah then proclaims that he is near, and not yet present, in order that he might judge the inhabited world in justice. Even now, perhaps, some individuals are divided in opinion; father is divided against son, and son against father. For one has believed in Christ, and the other is counted among the unbelievers. Still others stand apart from love for their neighbor; they were separated because of hatred, incessant wrath, and rivalries over whatever is of consequence in the world. For indeed the prophet will restore by gathering together again into one faith those who have been divided and by restoring "a man to his neighbor, lest I come," he says, "and smite the earth utterly," that is, completely and

entirely. You see therefore, the Lord of the universe's gentleness. He assures the people on earth in advance, and he all but solemnly affirms through the voice of Elijah that the judge will be present. [He does this] in order that those who are living on the earth at that time and who are amending their own lives with changes for the better might not fall in with a harsh judge who sends [them] to the flame and into outer darkness.[87]

Cyril places a good deal of emphasis upon Elijah's role as herald, announcing the second coming in advance. The purpose of this prior annunciation, it seems, is to provide the people of the earth with an opportunity for repentance. Once again, the theme of unity is present. Yet the discord which Elijah comes to address is not between Jew and Gentile specifically, but rather the general division between believer and unbeliever. In this text, Elijah's message does not seem to be directed at the Jewish people in particular.

Conclusion

During the first century of the Christian era, there was apparently some confusion as to the fulfillment of the promises in Malachi 3:1, 23. Thus, the author of Matthew attempted to settle the matter conclusively for the church with Jesus' statement regarding John the Baptist in Matthew 11:14, "if you are willing to accept it, he is Elijah who is to come." While the identification of John as the Elijah figure did, in fact, become the predominate Christian understanding of the Malachi prophecy, the explicit denial of this identification by John himself in John 1:21, coupled with the allusion to a returning Elijah in Revelation 11:3–13, served to keep diverse readings of the Elijah *redivivus* tradition current in the Christian community. That Matthew's statement did not conclusively settle the matter is demonstrated in the middle of the second century, as Justin Martyr is forced to take up the issue of the identification of the coming Elijah.[88]

In addressing the confusion, Justin first presents a line of interpretation that is followed by virtually all of the authors and texts included in this section. The solution calls for two advents—the first in humility and the second in glory—each with its own forerunner; thus, John the Baptist becomes the forerunner for the Incarnation while Elijah will be the forerunner for the Parousia.[89] Luke 1:17 proves to be the interpretive linchpin in defense of this reading, as John the Baptist is argued to have appeared only "in the spirit and power of Elijah," allowing for Elijah himself to return before the second advent.[90] A second interpretive option is advanced in favor of the concept of two advents and two forerunners. Theodoret makes a distinction between the identities of the figures in Malachi 3:1 and Malachi 3:23, understanding John the Baptist as the messenger of 3:1 while 3:23, as a separate prophecy, refers to the eschatological return of Elijah.[91]

In terms of the function that Elijah exercises upon his return, the earlier texts present him, in general terms, primarily as a forerunner or herald of the second coming.[92] Some of these specifically mention the role of preaching repentance.[93] Of the eleven authors cited here, six of them portray Elijah as having some role in Jewish salvation.[94] Victorinus, included in the previous section of this chapter, brings the total to seven. In these texts Elijah functions as an agent of Jewish salvation, and his activity is depicted in the following ways: he gathers the Jews;[95] he expounds the law to them;[96] he corrects Jewish unbelief,[97] and he persuades the Jews to believe in Christ.[98] Naturally, some authors will contain several of the elements above. It is interesting to observe that all four Antiochenes understand Elijah to have a role in the future salvation of the Jews, so it seems that such a reading could be regarded as an Antiochene tradition. Yet it also appears outside of that stream in Victorinus, Jerome, and Augustine, the latter of whom goes so far as to say, "It is a familiar theme in the conversation and heart of the faithful."[99] Cyril's presentation of the tradition does not mention Jews explicitly, but there are a number of parallels, particularly the call for religious unity.[100] In summation, the expectation that Elijah will return at the Parousia was widespread in early Christianity, and the idea that this Elijah *redivivus* will play a role in Jewish salvation was present both in the East and the West.

Summary of Chapters Four and Five

Chapter Four presented the Middle Jewish texts containing Elijah *redivivus* traditions according to their traditional division, in which Elijah is understood to be either a forerunner of the Day of the Lord or of the Messiah. The textual data has yielded no evidence of the expectation of Elijah as a forerunner of the messiah prior to the Christian era. The possibility that some Jews could have conceived of the returning Elijah functioning in a preparatory role in the early first century has not been discounted. Nevertheless, it has been demonstrated that the oft repeated assertion that the expectation of Elijah as the forerunner of the Messiah was widespread or universal runs contrary to the evidence of the extant primary texts.

In more positive terms, it would be appropriate to make the general statement that the return of Elijah was a feature of the eschatology of a number of Jews at the beginning of the Christian era. Drawing upon the prophecy of Malachi 3:23-24, Elijah's task was initially that of restoration, understood generally in terms of covenant renewal. This role was fluid, however, during the Middle Jewish period, as various texts present him as a herald, a witness, a judge, and possibly even a martyr.[101] Since the first clear evidence of an Elijah figure fulfilling a preparatory role with respect to a messiah is in the Christian gospels (John the Baptist as Elijah *redivivus*), it seems likely that the forerunner role for Elijah is a Christian innovation. A number of the Middle Jewish texts surveyed here, which serve to underscore the diversity of eschatological speculation during this period, present the Elijah *redivivus* figure himself in a messianic fashion.

Within the Christian tradition, outlined here in Chapter Five, there was continued speculation regarding the future role of Elijah owing to the Fourth Gospel's denial that John the Baptist was Elijah (John 1:21, 25) and to the presence in Revelation of an allusion to Elijah's return (Rev 11:3-13). The subsequent Christian uses of the Elijah *redivivus* tradition emerge into two broad streams: (1) those texts which present Elijah as an eschatological witness, and (2) those which present him as a forerunner of the Parousia. The traditions in the first category, in which Elijah is usually associated with the antichrist, are generally dependent upon the account in Revelation 11, whereas the texts of the second category seem to be heavily influenced by Malchi 3:23-24.

As an eschatological witness, Elijah's return is connected in some way to the antichrist. Furthermore, Elijah is generally accompanied by a second figure, who is typically Enoch; this pairing is likely a pre-Christian tradition. Heavily dependent upon the canonical account of the two-witness (Rev 11:3-13), these texts portray Elijah as performing various functions in relation to the antichrist such as witness, martyr, exposer of antichrist, vanquisher of antichrist, forerunner of antichrist, and sealer of believers before antichrist.

As the forerunner of the Parousia, Elijah's return is seen in light of the prophecy in Malachi 3:23-24. The apparent contradiction between the statement of Jesus ("he is Elijah who is to come," Matt 11:14) and the denial by John the Baptist ("I am not," John 1:21) created confusion as to the identity of the Elijah *redivivus* figure. The exegetical solution was to read Malachi 3:23-24 as a prophecy with a double fulfillment. Applying Luke 1:17, patristic interpreters in this category argued consistently that John the Baptist appeared "in the spirit and power of Elijah," leaving the door open for Elijah to return himself. Thus, John the Baptist served as the forerunner for the Incarnation, while Elijah will be the forerunner of the Parousia. Other exegetes argued for the two advent/two forerunner model by advocating a distinction between the figures of Malach 3:1 and 3:23, with the messenger of 3:1 understood to be

John the Baptist. In these texts, Elijah's role is consistently defined as that of a forerunner with additional functions being those of herald, preacher of repentance, and agent of Jewish salvation. Seven authors[102] portray Elijah as having some role in Jewish salvation, with his actions variously described as gathering the Jews, expounding the law to them, correcting their unbelief, and persuading them to believe in Christ. Thus, Theodoret's understanding of the Elijah *redivivus* tradition is not unique but rather part of larger stream of Christian tradition.

Notes

1. Or at least upon a common apocalyptic tradition.

2. Rev 11:3–13 (NRSV).

3. Haugg, *Die Zwei Zeugen*, 13–14.

4. While there is only one lampstand mentioned in Zech 4:2–3, 11, subsequent Jewish traditions depict the Temple as containing two. David E. Aune, *Revelation 6–16* (WBC 52B; Nashville: Thomas Nelson, 1998), 612.

5. Charles H. Talbert, *The Apocalypse: A Reading of the Revelation of John* (Louisville: Westminster John Knox, 1994), 45–46; Elisabeth Schüssler Fiorenza, *Revelation: A Vision of a Just World* (Minneapolis: Fortress, 1991), 77–9; Bruce M. Metzger, *Breaking the Code: Understanding the Book of Revelation* (Nashville: Abingdon, 1993), 70–71; J. S. Considine, "The Two Witnesses: Apoc 11:3–13," *CBQ* 8 (1946), 391; Markus Öhler, *Elia im Neuen Testament*, 295.

6. Aune adds that "the author modifies the expectation of Enoch and Elijah *redivivi* to Moses and Elijah *redivivi*" in order to serve his purpose. Aune, *Revelation*, 610.

7. Richard Bauckham, "The Martyrdom of Enoch and Elijah: Jewish or Christian?" *JBL* 95 (1976): 452.

8. Ibid., 458.

9. There is a Gnostic *Apocalypse of Peter*, which is found in the Nag Hammadi library, as well as a later Arabic *Apocalypse of Peter*.

10. It proved to be particularly influential, spawning a number of successors, including Dante's *Divine Comedy*.

11. Commentators frequently relate the Jewish Antichrist who persecutes the Christians to Bar Kokhba. C. Detlef G. Müller, "Apocalypse of Peter," in *New Testament Apocrypha: Writings Relating to the Apostles Apocalypses and Related Subjects* (Louisville: John Knox, 1992), 622.

12. It is mentioned in the Muratorian Fragment, which is generally dated at the end of the second century, F. F. Bruce, *The Canon of Scripture* (Downers Grove, Ill.: InnerVarsity, 1988), 158. According to Eusebius, Clement of Alexandria (150–215 CE) lists it as a disputed work in the canonical discussion contained in the *Hypotyposes*. Eusebius, *Historia ecclesiastica* 6:14:2 (*NPNF*² 1:261). It is also mentioned in *Codex Clarmontanus*, which scholars believe to represent an Alexandrian list *circa* 300 CE, Bruce, *Canon*, 218–19. Furthermore, citations from the document have been identified in Clement of Alexandria, Methodius, Macarius, and possibly in Theophilus of Antioch; Clement and Macarius name the source. J. K. Elliot, ed., *The Apocryphal New Testament: A Collection of Apocryphal Christian Literature in an English Translation* (Oxford: Clarendon, 1993), 593.

13. *Apocalypse of Peter*, 2 (Elliot).

14. Quasten, *Patrology*, 2:289.

15. Tertullian, *De anima* 50 (ANF 3:227–28).

16. Ibid., *De resurrectione carnis* 22 (ANF 3:561).

17. Quasten, *Patrology*, 2:170.

18. The texts in which this function is discussed will be presented in full in the next section of this chapter.

19. Hippolytus, *De antichristo*, 46 (ANF 5:213).

20. Ibid., 47 (ANF 5:213-14).

21. They are briefly referred to again without being named in *Antichr.* 64 as "the two prophets and forerunners of the Lord." After they have finished their course, nothing remains except for the return of Christ.

22. Hippolytus, *Commentarium in Danielem*, 2:22 (ANF 5:182).

23. Like Hippolytus, Pseudo-Hippolytus presents a synthesis of the two main streams of the Elijah *redivivus* tradition in Christianity. He states that there are two advents of the Christ, one in humiliation and another in glory. John the Baptist was the forerunner of the first, and the second advent will exhibit Enoch, Elijah, and a third forerunner—John the Theologian (θεολόγον)! According to Photius (cod. 229), Ephraem of Antioch also knows of such a tradition, which is rooted in John 21:22. Pseudo-Hippolytus then presents a version of the Elijah *redivivus* tradition that is heavily dependant upon Revelation, except that the three witnesses (Enoch, Elijah, and the author of the Fourth Gospel) proclaim to the world the advent of the antichrist figure before being martyred. Thus, like the *Apocalypse of Peter*, part of their function is to expose this figure. See Pseudo-Hippolytus, *De consummatione mundi* 21, 29 (ANF 5:247, 249-50).

24. J. B. Lightfoot, *The Apostolic Fathers* (London: Macmillan, 1889), 2:398.

25. Orval S. Wintermute, "Apocalypse of Elijah," ABD 2:466.

26. David Frankfurter, *Elijah in Upper Egypt: The Apocalypse of Elijah and Early Egyptian Christianity* (SAC; Minneapolis: Fortress, 1993), 55.

27. The date of the Hebrew *Apocalypse of Elijah*—around the mid-sixth or early seventh century—is beyond the purview of this study, although the work most certainly draws upon earlier material. Furthermore, Elijah's role in this apocalypse is different, as he is the seer through whom the future visions are related. Wintermute, "Apocalypse of Elijah," ABD 2:467.

28. Orval S. Wintermute, "Apocalypse of Elijah: A New Translation and Introduction," in *The Old Testament Pseudepigrapha* (vol. 1; ed. James H. Charlesworth; Garden City, NY: Doubleday, 1983), 730.

29. The martyrdom of Elijah and Enoch in chapter 4 is preceded by the martyrdom of Tabitha and followed by that of the sixty righteous ones.

30. *Apoc. El.* (C) 4:7-19 (Wintermute).

31. *Apoc. El.* (C) 5:32-35 (Wintermute).

32. Quasten, *Patrology* 2:411.

33. Victorinus, *Commentarium in Apocalypsim* 7:2 (ANF 7:351-52).

34. This phrase replaces the MT's "(to turn) the hearts of children to their parents" and the LXX's "(to turn) the heart of a person to his/her neighbor."

35. Victorinus, *Commentarium in Apocalypsim* 11:5 (ANF 7:354).

36. Hilary of Poitiers (d. 368) knows of the tradition regarding Jeremiah. He states that there are different opinions as to whether Enoch or Jeremiah is the one who must die with Elijah in Revelation 11. Hilary, *In Matthaeum* 20:10 (SC 258:114).

37. Victorinus, *Comm. Apoc.* 12:14 (ANF 7:356). In 14:8 the other witness is merely called "the associate of his prophesying."

38. Ibid., 12:6 (ANF 7:356).

39. This work will use the title *Acts of Pilate* to refer to the entire work while employing the conventional numbering of chapters that carries over into the Descent (which begins with chapter 17).

40. Elliot, *Apocryphal New Testament*, 164.

41. Clayton N. Jefford, "Acts of Pilate," *ABD* 5:371.

42. Felix Scheidweiler, "The Gospel of Nicodemus: Acts of Pilate and Christ's Descent into Hell," in *New Testament Apocrypha* (rev. ed.; vol. 1; ed. Wilhelm Schneemelcher; trans. R. McL. Wilson; Louisville: Westminster John Knox, 1991), 501.

43. Elliot, *Apocryphal New Testament*, 165. A fifth century date would be contemporaneous with Theodoret.

44. *Acts Pil.* 25 (Elliot).

45. Brian E. Daley, *The Hope of the Early Church: A Handbook of Patristic Eschatology* (Cambridge: Cambridge University Press, 1991), 162; Jean-Paul Brisson, *Autonomisme et christianisme dans l'afrique romaine de Septime Sévère à l'invasion vandale* (Paris: E. de Boccard, 1958), 390–94.

46. Commodian, *Instructiones* 41 (ANF 4:211).

47. The *Carmen* also mentions the advent of a second antichrist in the East; this false messiah outlives Nero, the first antichrist, and performs miracles in Judaea. Ibid., *Carmen apoligeticum* 825–64 (CCL 128:103–05).

48. Quasten, *Patrology*, 2:397.

49. Lactantius, *Divinarum institutionum* 7:17 (FC 49:517–18).

50. Bauckham, "Martyrdom of Enoch and Elijah," 452.

51. While Commodian mentions only Elijah in the *Instructiones*, he does refer to two prophets in the *Carmen*; see above.

52. Johannes Munck, *Petrus und Paulus in der Offenbarung Johannis* (Copenhagen: Rosenkilde og Bagger, 1950), 81–118.

53. Bauckham, "Martyrdom of Enoch and Elijah," 457.

54. Ibid., 451, 457; Jeremias, "Ηλ(ε)ίας," *TDNT* 2:939–40.

55. There are exceptions, of course. The figure does not appear to be Enoch in Revelation 11, and Elijah is paired with Jeremiah in Victorinus. Commodian and Lactantius present him as a single agent, while Pseudo-Hippolytus adds a third witness, John the Theologian. As for the martyrdom, it is absent in Victorinus and Commodian; while it is not explicit in *Apoc. Pet.*, it is likely implied.

56. Victorinus is distinct within this category, combining the antichrist tradition with forerunner role in which Elijah preaches repentance and is an agent of restoration with respect to both the churches and the salvation of the Jews.

57. Justin mistakenly attributes the quotation to Zechariah instead of Malachi.

58. Justin, *Dial.* 49:2–7 (ANF 1:219–20).

59. Hippolytus, *De antichristo* 43–44 (ANF 5:213).

60. Ibid., 46 (ANF 5:213).

61. Tertullian, *De anima* 35 (ANF 3:217).

62. Origen, *Commentarii in evangelium Joannis* 6:62 (FC 80:185).

63. Ibid., *Homiliae in Lucam* 4:5 (FC 94:19).

64. Ibid., *Commentarii in evangelium Joannis* 6:71 (FC 80:188).

65. Ibid., *Commentarium in evangelium Matthaei* (GCS 40, 176–83).

66. Jerome, *Commentariorum in Malachiam liber* 3:1 (CCSL 76A 927–28:4–34; 929:70–74).

67. Ibid., 3:6 (CCSL 76A 941–42:91–110).

68. Augustine, *In Evangelium Johannis tractatus* 4:5 (NPNF[1] 7:27).

69. Ibid., *De civitate Dei* 20:29 (NPNF[1] 2:448).

70. Ibid.

71. The second phrase in the LXX is "καὶ καρδίαν ἀνθρώπου πρὸς τὸν πλησίον αὐτοῦ." Augustine comments that God took on human flesh, becoming our πλησίον. Ibid.

72. Augustine, *Sermones* 122:5 (WSA III/4:241); *Quaestionum evangelicarum* 2:23 (CCSL 44B: 66–67).

73. Karl Staab, *Pauluskommentare aus der Griechischen Kirche: aus Katenen–handschriften gesammelt und herausgegeben* (NTAbh 15; Münster i.W.: Aschendorff, 1933).

74. Ibid., 104.

75. Quasten, *Patrology*, 3:437.

76. John Chrysostom, *Homiliae in Mattheum* 37 (PG 57:422).

77. Ibid., *Homiliae in Mattheum* 55 (PG 58:557–59).

78. Ibid., (PG 58:559).

79. He is obviously using the LXX, which omits the reversal of the phrase.

80. Ibid.

81. Williston Walker *et al.*, *A History of the Christian Church* (New York: Charles Scribner's Sons, 1985), 178–79.

82. Theodore, *Commentarius in Malachiam* 3:1–2 (PG 66:620–21).

83. Ibid., 4:4–6 (PG 66:632).

84. Luke 1:17b—"to turn the hearts of the fathers back to the children, and *the disobedient to the attitude of the righteous*"—may be behind the εὐσέβεια /ἀσέβεια language here.

85. Theodoret, *Enarratio in Malachiam* 3:1–2 (PG 81:1977).

86. Ibid., 4:4–6 (PG 81:1985).

87. Cyril, *In Malachiam Phophetam Commentarious* 4:5–6 (PG 72:361, 364).

88. Öhler, *Elia im Neuen Testament*, 298.

89. Every text in this section presents this two advent/two forerunner view except for Diodore and Theodore. Diodore is commenting specifically upon Romans 11:25–26. Since he is focusing on the second coming, he makes no reference at this point to an earlier advent or

forerunner. Theodore's comments, likewise, focus exclusively on the Parousia. If he knows of the two forerunners tradition (his fellow Antiochene's Chrysostom and Theodoret do), he does not mention it at this point.

90. Every author in this section employs the language of Luke 1:17 except for the four Antiochenes: Diodore, Chrysostom, Theodore, and Theodoret.

91. Cyril makes this distinction as well.

92. Justin, Hippolytus, Tertullian, Origen, and Cyril (who is later).

93. Hippolytus and Cryil. Origen states that he prepares for restoration, which could be understood as repentance.

94. Jerome, Augustine, Diodore, Chrysostom, Theodore, and Theodoret.

95. Diodore.

96. Augustine.

97. Chrysostom and Theodore.

98. Victorinus, Chrysostom, Theodoret, and Jerome. Jerome is the only author in the forerunner category who does not present Elijah as coming alone; rather, Elijah comes with the prophets, Isaac, Jacob, and all of the patriarchs.

99. Augustine, *De civitate Dei* 20:29 (*NPNF*[1] 2:448).

100. The question with respect to Cyril is: Is he speaking about Jewish–Gentile unity or theological unity within the church itself?

101. The martyriological function here is dependant upon the identification of Elijah with the Phinehas of Pseudo–Philo.

102. Including Victorinus for the eschatological witness category.

• C H A P T E R   S I X •

Conclusion

Summary of Findings

In keeping with the recent revival of interest in patristic studies, this study
has attempted to listen seriously to an oft unknown ancient voice. In commenting on the salvation of all Israel in Romans 11:26, Theodoret of
Cyrus (c. 393–466) writes, "And he [Paul] urges them not to despair of the salvation of the other Jews; for when the Gentiles have received the message,
even they, the Jews, will believe, when the excellent Elijah comes, bringing to
them the doctrine of faith. For even the Lord said this in the sacred gospels:
'Elijah is coming, and he will restore all things.'"[1] This interesting reading of
Romans 11:26, depicting Elijah as the agent of Jewish salvation, is virtually
unknown to modern scholarship on Romans.[2] The initial purpose of this
study is to ascertain if this distinct reading is unique. It has been determined
that it is not. Rather, it is part of a larger stream of early Christian Elijah *redivivus* traditions. An additional purpose of this project is the categorization of
the broad trajectories within the development of these Christian traditions.[3] It
has been determined that the Christian Elijah *redivivus* traditions can be
grouped into two general categories: (1) Elijah as eschatological witness, and
(2) Elijah as forerunner of the Parousia.

Those texts which present Elijah as an eschatological witness are heavily
dependent upon the pericope of the two witnesses in Revelation 11:3–13, although elements of the tradition may derive from the larger Middle Jewish
apocalyptic milieu. One such element is the association of Elijah with a second
figure, usually Enoch, which is a feature of the majority of these texts. All of
the texts in this category associate the returning Elijah with the antichrist in
some way, and his function is usually defined in relation to that antichrist figure. Elijah is variously presented as a witness, martyr, exposer of antichrist,
vanquisher of antichrist, forerunner of antichrist, and a sealer of believers before antichrist.

Those texts which present Elijah as a forerunner of the Parousia are
rooted in the interpretation of Malachi 3:23–24. There was apparently some
confusion that early Christian writers had to address regarding the fulfillment

of this prophecy. This perplexity can be attributed to the discrepancy between Jesus' statement regarding John the Baptist in Matthew 11:14 ("If you are willing to accept it, he is Elijah who is to come.") and John's own denial of that identification in John 1:21 ("'Are you Elijah?' He said, 'I am not.'"). Moreover, the allusion to Elijah in Revelation 11 also served to keep diverse readings of the Elijah *redivivus* tradition current in the Christian community.

In addressing this uncertainty as to the identity of the returning Elijah, virtually all of the authors in this second category pursue the following line of interpretation. The solution calls for two advents—the first in humility and the second in glory—each with its own forerunner; thus, John the Baptist becomes the forerunner for the Incarnation while Elijah will be the forerunner for the Parousia. At this point appeal is made to Luke 1:17 as the interpreters note that John the Baptist appeared only "in the spirit and power of Elijah," thus allowing for Elijah himself to return before the second advent. Theodoret himself presents a second exegetical argument for the concept of two advents and two forerunners. Making a distinction between the identities of the figures in Malachi 3:1 and 3:23, Theodoret asserts that the Baptist is the messenger of 3:1, while 3:23, as a separate prophecy, refers to the eschatological return of Elijah.

The texts of this second category present Elijah, in general terms, as a forerunner of the Parousia of Christ. In the earliest texts his function is limited, such as merely announcing the second coming as a herald, while other texts specifically mention the role of preaching repentance. Of the eleven authors cited in this category, six of them depict Elijah as having some role in Jewish salvation. Victorinus, a representative of the first category, brings the total to seven. These texts present Elijah as an agent of Jewish salvation, and his role is described in the following ways: he gathers the Jews, he expounds the law to the Jews, he corrects Jewish unbelief, and he persuades the Jews to believe in Christ. All four of the Antiochene interpreters in this category mention Elijah in relation to the salvation of the Jews, yet a similar role appears outside of this school as well, as evidenced by the readings of Victorinus, Jerome, and Augustine. Augustine even observes, "It is a familiar theme in the conversation and heart of the faithful."[4]

In conclusion, this study has demonstrated that Theodoret of Cyrus' expectation of the eschatological return of Elijah in order to address the issue of Jewish salvation is not an isolated reading but rather part of a larger, widespread Elijah *redivivus* expectation in early Christianity. This expectation is manifested in two trajectories: one in which Elijah is presented as an eschatological witness who confronts the antichrist, and another in which Elijah is expected as the forerunner of the return of Christ. Within this latter category, there is a subset of texts that depict Elijah as an agent of Jewish salvation, and it is to this group that Theodoret of Cyrus' reading belongs.

As indicated at the outset, it is hoped that the recovery of this ancient Christian tradition has yielded a collection of data that may subsequently be used to bring an ancient yet fresh perspective to bear upon the impasse regarding the interpretation of Romans 11:26. Franz Mussner, eschewing both the traditional christological and the two-covenant theological interpretations of "the Deliverer from Zion," asserts that the Jews will be saved via a *Sonderweg*, i.e., they will be saved by Christ at the Parousia apart from traditional conversion to the Christian gospel. While some of the texts presented in this study employ language indicative of conversion, others speak more subtly of Elijah establishing agreement and unity between the groups. These texts in which Elijah acts as an agent of Jewish salvation, drawing upon early Christian and Jewish traditions, demonstrate what one type of *Sonderweg* might look like.

Charles Talbert is the only modern commentator that I know who cites Theodoret's treatment of Romans 11:26.[5] In addressing the issue of when the salvation of Israel—understood as a corporate ethnic designation—will take place, Talbert favors the reading which places it, possibly in a great event, prior to the Parousia. As evidence in support of this, he notes that Romans 11:12 and 11:15 point to an interval, no matter how brief, between the inclusion of the Jews and the Parousia. Furthermore, Romans 11:15 echoes the belief that Israel's faithfulness would be a catalyst for the End.[6] Yet Talbert is unable to say how this mass ingathering before the end of history will transpire. He seems dubious that it could be due to Christian preaching alone. Then after pointing out the surprising twists of grace in salvation history, Talbert exclaims, "Saving grace seems to surprise its recipients! Perhaps, alongside Christian preaching God has some surprises yet in store for Gentiles and Jews about the way unbelieving Israel will be brought to faith in their Messiah."[7] Recalling his earlier citation of Theodoret's intriguing application of the Elijah *redivivus* tradition, the attentive reader will recognize that Talbert is actually entertaining the notion of Elijah's return as the catalyst for that mass ingathering of the Jews prior to the Parousia. He cannot, however, quite bring himself to make such an interpretation explicit. This study is significant in that it has marshaled an array of texts that may be utilized to support just such a reading.

Avenues for Future Research

The findings of this study have opened several promising avenues of research. First, there is more work to be done in mapping out the trajectories of the Christian Elijah *redivivus* traditions. In his investigation of the martyrdom of Enoch and Elijah, Richard Bauckham presents a list of Elijah *redivivus* texts (corresponding to the eschatological witness category of this study) that continues through the Byzantine period up until the tenth century, concluding with Adso (d. 992), abbot of the Cluniac monastery of Moutier-en-Der. Bauckham observes in a footnote that "Adso—and thence the whole Western medieval tradition—gives them [Enoch and Elijah] the additional role of converting the Jews to Christianity."[8] Thus, the tradition of Elijah's return as an agent of Jewish salvation has a long history in Christian interpretation. It was likely lost to modern scholarship, which has been predominantly Protestant, as a result of the Reformation. Bauckham's general statement needs to be verified by tracing and documenting the historical trajectories of Elijah's role in the salvation of Israel.

Second, the functions of Elijah *redivivus* in Christian tradition need to be examined in relation to those found within the rabbinic tradition.[9] Addressing the influence of the Jewish presence on Theodoret's exegesis, Thomas McCollough states, "What Theodoret well knew...was that because Jews continued to exist alongside Christians—and there is ample evidence now that attests to an ongoing and vital Jewish presence—as long as this was the situation, the appropriation of the Jewish Scriptures was always to be a problematic task."[10] John Chrysostom, the bishop of Theodoret's youth, preached against those members of his flock who sought out the synagogue almost as a talisman; the synagogues' sanctity and power, according to Chrysostom, derived from the fact of their possession of the law and the prophets.[11] Such an environment would provide fertile ground for the cross-pollination of traditions.

Some of the Christian traditions presented in this study appear to have affinities with a few of the rabbinic categories. One rabbinic category in particular—*Elijah as arbiter of interpretation*[12]—evinces similarities with Theodoret's reading, in which Elijah returns bringing "the doctrine of faith."[13] This teaching function is also reflected in Augustine's portrayal of Elijah as expounding the law to the Jews. An additional rabbinic category—*Elijah as adjudicator of communal membership*[14]—could shed light on the Christian texts in which Elijah *redivivus* in mentioned in relation to the Jews.

Notes

1. Theodoret of Cyr, *Interpretatio in xiv epistulas sancti Pauli* (Migne, PG 82:180).
2. To our knowledge it is acknowledged only by Charles Talbert, *Romans*, 242. It is, however, listed in the catena style commentary of the ACC; Gerald Bray, *Romans*, 299.
3. The concern here is with those Christian traditions in which the role of Elijah *redivivus* is seen to be as yet unfulfilled.
4. Augustine, *De civitate Dei* 20:29 (NPNF1 2:448).
5. Talbert, *Romans*, 242.
6. Ibid., 265.
7. Ibid., 267.
8. Bauckham, "Martrydom of Enoch and Elijah," n. 21 453.
9. Several broad categories of rabbinic Elijah *redivivus* traditions will be introduced in the Appendix.
10. Thomas McCollough, "Theodoret of Cyrus as Biblical Interpreter," in *Studia Patristica XVIII* (ed. Elizabeth A. Livingstone; Kalamazoo, Mich.: Cistercian Publications, 1986), 331.
11. John Chrysostom, *Homilia adversus Judaeos* 1:3, 5 (PG 48:847-50).
12. Category one in the Appendix.
13. Augustine, *De civitate Dei* 20:29 (NPNF1 2:448).
14. Category two in the Appendix.

Appendix

Functions of Elijah in the Rabbinic Literature

The tasks performed by Elijah *redivivus* in the rabbinic literature are so diverse as to almost defy systematic categorization. It is the intent of this appendix merely to present a general introduction to the types of activities in which he engages in order to uncover avenues that may be promising for comparison with the Christian developments. This treatment is by no means exhaustive.

1. Elijah as Arbiter of Interpretation

One of the more frequently observed functions of Elijah in the rabbinic literature is his return to settle disputes between the schools over interpretation of the law. In a treatment of passages on Ezekiel, several Rabbis are quoted as saying, "This passage will be interpreted by Elijah in the future."[1] One question often resolved by Elijah is that of ritual cleanliness, as indicated in *b. Bekhorot* 33b:

> And it may be that R. Eliezer holds this view only [in connection with doubtful *terumah*], in case Elijah should come and pronounce it clean, but in this case, where if you leave it the animal dies, he holds the view of the Rabbis! And [perhaps] the Rabbis hold their view only here, for if he leaves it, it dies, but there, in case Elijah should come and pronounce it clean, they hold with R. Eliezer![2]

Having been asked whether *tefillin* may be written upon the skin of a clean fish, Rabbi Nahman ben Isaac responded:

> If Elijah will come and declare, he replied. What does 'if Elijah will come and declare' mean. Shall we say, whether it has a [separate] skin or not,—but we see that it has a skin? Moreover we learned: The bones of a fish and its skin afford protection in the tent wherein is a corpse! Rather [he meant]: If Elijah comes and tells [us] whether its foul smell evaporates or not.[3]

This is hardly as exciting work as dissolving antichrist like ice (Coptic *Apoc. El.* 5:32–35), but it is indicative of the more trivial nature of some of the issues addressed by the prophet upon his return.

In the Mishnah tractate *Bava Metzi'a*, Elijah returns to resolve such issues as disputes over loan repayments (*m. Bava Metzi'a* 3:4–5), what to do with found vessels of gold or glass (*m. Bava Metzi'a* 2:8), and what to do with a found document of unknown nature (*m. Bava Metzi'a* 1:8). To these and other such issues, the response is given, "It must be left until Elijah comes."[4] Faierstein comments that this concept is epitomized by the term *teyqu*—meaning "the Tishbite will resolve difficulties and problems"—which is used to conclude eighteen talmudic discussions.[5]

2. Elijah as Adjudicator of Communal Membership

According to Rabbi Hama bar Hanina, when God causes his divine presence to rest, it rests only upon the families of pure birth in Israel (*b. Qiddushin* 70b). M. *Eduyyot* 8:7 portrays Elijah as the one who determines a family's rightful place in Israel:

> R. Joshua said: I have received as a tradition from Rabban Johanan b. Zakkai, who heard from his teacher, and his teacher from his teacher, as a *Halakah* given to Moses from Sinai, that Elijah will not come to declare unclean or clean, to remove afar or to bring nigh, but to remove afar those [families] that were brought nigh by violence and to bring nigh those [families] that were removed afar by violence. The family of Beth Zerepha was in the land beyond Jordan and Ben Zion removed it afar by force. The like of these Elijah will come to declare unclean or clean, to remove afar or to bring nigh. R. Judah says: To bring nigh but not to remove afar.[6]

This role of monitor of familial purity is further in evidence in *b. Qiddushin* 70a, where Elijah exercises a punitive function: "He who marries a wife who is not fit for him, Elijah binds him and the Holy One, blessed be He, flagellates him."[7]

3. Elijah as High Priest

Elijah is associated with a priestly function by virtue of being designated as the one who restores the implements of the Temple:

> And this is one of the three things which Elijah will, in the future, restore to Israel: The bottle of manna, the bottle of sprinkling water, and the bottle of anointing oil. And some say: Also the rod of Aaron with its ripe almonds and blossoms, for it is said: 'Bring back the rod of Aaron,' etc. (Num. 17:25).[8]

Elijah is identified as a Levite by some rabbinic texts. *Tanhuma* calls him the second prophet, after Moses, of the tribe of Levi. Another priestly connection is found in *Targum Yerusalmi*, in which Elijah is identified with John Hyrcanus. The suggestion that Phinehas is still alive in *Rabbah* Numbers 21:3 led to speculation that eventually identified Elijah with Phinehas.[9]

4. Elijah as the Forerunner of the Messiah

This is not a frequent function for Elijah, but it is particularly relevant to the study at hand. The earliest reference is an anonymous *baraitha* in *b. Eruvin* 43b:[10]

> Why [it may be asked] is it permitted [for the man to drink wine] on Sabbaths and festival days?—There the case is different since Scripture said, *Behold I will send you Elijah the prophet* etc. and Elijah, surely, did not come on the previous day. If so, even in the case of weekdays, [the drinking of wine] should be permitted on any day since Elijah did not come on the previous day." But the fact is that we assume that he appeared before the high court, then why should we not here also assume that he appeared before the high court?—Israel has long ago been assured that Elijah would not come either on Sabbath eves or on festival eves owing to the people's preoccupation.
>
> Assuming that as Elijah would not come the Messiah also would not come, why should not [the drinking of wine] be permitted on a Sabbath eve? Elijah would not, but the Messiah might come because the moment the Messiah comes all will be anxious to serve Israel. [But why should not the drinking of wine] be permissible on Sunday? May it then be derived from this that the law of Sabbath limits is inapplicable, for had it been applicable [the drinking of wine] should have been permissible on a Sunday since Elijah did not arrive on the preceding Sabbath?[11]

In the view of this text, Elijah is the precursor of the Messiah by one day. An additional text is sometimes cited as example of Elijah as a messianic forerunner, but the particular role he performs and the time of its execution are unclear:

> *And the Lord showed me four craftsmen.* Who are these *'four craftsmen'*?—R. Hana b. Bizna citing R. Simeon Hasida replied: The Messiah the son of David, the Messiah the son of Joseph, Elijah and the Righteous Priest...*These then are come to frighten them, to cast down the horns of the nations, which lifted up their horn against the Land of Judah, to scatter it.*

There are other rabbinic texts that present Elijah as the forerunner of the Messiah, but they are very late (*Pirqe Rabbi Eliezar* and *Pesiqta Rabbati*).

5. Elijah as Supernatural Mediator

In the Babylonian Talmud, Elijah is presented in a manner reminiscent of the angels, possessing supernatural knowledge and traveling freely between heaven and earth; even so, he interacts with individuals in a personal way. This supernatural interaction is evident in three generic patterns: (1) Elijah appears in disguise to help or rescue; (2) Elijah appears to the rabbis, and (3) Elijah refuses to visit one who has done wrong.[12] Examples of these patterns are provided below.

Elijah appears in disguise to help or rescue. In b. Avodah Zarah 18a–b Elijah appears as a prostitute to aid Rabbi Meir's escape from the Romans. Elijah appears before the Roman Emperor, disguised as a Roman advisor, in order to save Nahum of Gimzo from execution (b. Sanhedrin 108b–109a).

Elijah appears to the rabbis. In *b. Megillah* 15b Rabbah b. Abbuha comes across Elijah and inquires about Esther's motives. Rabbi Nathan, in *b. Bava Metzi'a* 59b, met Elijah and asked him what God was doing during the Sages debate on the oven of Aknai; Elijah responds, "He laughed [with joy], saying, 'My sons have defeated Me, My sons have defeated Me.'"[13]

Elijah refuses to visit one who has done wrong. B. Sanhedrin 113a–b relates this story:

> R. Jose taught in Sephhoris: Father Elijah was a hot tempered man. Now, he [Elijah] used to visit him, but [after this] he absented himself three days and did not come. When he came on the fourth day, he [R. Jose] said to him, "Why did you not come before?' He replied, '[Because] you called me hot tempered.' He retorted, 'But before us Master has displayed [your] temper!'"[14]

Miscellaneous

The rabbinic texts present Elijah performing a wide range of miscellaneous functions, including making peace in the world (*m. Eduyyot* 8:7) and the resurrection of the dead (*m. Sotah* 9:15). He is also seen acting with other figures, such as Moses (*Deut. Rab.* 3:17). For a fuller treatment, see the references below.[15]

Notes

1.   *b. Menahot* 45 a, in *Seder Kodashim* 1 (Soncino), 271.

2.   *b. Bekhorot* 33b, in *Seder Kodashim* 3 (Soncino), 214. See also *b. Pesahim* 13a, 20b, 70b.

3.   *b. Shabbat* 108a, in *Seder Moed* 1 (Soncino), 523.

4.   *m. Bava Metzi'a* 1:8 (Danby), 348. The surplus of money collected to pay for someone's burial must also be left until Elijah comes, *m. Sheqalim* 2:5.

5.   Faierstein, "Elijah Must Come First?," 82. For a list of these eighteen references see Louis Ginzberg, *An Unknown Jewish Sect* (New York: The Jewish Theological Seminary of America, 1970), 212 n. 14.

6.   *m. Eduyyot* 8:7 (Danby), 436.

7.   *b. Qiddushin* 70, in *Seder Nashim* 4 (Soncino), 354.

8.   *Mekilta de-Rabbi Ishmael, Vayassa* 6 (vol. 2; trans. Jacob Z. Lauterbach; Philadelphia: Jewish Publication Society of America, 1961), 126.

9.   For further information on this development see Robert Hayward, "Phinehas—the same as Elijah: The Origins of a Rabbinic Tradition," *JJS* 29 (1978): 22-34; David G. Clark, "Elijah as Eschatological High Priest: An Examination of the Elijah Tradition in Mal. 3:23-24" (Ph.D. diss., University of Notre Dame, 1975).

10. The question being addressed in this text is the permissibility of drinking wine on the Sabbath if one has vowed to be a nazirite on the day on which the Son of David comes.

11. *b. Eruvin* 43b, in *Seder Moed* 2 (Soncino), 299-300.

12. Kristen Lindbeck, "Story and Theology: Elijah's Appearances in the Babylonian Talmud," (Ph.D. diss., The Jewish Theological Seminary of America, 1999), 156-62.

13. *b. Bava Metzi'a* 59b, in *Neziqin* 1 (Soncino), 353.

14. *b. Sanhedrin* 113a-b, in *Neziqin* 3 (Soncino), 780-81.

15. Str-B IV 4/2:779-98; Louis Ginzberg, *An Unknown Jewish Sect* (New York: The Jewish Theological Seminary of America, 1970); *Legends of the Jews* (vol. 4; Philadelphia: The Jewish Publication Society of America, 1913).

Bibliography

Allenbach, Jean et al., eds. *Biblia patristica: index des citations et allusions bibliques dans la littérature patristique*. 7 vols. Paris: Editions du Centre national de la recherche scientifique, 1975–2000.

Allison, Dale C. Jr. "Elijah Must Come First." *Journal of Biblical Literature* 103 (1984): 256–8.

Altaner, Berthold. *Patrology*. Translated by Hilda C. Graef. New York: Herder & Herder, 1961.

Althaus, Paul. *The Theology of Martin Luther*. Translated by Robert C. Schultz. Philadelphia: Fortress, 1966.

————. *Der Brief an die Römer*. Das Neue Testament Deutsch 6. Göttingen: Vandenhoeck & Ruprecht, 1959.

Anastos, M. V. "Nestorius Was Orthodox." *Dumbarton Oaks Papers* 16 (1962): 119–140.

Arminius, Jacobus. *The Writings of James Arminius*. Vol. 1. Translated by James Nichols. Grand Rapids, Mich.: Baker, 1977.

Ashby, G. W. *Theodoret of Cyrrhus as exegete of the Old Testament*. Grahamstown: Rhodes University Press, 1972.

————. "The Hermeneutic Approach of Theodore of Cyrrhus to the Old Testament." Pages 131–135 in *Studia Patristica* 15.1. Edited by Elizabeth A. Livingstone. Berlin: Akademie Verlag, 1984.

Augustine. *Quaestiones evangeliorum*. Corpus Christianorum: Series Latina 44B. Turnhout, 1980.

————. *Letters 100–150*. The Works of Saint Augustine: A Translation for the 21ˢᵗ Century II/2. Edited by Boniface Ramsey. Translated by Roland Teske. Hyde Park, NY: New City, 2003.

————. *Sermons*. The Works of Saint Augustine: A Translation for the 21ˢᵗ Century III/4. Edited by John E. Rotelle. Translated by Edmund Hill. Brooklyn, NY: New City, 1992.

Aune, David E. *Revelation 6–16*. Word Biblical Commentary 52B. Nashville: Thomas Nelson, 1998.

Azéma, Y. "Citations d'auteurs et allusions profanes dans la Correspondance de Théodoret." Pages 5–13 in *Überlieferungsgeschichtliche Untersuchungen*. Texte und Untersuchungen zur Gesch der altchristlichen Literatur 125. Berlin: Akademie Verlag, 1981.

Babcock, William S. "MacMullen on conversion: a response." *Second Century* 5 (1985): 82–89.

Bardenhewer, Otto. *Geschichte der Altkirchlichen Literatur*. Darmstadt: Wissenschaftliche Buchgesellschaft, 1962.

Bardy, Gustave. "Théodoret." *Dictionnaire de théologie catholique* 15 (1946): 299–325.

————. "Interprétation chez les pères." *Dictionnaire de la Bible: Supplément* 4 (1949): 569–91.

————. ed. *Élie le prophète: selon les écritures et les traditions chrétiennes*. Vol. 1. Paris: Desclée de

Brouwer, 1956.

Barrett, C. K. A *Commentary on the Epistle to the Romans*. New York: Harper and Brothers, 1957.

Barth, Karl. *The Epistle to the Romans*. Translated by Edwyn C. Hoskyns. Oxford: Oxford University Press, 1968.

Bate, H. N. "Some Technical Terms of Greek Exegesis." *Journal of Theological Studies* 24 (1922–23).

Bauckham, Richard. "The Martyrdom of Enoch and Elijah: Jewish or Christian?" *Journal of Biblical Literature* 95 (1976): 447–58.

Baur, Ferdinand Christian. "Über Zweck und Gedankengang des Römerbriefs," *Theologische Jahrbücher* 16 (1857).

Beare, Frank W. *St. Paul and His Letters*. New York: Abingdon, 1962.

Beck, Johann Tobias. *Versuch einer pneumatisch hermeneutischen Entwicklung des neunten Kapitels im Briefe an die Römer*. Stuttgart: C. Hoffmann, 1833.

Beker, J. Christiaan. *Paul the Apostle: The Triumph of God in Life and Thought*. Philadelphia: Fortress, 1980.

Berkouwer, G. C. *The Return of Christ*. Grand Rapids, Mich.: Eerdmans, 1972.

Beyschlag, Willibald. *Die paulinische Theodicee, Römer IX–XI: Ein Beitrag zur biblischen Theologie*. Halle: Eugen Strien, 1868.

Bishop, David Lynn. *The Doctrine of Providence in Selected Writings of Theodoret of Cyrus*. Ph.D. diss., The Southern Baptist Theological Seminary, 1995.

Black, Matthew, ed. *The Book of Enoch or 1 Enoch*. Studia in Veteris Testamenti pseudepigraphica. Leiden: E. J. Brill, 1985.

Blaising, Craig A. "Dispensationalism: The Search for Definition." Pages 13–34 in *Dispensationalism, Israel and the Church: The Search for Definition*. Edited by Craig A. Blaising and Darrell L. Bock. Grand Rapids, Mich.: Zondervan, 1992.

Blenkinsopp, Joseph. *Prophecy and Canon: A Contribution to the Study of Jewish Origins*. Notre Dame: Notre Dame University Press, 1977.

Bloesch, Donald G. "'All Israel will be saved:' supersessionism and the biblical witness." *Interpretation* 43 (1989): 130–142.

Boccaccini, Gabriele. *Middle Judaism: Jewish thought, 300 B.C.E.–200 C.E.* Minneapolis: Fortress, 1991.

Boismard, M.-E. Review of Franz-J. Leenhardt, *L' Épître de saint Paul aux Romains*, *Revue Biblique* 65 (1958): 432–436.

Bornkamm, Günther. *Paul*. Translated by D. M. G. Stalker. San Francisco: Harper & Row, 1971.

Bousset, Wilhelm. *The Antichrist Legend: A chapter in Christian and Jewish folklore*. Translated by A. H. Keane. 1896. Repr., Atlanta: Scholars Press, 1999.

Bouyer, Louis. *The Spirituality of the New Testament and the Fathers*. London: Burns & Oates, 1963.

Bovon, François. *Luke 1: A Commentary on the Gospel of Luke 1:1–9:50*. Translated by Christine M. Thomas. Minneapolis: Fortress, 2002.

Braaten, Carl E. *History and Hermeneutics*. Vol. 2 of *New Directions in Theology Today*. Edited by William Hordern. Philadelphia: Westminster, 1966.

Bray, Gerald, ed. *Romans.* Ancient Christian Commentary on Scripture, New Testament 6. Downers Grove, Ill.: InterVarsity, 1998.

Breck, John. "Theoria and Orthodox Hermeneutics." *St. Vladimir's Theological Quarterly* 20 (1976).

———. *The Power of the Word in the Worshiping Church.* Crestwood, NY: St. Vladimir's Seminary, 1986.

Brisson, Jean-Paul. *Autonomisme et christianisme dans l'afrique romaine de Septime Sévère à l'invasion vandale.* Paris: E. de Boccard, 1958.

Brown, Raymond E. *The Sensus plenior of Sacred Scripture.* Baltimore: St. Mary's University, 1955.

Bruce, F. F. *The Letter of Paul to the Romans: An Introduction and Commentary.* Tyndale New Testament Commentaries. Grand Rapids, Mich.: Eerdmans, 1985.

———. *The Canon of Scripture.* Downers Grove, Ill.: InnerVarsity, 1988.

Bultmann, Rudolf. "History and Eschatology in the New Testament." *New Testament Studies* 1 (1954): 5–16.

———. *Theology of the New Testament.* Translated by Kendrick Grobel. 2 vols. New York: Charles Scribner's Sons, 1951–1955.

Burns, J. Lanier. "The Future of Ethnic Israel in Romans 11." Pages 188–229 in *Dispensationalism, Israel and the Church.* Edited by Craig A. Blaising and Darrell L. Bock. Grand Rapids, Mich.: Zondervan, 1992.

Buttenwieser, Moses. *Outline of the Neo-Hebraic Apocalyptic Literature.* Cincinnati: Jennings and Pye, 1901.

Calvin, John. *Institutes of the Christian Religion.* Edited by John T. McNeill. Translated by Ford Lewis Battles. 2 vols. Philadelphia: Westminster, 1960.

———. *The Epistles of Paul the Apostle to the Romans and to the Thessalonians.* Edited by David W. Torrance and Thomas F. Torrance. Translated by Ross Mackenzie. Grand Rapids, Mich.: Eerdmans, 1961.

Canivet, Pierre. *Histoire d'une enterprise apologétique de Ve siècle.* Paris: Bloud & Gay, 1958.

Cavalcanti, E. "Theodoret of Cyrrhus." Pages 827–28 in vol. 2 of *Encyclopedia of the Early Church.* Edited by Angelo Di Berardino. Translated by Adrian Walford. 2 vols. New York: Oxford University Press, 1992.

Cayré, Fulbert. *Manual of Patrology and History of Theology.* Translated by H. Howitt. 2 vols. Paris: Desclée & Co., 1936.

Cerfaux, Lucien. *The Church in the Theology of St. Paul.* Translated by Geoffrey Webb and Adrian Walker. Freiburg: Herder & Herder, 1959.

———. *Une Lecture de L'Épitre aux Romains.* Tournai: Casterman, 1947.

Chafer, Lewis Sperry. *Systematic Theology.* 8 vols. Dallas: Dallas Seminary Press, 1948.

Charles, R. H., ed. *The Apocrypha and Pseudepigrapha of the Old Testament in English, with introductions and critical and explanatory notes to the several books.* Oxford: Clarendon, 1913.

Charlesworth, James H. "Christian and Jewish Self-Definition in Light of the Christian Additions to the Apocryphal Writings." Pages 27–55 in *Jewish and Christian Self-Definition,* vol. 2. Edited by E. P. Saunders. Philadelphia: Fortress, 1981.

———, ed. *The Old Testament Pseudepigrapha.* 2 vols. Garden City, NY: Doubleday, 1983–85.

Charry, Ellen T. *By the renewing of your minds: the pastoral function of Christian doctrine.* New York: Oxford University Press, 1997.

Chary, Théophane. *Aggée-Zacharie-Malachie*. Sources bibliques. Paris: Gabalda, 1969.

Chesnut, Glenn F. *The First Christian Histories: Eusebius, Socrates, Sozomen, Theodoret and Evagrius*. Macon, Ga.: Mercer University Press, 1986.

Chesnut, R. C. "The Two Prosopa in Nestorius' Bazaar of Heraclides." *Journal of Theological Studies* 29 (1978): 392-409.

Childs, Brevard. "The *Sensus Literalis* of Scripture: An Ancient and Modern Problem." Pages 80-93 in *Beiträge zur Alttestamentlichen Theologie*. Edited by Herbert Donner et al. Göttingen: Vandenhoeck & Ruprecht, 1977.

———. "The Canonical Shape of the Prophetic Literature." *Interpretation* 32 (1978): 46-55.

Clark, David G. "Elijah as Eschatological High Priest: An Examination of the Elijah Tradition in Mal. 3:23-24." Ph.D. diss., University of Notre Dame, 1975.

Collins, John J. "The Sibylline Oracles." Pages 317-472 in *The Old Testament Pseudepigrapha*. Vol. 1. Edited by James H. Charlesworth. Garden City, NY: Doubleday, 1983.

———. "Sibyllene Oracles." Pages 2-6 in vol. 6 of *The Anchor Bible Dictionary*. Edited by David Noel Freedman. 6 vols. New York: Doubleday, 1992.

———. "The Works of the Messiah." *Dead Sea Discoveries* 1 (1994): 98-112.

Colson, Charles and Richard John Neuhaus. *Evangelicals and Catholics Together: Toward a Common Mission*. Dallas: Word, 1995.

Commodian. *Commodiani Carmina*. Corpus Christianorum: Series Latina 128. Turnhout, 1960.

Considine, J. S. "The Two Witnesses: Apoc 11:3-13." *Catholic Biblical Quarterly* 8 (1946): 377-92.

Cordasco, Francesco. *A Brief History of Education*. Paterson, NJ: Littlefield, Adams, 1963.

Corley, Bruce. "The Significance of Romans 9-11: A Study in Pauline Theology." Ph.D. diss., Southwestern Baptist Theological Seminary, 1975.

Craigie, Peter C. *Twelve Prophets*. Philadelphia: Westminster, 1985.

Cranfield, C. E. B. *A Critical and Exegetical Commentary on the Epistle to the Romans*. 2 vols. The International Critical Commentary. Edinburgh: T & T Clark, 1975-1979.

Crutchfield, Larry V. *The Origins of Dispensationalism: The Darby Factor*. Lanham, Md.: University Press of America, 1991.

Cullmann, Oscar. "Le caractère eschatologique du devoir missionnaire et de la conscience apostolique de S. Paul. Étude sur le κατέχον (-ων) de 2 Thess. 2:6-7." *Revue d'Histoire et de Philosophie Religieuses* 16 (1936): 210-245.

———. *Salvation in History*. Translated by Sidney G. Sowers. London: SCM, 1967.

———. *Christ and Time: The Primitive Christian Conception of Time and History*. Translated by Floyd V. Filson. Philadelphia: Westminster, 1950.

Cutsinger, James S., ed. *Reclaiming the Great Tradition: Evangelicals, Catholics and Orthodox in Dialogue*. Downers Grove, Ill.: InterVarsity, 1997.

Daly, Anthony Chrisitan. *Nestorius in the Bazaar of Heracleides: a Christology compatible with the third letter and anathemas of Cyril of Alexandria*. Ph.D. diss., University of California, Los Angeles, 1983.

Daley, Brian E. "Is Patristic Exegesis Still Usable? Some Reflections on Early Christian Interpretations of the Psalms." Pages 69-88 in *The Art of Reading Scripture*. Edited by Ellen F. Davis and Richard B. Hays. Grand Rapids, Mich.: Eerdmans, 2003.

———. *The Hope of the Early Church: A Handbook of Patristic Eschatology.* Cambridge: Cambridge University Press, 1991.

Dalman, Gustaf. *Jesus–Jeshua.* Translated by Paul P. Levertoff. New York: Ktav, 1971.

Danby, Herbert, trans. *The Mishnah.* London: Oxford University Press, 1933.

Danker, Frederick William, ed. *A Greek-English Lexicon of the New Testament and other Early Christian Literature.* Chicago: University of Chicago Press, 2000.

Danielou, Jean, A. H. Couratin, and John Kent. *Historical Theology.* Vol. 2 of The Pelican Guide to Modern Theology. Edited by R. P. C. Hanson. Harmondsworth: Penguin, 1969.

———. *The Theology of Jewish Christianity.* Translated by John A. Baker. London: Darton, Longman & Todd, 1964.

Davies, Alan T. *Anti-Semitism and the Christian Mind: The Crisis of Conscience After Auschwitz.* New York: Herder and Herder, 1969.

Davies, W. D. *Paul and Rabbinic Judaism.* New York: Harper, 1967.

———. "Paul and the People of Israel." *New Testament Studies* 24 (1977–78): 4–39.

———. *The Sermon on the Mount.* Cambridge: Cambridge University Press, 1966.

Deissler, Alfons. *Zwölf Propheten III: Zefanja. Haggai. Sacharja. Maleachi.* Neue Echter Bibel 21. Wurzburg: Echter, 1988.

de Margerie, Bertrand. *An Introduction to the History of Exegesis.* 3 vols. Petersham: St. Bede's, 1993–94.

Denis, Albert-Marie. *Introduction aux pseudégraphs grecs d'ancien testament.* Studia in Veteris Testamenti pseudepigraphica 1. Leiden: Brill, 1970.

Di Berardino, Angelo, and Basil Studer, eds. *History of Theology: The Patristic Period.* Vol. 1 of *The History of Theology.* Translated by Matthew J. O'Connell. Collegevill, Minn.: Liturgical Press, 1996.

Di Lella, Alexander A. "Wisdom of Ben-Sira." Pages 931–945 in vol. 6 of *The Anchor Bible Dictionary.* Edited by David Noel Freedman. 6 vols. New York: Doubleday, 1992.

Dodd, C. H. *The Epistle of Paul to the Romans.* New York: Harper and Brothers, 1932.

Downey, Glanville. *A History of Antioch in Syria: from Seleucus to the Arab Conquest.* Princeton: Princeton University Press, 1961.

Dunn, James D. G. *Romans 9–16.* Word Biblical Commentary 38B. Dallas: Word, 1988.

Ehrhard, Albert. *Die Cyrill von Alexandrien zugeschriebene Schrift Περὶ τῆς τοῦ Κυρίου ἐνανθρωπήσεως, ein Werk des Theodoret von Cyrus.* Tübingen: H. Laupp, Jr., 1888.

Eissfeldt, Otto. *The Old Testament: An Introduction, including the Apocrypha and Pseudepigrapha, and also the works of similar type from Qumran: the history of the formation of the Old Testament.* Translated by Peter Ackroyd. New York: Harper & Row, 1965.

Elliot, J. K., ed. *The Apocryphal New Testament: A Collection of Apocryphal Christian Literature in an English translation.* Oxford: Clarendon, 1993.

Epstein, I., ed. *The Babylonian Talmud: Translated into English with notes, glossary, and indices.* London: Soncino Press, 1961.

Erickson, Millard J. *Christian Theology.* 3 vols. Grand Rapids, Mich.: Baker, 1985.

Escolan, Philippe. *Monachisme et Eglise: Le monachisme syrien du IVe au VIIe siècle, un ministère charismatique.* Théologie historique 109. Paris: Beauchesne, 1999.

Faierstein, Morris M. "Why Do the Scribes Say that Elijah Must Come First?" *Journal of Biblical*

Literature 100 (1981): 75–86.

Farrar, Frederic W. *History of Interpretation*. London: Macmillan, 1886.

Feuillet, André. "Le plan salvifique de Dieu d'après L'Épitre aux Romains. Deuxieme Partie: Le plan salvifique de Dieu et le sort d'Israel." *Revue Biblique* 57 (1950): 489–506.

Fiorenza, Elisabeth Schüssler. *Revelation: A Vision of a Just World*. Minneapolis: Fortress, 1991.

Fitzmyer, Joseph A. "More About Elijah Coming First." *Journal of Biblical Literature* 104 (1985): 295–96.

———. *Romans: A New Translation with Introduction and Commentary*. The Anchor Bible 33. New York: Doubleday, 1993.

———. *Essays on the Semitic Background of the New Testament*. London: Chapman, 1971.

Fives, D. C. *The use of the optative mood in the works of Theodoret, bishop of Cyrus*. Washington, D.C.: The Catholic University of America, 1937.

Frankfurter, David. *Elijah in Upper Egypt: The Apocalypse of Elijah and Early Egyptian Christianity*. Studies in Antiquity and Christianity. Minneapolis: Fortress, 1993.

Fuller, R. H. *The Foundations of New Testament Christology*. London: Collins, 1965.

Gadamer, Hans-Georg. *Truth and Method*. New York: Continuum, 1995.

Gager, John G. *The Origins of Anti-Semitism: Attitudes Toward Judaism in Pagan and Christian Antiquity*. New York: Oxford University Press, 1983.

Garrett, Duane Andrew. "Chrysostom's Interpretatio in Isaiam: An English Translation with an Analysis of its Hermeneutics." Ph.D. diss., Baylor University, 1981.

Gaston, Lloyd. *Paul and the Torah*. Vancouver: University of British Columbia Press, 1987.

Geffcken, Johannes. *Komposition und Entstehungszeit der Oracula sibylline*. Texte und Untersuchungen zur Geschichte der altchristlichen Literatur 23, 1. Leipzig: J.C. Hinrichs, 1902.

Getty, Mary Ann. "Paul and the Salvation of Israel: A Perspective on Romans 9–11." *Catholic Biblical Quarterly* 50 (1988): 456–469.

Ginzberg, Louis. *An Unknown Jewish Sect*. New York: The Jewish Theological Seminary of America, 1970.

Glazier-McDonald, Beth. *Malachi: The Divine Messenger*. SBL Dissertation Series 98. Atlanta: Scholars, 1987.

Goodenough, E. R. *Jewish Symbols in the Greco-Roman Period*. 12 vols. New York: Pantheon Books, 1953–1965.

Gorday, Peter. *Principles of Patristic Exegesis: Romans 9–11 in Origin, John Chrysostom, and Augustine*. New York: E. Mellen, 1983.

Grant, Robert M., and David Tracy. *A Short History of the Interpretation of the Bible*. Philadelphia: Fortress Press, 1984.

———. "The Appeal to the Early Fathers." *Journal of Theological Studies* 11 (1960): 13–24.

Grillmeier, Aloys. *Christ in Christian Tradition*. 2 vols. Translated by J. Bowden. Atlanta: John Knox, 1975.

Guinot, Jean Noël. *L'Exégèse de Théodoret de Cyr*. Théologie Historique 100. Paris: Beauchesne, 1995.

———. "Theodoret of Cyrus: bishop and exegete." In *The Bible in Greek Christian Antiquity*. Edited by Paul M. Blowers. South Bend, Ind.: University of Notre Dame Press, 1997.

———. "Les sources de l'exégèse de Theodoret de Cyr." In *Studia Patristica* 25. Edited by

Elizabeth A. Livingstone. Louvain: Peeters, 1993.

Gundry, Robert H. *The Church and the Tribulation.* Grand Rapids, Mich.: Zondervan, 1973.

Hall, Christopher A. *Reading Scripture with the Church Fathers.* Downers Grove, Ill.: InterVarsity, 1998.

Hamell, Patrick J. *Handbook of Patrology.* Staten Island, N.Y.: Alba House, 1968.

Hanson, Paul D. *The Dawn of Apocalyptic: The Historical and Sociological Roots of Jewish Apocalyptic Eschatology.* Revised edition. Philadelphia: Fortress, 1979.

Hare, Douglas R. A. "The Lives of the Prophets." Pages 502–03 in vol. 5 of *The Anchor Bible Dictionary.* Edited by David Noel Freedman. 6 vols. New York: Doubleday, 1992.

———. "The Lives of the Prophets: A New Translation and Introduction." Pages 379–99 in *The Old Testament Pseudepigrapha.* Vol. 2. Edited by James H. Charlesworth. Garden City, NY: Doubleday, 1985.

Harmon, Steven R. "A Note on the Critical Use of Instrumenta for the Retrieval of Patristic Biblical Exegesis." *Journal of Early Christian Studies* 11 (2003): 95–107.

Harrington, Daniel J. "Pseudo-Philo." Pages 344–345 in vol. 5 of *The Anchor Bible Dictionary.* Edited by David Noel Freedman. 6 vols. New York: Doubleday, 1992.

———. "Pseudo-Philo: A New Translation and Introduction." Pages 297–377 in *The Old Testament Pseudepigrapha.* Vol. 2. Edited by James H. Charlesworth. Garden City, NY: Doubleday, 1985.

Haugg, Donatus. *Die Zwei Zeugen: Eine exegetische Studie über Apok 11, 1–13.* Neutestamentliche Abhandlungen 17.1. Münster: Aschendorffschen, 1936.

Hauschild, Wolf-Dieter. "Der Ertrag der neueren auslegungsgeschichtlichen Forschung für die Patristik." *Verkündigung und Forschung* 16 (1971): 5–25.

Hayward, Robert. "Phinehas—the same as Elijah: The Origins of a Rabbinic Tradition." *Journal of Jewish Studies* 29 (1978): 22–34.

Hendriksen, William. *Israel in Prophecy.* Grand Rapids, Mich.: Baker, 1968.

Hidal, Sten. "Apocalypse, persecution and exegesis: Hippolytus and Theodoret of Cyrrhus on the Book of Daniel." Pages 49–53 in *In the Last Days: On Jewish and Christian apocalyptic and its period.* Edited by Knud Jeppesen, Kirsten Nielsen, and Bent Rosendal. Aarhus, Denmark: Aarhus University Press, 1994.

Higgins, A. J. B. "Jewish Messianic Belief in Justin Martyr's Dialogue with Trypho." *Novum Testamentum* 9 (1967): 298–305.

Hilary of Poitiers. *Sur Matthieu.* Sources chrétiennes 258. Edited by Jean Doignon. Paris: Editions du Cerf, 1979.

Hill, Andrew E. *Malachi: A New Translation with Introduction and Commentary.* The Anchor Bible 25D. New York: Doubleday, 1998.

Hill, Robert C. "Theodoret's Commentary on Paul." *Estudios Bíblicos* 58 (2000): 79–99.

———. "Theodoret wrestling with Romans." Pages 347–52 in *Studia Patristica* 34. Texte und Untersuchungen zur Geschichte der altchristlichen Literatur. Berlin: Akademie-Verlag, 2001.

———. "On looking again at *synkatabasis.*" *Prudentia* 13 (1981): 3–11.

Hodge, Charles. *Commentary on the Epistle to the Romans.* Grand Rapids, Mich.: Eerdmans, 1950.

Hofius, Otfried. "'All Israel Will be Saved': Divine Salvation and Israel's Deliverance in Romans 9–11." *The Princeton Seminary Bulletin, Supplementary Issue* 1 (1990): 19–39.

———. "Das Evangelium und Israel. Erwägungen zu Römer 9-11," *Zeitschrift für Theologie und Kirche* 83 (1986): 297-324.

Hofmann, J. Chr. K. *Der Schriftbeweis: Ein theologischer Versuch.* 2 vols. Nördlingen: C. H. Beck, 1852.

Honigmann, Ernst. "Theodoret of Cyrrhus and Basil of Seleucia. The Time of their Death." *Patristic Studies* 173 (1953): 174-84.

Horne, C. M. "The Meaning of the Phrase 'And All Israel Will Be Saved' (Romans 11:26)." *Journal of the Evangelical Theological Society* 21 (1978): 329-334.

Horst, Friedrich. *Die zwölf kleinen Propheten: Nahum bis Maleachi.* Handbuch zum Alten Testament 1/14, 2. Tübingen: Mohr, 1954.

Hvalvik, Reidar. "A 'Sonderweg' for Israel: A Critical Examination of a Current Interpretation of Romans 11:25-27." *Journal for the Study of the New Testament* 38 (1990): 87-107.

Irons, Misty S., James T. Dennison, Jr., Catherine T. Drown, and Lee Irons. "Theodoret of Cyrhus; The Epistle of Paul to Philemon." *Westminster Theological Journal* 61 (1999): 111-17.

Isaac, E. "1 (Ethiopic Apocalypse of) Enoch: New Translation and Introduction." Pages 5-89 in *The Old Testament Pseudepigrapha.* Vol. 1. Edited by James H. Charlesworth. Garden City, NY: Doubleday, 1983.

Jefford, Clayton N. "Acts of Pilate." Pages 371-372 in vol. 5 of *The Anchor Bible Dictionary.* Edited by David Noel Freedman. 6 vols. New York: Doubleday, 1992.

Jenks, Gregory C. *The Origins and Early Development of the Anti-Christ Myth.* Beihefte zur Zeitschrift für die Neutestamentliche Wissenschaft und die Kunde der älteren Kirche 59. Berlin: Walter de Gruyter, 1991.

Jeremias, Joachim. "Einige vorwiegend sprachliche Beobachtungen zu Römer 11:25-36." Pages 193-203 in *Die Israelfrage nach Röm 9-11.* Edited by Lorenzo De Lorenzi. Rome: Abtei von St Paul von den Mauern, 1977.

———. "Ηλ(ε)ίας." Pages 928-41 in vol. 2 of *Theological Dictionary of the New Testament.* Edited by Gerhard Kittel. 10 vols. Grand Rapids, Mich.: Eerdmans, 1964.

Jerome. *Commentarii in Prophetas Minores.* Corpus Christianorum: Series Latina 76A. Turnhout: 1970.

Johnson, E. Elizabeth. *The Function of Apocalyptic and Wisdom Traditions in Romans 9-11.* Atlanta: Scholars, 1989.

Johnson, Luke Timothy. *Reading Romans: A Literary and Theological Commentary.* Macon, Ga.: Smyth & Helwys, 2001.

Jones, A. H. M. *The Later Roman Empire, 284-602: A Social, Economic, and Administrative Survey.* 2 vols. Norman: University of Oklahoma Press, 1964.

Josephus. *The Works of Josephus: Complete and Unabridged.* Translated by William Whiston. Peabody, Mass.: Hendrickson, 1987.

Jülicher, Adolf. *Der Bief an die Römer.* Die Schriften des neuen Testaments. Göttingen: Vandenhoeck & Ruprecht.

Justin Martyr. *Iustini Martyris Dialogus cum Tryphone.* Patristische Texte und Studien. Edited by Miroslav Marcovich. Berlin: Walter de Gruyter, 1997.

Käsemann, Ernst. *Commentary on Romans.* Translated and edited by Geoffrey W. Bromiley. Grand Rapids, Mich.: William B. Eerdmans, 1980.

Kelly, J. N. D. *Early Christian Doctrines*. Rev. ed. London: Adam & Charles Black, 1977.

Kepple, Robert J. "An Analysis of Antiochene Exegesis of Galatians 4:24-6." *Westminster Theological Journal* 39 (1977): 239-49.

Kittel, G., and G. Friedrich, eds. *Theological Dictionary of the New Testament*. Translated by G. W. Bromiley. 10 vols. Grand Rapids: Eerdmans, 1964-1976.

Kihn, Heinrich. "Über θεωρία und ἀλλεγορία nach den verlorenen hermeneutischen Schriften der Antiochener." *Theologische Quartalschrift* 20 (1880): 531-82.

Klausner, Joseph. *The Messianic Idea in Israel: From Its Beginning to the Completion of the Mishnah*. Translated by W. F. Stinespring. New York: Macmillan, 1955.

Knibb, M. A., ed. *The Ethiopic Book of Enoch: A New Edition in the Light of the Aramaic Dead Sea Fragments*. Oxford: Clarendon, 1978.

Koch, Deitrich-Alex. "Beobachtungen zum christologischen Schriftgebrauch in den vor-paulinischen Gemeinden." *Zeitschrift für neutestamentliche Wissenschaft und die Kunde der älteren Kirche* 71 (1980): 174-191.

Koch, G. *Strukturen und Geschichte des Heils in der Theologie des Theodoret von Kyros: ein dogmen- und theologieschichtliche Untersuchung*. Frankfurt am Main: J. Knecht, 1974.

Krueger, Derek. "Typological Figuration in Theodoret of Cyrrhus's Religious History and the Art of Postbiblical Narrative." *Journal of Early Christian Studies* 5 (1997): 393-419.

Kruse-Blinkenberg, Lars. "The Book of Malachi according to Codex Syro-Hexaplaris Ambrosianus." *Studia theologica* 21 (1967): 62-82.

Kühl, Ernst. *Der Brief des Paulus an die Römer*. Leipzig: Qeulle & Meyer, 1913.

Kurfess, Alfons. "Oracula Sibyllina." *Zeitschrift für Neutestamentliche Wissenschaft* 40 (1941): 151-65.

Kyle, Richard. "Nestorius: The Partial Rehabilitation of a Heretic." *Journal of the Evangelical Theological Society* 32 (1989): 73-83.

Lactantius. *The Divine Institutes: Books I-VII*. The Fathers of the Church 49. Translated by Sister Mary Francis McDonald. Washington: The Catholic University of America Press, 1964.

Lagrange, Marie-Joseph. *Saint Paul: Épitre aux Romains*. Paris: J. Gabalda, 1950.

Lakeland, Paul. *Post Modernity: Christian Identity in a Fragmented Age*. Minneapolis: Fortress, 1997.

Lampe, G. W. H., ed. *A Patristic Greek Lexicon*. 5 vols. Oxford: Clarendon Press, 1961-68.

Lapide, Pinchas, and Peter Stuhlmacher. *Paul: Rabbi and Apostle*. Translated by Lawrence W. Denef. Minneapolis: Augsburg, 1984.

Lenski, R. C. H. *The Interpretation of St. Paul's Epistle to the Romans*. Columbus: Wartburg, 1945.

Levi, Israel, ed. *The Hebrew Text of the Book of Ecclesiasticus*. Leiden: E. J. Brill, 1969.

Libanius, *Oration in Praise of Antioch*. Translated by Glanville Downey. Pages 652-687 in *The Proceedings of the American Philosophical Socity* 103 (1959).

Lightfoot, J. B. *The Apostolic Fathers*. 2 vols. London: Macmillan, 1889.

Lindbeck, Kristen Harriet. *Story and Theology: Elijah's Appearances in the Babylonian Talmud*. Ph.D. diss., The Jewish Theological Seminary of America, 1999.

Lübking, Hans-Martin. *Paulus und Israel im Römerbrief: Eine Untersuchung zu Römer 9-11*. Frankfort am Main: Peter Lang, 1986.

Luz, Ulrich. *Matthew 1-7: A Commentary*. Translated by Wilhelm C. Linss. Minneapolis:

Fortress, 1989.

———. *Das Geschichtsverständnis des Paulus*. Beiträge zur evanglischen Theologie 49. München: C. Kaiser, 1968.

Margerie, Bertrand de. "θεωρία et tradition dans l'École d'Antioch." Pages 188–213 in *Introduction à l'histoire de L'exégèse*. Vol. 1. Paris: Cerf, 1980.

Marshall, Bruce D. *Trinity and Truth*. Cambridge: Cambridge University Press, 2000.

Martyn, J. Louis. "We Have Found Elijah." Pages 181–219 in *Jews, Greeks and Christians: Religious Cultures in Late Antiquity. Essays in Honor of William David Davies*. Edited by Robert Hamerton-Kelly and Robin Scroggs. Leiden: E. J. Brill, 1976.

Mason, Rex. *The Books of Haggai, Zechariah and Malachi*. Cambridge Bible Commentary. Cambridge: Cambridge University Press, 1977.

Mayer, Bernhard. *Unter Gottes Heilsratschluss: Prädestinationsaussagen bei Paulus*. Forshung zur Bibel. Würzburg: Echter, 1974.

McCollough, C. Thomas. "Theodoret of Cyrus as Biblical Interpreter," Pages 327–334 in *Studia Patristica XVIII*. Edited by Elizabeth A. Livingstone. Kalamazoo, Mich.: Cistercian Publications, 1986.

———. "A Christianity for an age of crisis: Theodoret of Cyrus' Commentary on Daniel [especially Dan 2]." Pages 157–174 in *Religious Writings and Religious Systems*. Brown Studies in Religion 1. Edited by Jacob Neusner, Ernest S. Frerichs, and A. J. Levine. Atlanta: Scholars Press, 1989.

McGuckin, J. A. "Nestorius and the Political Factions of Fifth-century Byzantium: Factors in His Personal Downfall." *Bulletin of the John Rylands University Library of Manchester* 78 (1996): 7–21.

Maier, F. W. *Israel in der Heilsgeschichte nach Röm. 9–11*. Biblische Zeitfragen 12.11–12. Münster in Westfalen: Aschendorff, 1929.

Bruce M. Metzger. "The Fourth Book of Ezra." Pages 516–559 in *The Old Testament Pseudepigrapha*. Vol. 1. Edited by James H. Charlesworth. Garden City, NY: Doubleday, 1983.

———. *Breaking the Code: Understanding the Book of Revelation*. Nashville: Abingdon, 1993.

Meyer, Heinrich August Wilhem. *Critical and Exegetical Handbook to the Epistle to the Romans*. Edited by William P. Dickson. Translated by John C. Moore and Edwin Johnson. New York: Funk & Wagnalls, 1884.

Michel, Otto. *Der Brief an die Römer*. Kritisch-exegetischer Kommentar über das Neue Testament. Göttingen: Vandenhoeck & Ruprecht, 1963.

Milbank, John. *The Word Made Strange: Theology, Language, Culture*. Oxford: Blackwell, 1997.

Milik, Jozef T. "Problèmes de la littérature Hénochique à la lumière des fragments araméens de Qumrân." *Harvard Theological Review* 64 (1971): 333–78.

Montefiore, G. C., and H. Loewe, eds. *A Rabbinic Anthology*. Repr. New York: Schocken Books, 1974.

Moore, George Foot. *Judaism in the First Centuries of the Christian Era, the Age of the Tannaim*. 3 vols. Cambridge: Harvard University Press, 1927–1930.

Moule, Handley C. G. *The Epistle of St. Paul to the Romans*. New York: A. C. Armstrong & Son, 1905.

Mowinckel, Sigmund. *He That Cometh*. Translated by G. W. Anderson. New York: Abingdon

Press, 1954.

Müller, C. Detlef G. "Apocalypse of Peter." Pages 620–38 in *New Testament Apocrypha*. Revised Edition. Vol 2. Edited by Wilhelm Schneemelcher. Translated by R. McL. Wilson. Louisville: Westminster John Knox, 1992.

Müller, Christian. *Gottes Gerechtigkeit und Gottes Volk: Eine Untersuchung zu Römer 9–11*. Forschungen zur Religion und Literatur des Altens und Neuen Testaments 86. Göttingen: Vandenhoeck & Ruprecht, 1964.

Munck, Johannes. *Christ & Israel: An Interpretation of Romans 9–11*. Translated by Ingeborg Nixon. Philadelphia: Fortress Press, 1967.

———. *Paul and the Salvation of Mankind*. Translated by Frank Clarke. Richmond: John Knox, 1959.

———. *Petrus und Paulus in der Offenbarung Johannis*. Copenhagen: Rosenkilde og Bagger, 1950.

Murray, John. *The Epistle to the Romans: The English Text with Introduction, Exposition and Notes*. 2 vols. Grand Rapids, Mich.: Eerdmans, 1965.

Mussner, Franz. *Traktat über die Juden*. München: Kösel, 1979.

Nassif, Bradley. "'Spiritual Exegesis' in the School of Antioch." Pages 343–77 in *New Perspectives on Historical Theology: Essays in Memory of John Meyendorff*. Edited by Bradley Nassif. Grand Rapids, Mich.: Eerdmans, 1996.

Nestorius, *The Bazaar of Heracleides*. Translated by G. R. Driver and Leonard Hodgson. Oxford: Clarendon, 1925.

Nickelsburg, George W. E. "Enoch, First Book of." Pages 508–516 in vol. 2 of *The Anchor Bible Dictionary*. Edited by David Noel Freedman. 6 vols. New York: Doubleday, 1992.

Nygren, Anders. *Commentary on Romans*. Translated by Carl C. Rasmussen. Philadelphia: Muhlenberg, 1949.

Oden, Thomas C. "The Long Journey Home." *Journal of the Evangelical Theological Society* 34 (1991): 77–92.

———. *Systematic Theology*. 3 vols. San Francisco: Harper & Row, 1987–1992.

Öhler, Markus. *Elia im Neuen Testament: Untersuchungen zur Bedeutung des alttestamentlichen Propheten im frühen Christentum*. Beihefte zur Zeitschrift für die neutestamentliche Wissenschaft und die Kunde der älteren Kirche 88. Berlin: Walter de Gruyter, 1997.

O'Keefe, John J. "A Letter that Killeth: Toward a Reassessment of Antiochene Exegesis, or Diodore, Theodore, and Theodoret on the Psalms." *Journal of Early Christian Studies* 8 (2000): 83–104.

———. "Interpreting the Angel: Cyril of Alexandria and Theodoret of Cyrus, Commentators on the Book of Malachi." Ph.D. diss. The Catholic University of America, 1993.

Otto, J. C. T., ed. *Justini philosophi et martyris opera quae feruntur omnia*. Corpus apologetarum Christianorum saeculi secundi. Vols. 4–5. Jenae: Libraria Hermanni Dufft, 1880–1881.

Parmentier, Martin. "Greek Church Fathers on Romans 9." *Bijdragen tijdschrift voor filosofie en theologie* 50 (1989): 139–154.

———. "Greek Church Fathers on Romans 9. Part II." *Bijdragen tijdschrift voor filosofie en theologie* 51 (1990): 2–20.

Patrologia graeca. Edited by J.-P. Migne. 162 vols. Paris, 1857–1886.

Petersen, David L. *Zechariah 9–14 and Malachi: A Commentary*. The Old Testament Library. Louisville: Westminster John Knox, 1995.

Photius, *The Bibliotheca*. Translated by N. G. Wilson. London: Duckworth, 1994.

Piper, Otto. "Heilsgeschichte." Pages 156–59 in *A Handbook of Christian Theology*. Edited by Marvin Halverson and Arthur Cohen. New York: Meridian, 1958.

Plag, Christoph. *Israels Wege zum Heil: eine Untersuchung zu Römer 9 bis 11*. Arbeiten zur Theologie Reihe 1, Heft 40. Stuttgart: Calwer, 1969.

Pleasants, Phyllis Rodgerson. "Making Antioch Christian: The City in the Pastoral Vision of John Chrysostom." Ph.D. diss., The Southern Baptist Theological Seminary, 1991.

Plummer, W. S. *Commentary on Romans*. Grand Rapids, Mich.: Kregel, 1971.

Poirier, John C. "The Endtime Return of Elijah and Moses at Qumran." *Dead Sea Discoveries* 10 (2003): 221–42.

Prosser, Peter E. *Dispensationalist Eschatology and Its Influence on American and British Religious Movements*. Texts and Studies in Religion 81. Lewiston, N.Y.: Edwin Mellen, 1999.

Quasten, Johannes. *Patrology*. 3 vols. Utrecht: Spectrum, 1950–1960.

Reddish, Mitchell G., ed. *Apocalyptic Literature: A Reader*. Peabody, Mass.: Hendrickson, 1995.

Redditt, Paul L. *Haggai, Zechariah, Malachi*. New Century Bible. Grand Rapids, Mich.: Eerdmans, 1995.

Refoulé, François. "Unité de la L'Épitre aux Romains et histoire du salut." *Revue des Sciences Philosophiques et Théologiques* 71 (1987): 243–59.

———. *"...et ainsi tout Israël sera sauvé": Romains 11, 25–32*. Lectio Devina 117. Paris: Editions due Cerf, 1984.

Räisänen, Heikki. "Römer 9–11: Analyse eines geistigen Ringens," *ANRW* 25.4:2891–2936. Part 2, *Principat*, 25.4. Edited by H. Temporini and W. Haase. New York: de Gruyter, 1989.

Rese, Martin. "Die Rettung der Juden nach Römer 11." Pages 422–430 in *L'Apôtre Paul*. Edited by A. Vanhoye. Leuven: University Press/Peeters, 1986.

Robinson, J. A. T. "Elijah, John and Jesus: An Essay in Detection." *New Testament Studies* 4 (1957–58): 263–81.

Rossiter, Francis. "Messianic Prophecy according to Theodoret of Cyrus." Ph.D. diss., The Pontifical Gregorian University, 1949.

Rottenberg, Isaac C. *Redemption and Historical Reality*. Philadelphia: Westminster, 1964.

Rosenweig, Franz. *Der Stern der Erlösung*. Heidelberg: Lambert Schneider, 1954.

Rupp, Gordon. *The Righteousness of God: Luther Studies*. New York: Philosophical Library, 1953.

Ryrie, Charles Caldwell. *Dispensationalism Today*. Chicago: Moody, 1965.

Sanday, William and Arthur C. Headlam. *A Critical and Exegetical Commentary on the Epistle to the Romans*. The International Critical Commentary. New York: Charles Scribner's Sons, 1896.

Sanders, E. P. *Paul, the Law, and the Jewish People*. Minneapolis: Fortress, 1983.

Sauer, Erich. *From Eternity to Eternity: An Outline of the Divine Purposes*. Translated by G. H. Lang. Grand Rapids, Mich.: Eerdmans, 1957.

Schaller, Berndt. "ΗΞΕΙ ΕΚ ΣΙΟΝ Ο ΡΥΟΜΕΝΟΣ: Zur Textgestalt von Jes. 59.20–21 in Rom. 11.26–27." Pages 201–206 in *De Septuaginta: Studies in Honour of John William Wevers on his Sixty-Fifth Birthday*. Edited by A. Pietersma and C. Cox. Missisauga, Ontario: Benben, 1984.

Schäublin, Christoph. *Untersuchengen zu Methode und Herkunft der Antiochenischen Exegese*. Köln-

Bonn: Peter Hanstein, 1974.

Scheidweiler, Felix. "The Gospel of Nicodemus: Acts of Pilate and Christ's Descent into Hell." Pages 501–36 in *New Testament Apocrypha*. Revised Edition. Vol. 1. Edited by Wilhelm Schneemelcher. Translated by R. McL. Wilson. Louisville: Westminster John Knox, 1991.

Schelkle, Karl Hermann. "Kirche und Synagoge in der frühen Auslegung des Römerbriefes." Pages 282–299 in *Wort und Schrift*. Düsseldorf, 1966.

———. "Erwählung und Freiheit im Römerbrief nach Auslegung der Väter." Pages 251–272 in *Wort und Schrift*. Düsseldorf, 1966.

———. *Paulus Lehrer der Väter: Die altkirchliche Auslegung von Römer 1–11*. Düsseldorf: Patmos, 1956.

Schmidt, Hans Wilhelm. *Der Brief des Paulus an die Römer*. Theologischer Handkommentar zum Neuen Testament. Berlin: Evangelische, 1966.

Schmidt, Karl Ludwig. *Die Judenfrage im Lichte der Kapitel 9–11 des Römerbriefes*. Theologische Studien 13. Zollikon-Zurich: Evangelischer, 1947.

Schneemelcher, Wilhelm, ed. *New Testament Apocrypha*. Revised Edition. 2 vols. Translated by R. McL. Wilson. Louisville: Westminster John Knox, 1991–1992.

Schoeps, H. J. *Paul: The Theology of the Apostle in the Light of Jewish Religious History*. Translated by Harold Knight. Philadelphia: Westminster, 1959.

———. *The Jewish-Christian Argument: A History of Theologies in Conflict*. Translated by David E. Green. New York: Holt, Rinehart and Winston, 1963.

Scholem, G. *The Messianic Idea in Judaism*. New York: 1971.

Schulte, Joseph. *Theodoret von Cyrus als Apologet: Ein Beitrag zur Geschichte der Apologetik*. Theologische Studiën. Vienna: Mayer, 1904.

Schürer, Emil. *The History of the Jewish People in the Age of Jesus Christ*. 3 vols. Rev. ed. by Geza Vermes, Fergus Millar, and Matthew Black. Edinburgh: T & T Clark, 1973–1987.

Scofield, Cyrus I., ed. *The Scofield Reference Bible*. New York: Oxford University Press, 1909.

Segal, Samuel M. *Elijah: A Study in Jewish Folklore*. New York: Behrman's, 1935.

Sharot, S. *Messianism, Mysticism and Magic*. Chapel Hill, 1982.

Silver, Abba Hillel. *Messianic Speculation in Israel*. Boston: 1959.

Smith, Ralph L. *Micah-Malachi*. Word Biblical Commentary 32. Waco, Texas: Word, 1984.

Staab, Karl. *Pauluskommentare aus der Griechischen Kirche: aus Katenen-handschriften gesammelt und herausgegeben*. Neutestamentliche Abhandlungen 15. Münster i.W.: Aschendorff, 1933.

Stanley, Christopher D. "'The Redeemer Will Come ἐκ Σιών': Romans 11:26–27 Revisited." Pages 118–142 in *Paul and the Scriptures of Israel*. Edited by Craig A. Evans and James A. Sanders. Sheffield: JSOT, 1993.

Starcky, Jean. "Les quatres étapes du messianique à Qumran." *Revue Biblique* 70 (1963): 489–505.

Steinmetz, David. "The Superiority of Pre-critical Exegesis." Pages 65–77 in *A Guide to Contemporary Hermeneutics*. Edited by Donald K. McKim. Grand Rapids: Eerdmans, 1986.

Stendahl, Krister. *Paul Among Jews and Gentiles and Other Essays*. Philadelphia: Fortress, 1976.

———. *Meanings: The Bible as Document and as Guide*. Philadelphia: Fortress, 1984.

Stone, Michael E. "Second Book of Esdras." Pages 611–614 in vol. 2 of *The Anchor Bible Dictionary*. Edited by David Noel Freedman. 6 vols. New York: Doubleday, 1992.

Strack, Hermann L., and Paul Billerbeck. *Kommentar zum Neuen Testament aus Talmud und Midrasch*. 6 vols. Munich: C. H. Beck, 1922–1961.

———, and G. Stemberger. *Introduction to the Talmud and Midrash*. Minneapolis: Fortress, 1992.

Strugnell, John. "Moses-Pseudepigrapha at Qumran: 4Q375, 4Q376, and Similar Works." Pages 221–56 in *Archaeology and History in the Dead Sea Scrolls: The New York University Conference in Memory of Yigael Yadin*. Edited by Lawrence H. Schiffman. Journal for the Study of the Pseudepigrapha: Supplement Series 8. Sheffield: JSOT Press, 1990.

Stuhlmacher, Peter. *Paul's Letter to the Romans: A Commentary*. Translated by Scott J. Hafemann. Louisville, Ky.: Westminster/John Knox, 1994.

———. "Zur Interpretation von Römer 11:25–32." Pages 555–570 in *Probleme biblischer Theologie: Gerhard von Rad zum 70. Geburtstag*. Edited by Hans Walter Wolff. München: Chr. Kaiser, 1971.

Talbert, Charles H. *Romans*. Smyth & Helwys Bible Commentary. Macon, Ga.: Smyth & Helwys, 2002.

———. *The Apocalypse: A Reading of the Revelation of John*. Louisville: Westminster John Knox, 1994.

Ternant, Paul. "La θεωρία d'Antioche dans le cadre des sens de l'Eriture." *Biblica* 34 (1953): 135–58; 354–83; 456–86.

Theodore of Mopsuestia. *Commentary on the Twelve Prophets*. The Fathers of the Church 108. Translated by Robert C. Hill. Washington: The Catholic University of America Press, 2004.

Theodoret of Cyrus. *Commentary on the Psalms*. Translated by Robert C. Hill. 2 vols. The Fathers of the Church. Washington, D.C.: The Catholic University of America Press, 2000.

———. *Commentario alla lettera ai Romani*. Translated by L. Scarampi, et al. Roma: Borla, 1998.

———. *Théodoret de Cyr, Correspondance*. Sources chrétiennes 40, 98, 111. Edited by Yvan Azéma. Paris: Editions du Cerf, 1955–1965.

———. *Théodoret de Cyr, Commentaire sur Isaie*. Sources chrétiennes 276. Edited by Jean Noël Guinot. Paris: Editions du Cerf, 1980.

———. *Théodoret de Cyr, Histoire des Moines de Syrie*. Sources chrétiennes 234, 257. Edited by Pierre Canivet and Alice Leroy-Molinghen. Paris: Editions du Cerf, 1977–1979.

———. *Théodoret de Cyr, Thérapeutique des Maladies Helléniques*. Sources chrétiennes 57. Edited by P. Canivet. Paris: Editions du Cerf, 1958.

———. *Eranistes*. Translated by Gérard H. Ettlinger. Oxford: Clarendon Press, 1975.

———. *A History of the Monks in Syria*. Translated by R. M. Price. Kalamazoo, Mich.: Cistercian Publications, 1985.

———. *On Divine Providence*. Translated by Thomas Halton. New York: Newman, 1988.

———. *Commentarius in omnes B. Pauli Epistolas*. Edited by C. Marriott. Oxford: J. Parker, 1852.

———. *Opera omnia in quatuor tomos distributa, quorum plurima, Graece, quaedam etiam Latine nunc primum prodeunt: Graeca cum manuscriptis exemplaribus...collata, Latinae versiones ad Graecorum normam exactae & recognitae*. Edited by Jacques Sirmond. Paris: Sumptibus S. Cramoisy, 1642.

———. *B. Theodoreti Opera Omnia*. Edited by Johann Ludwig Schulze. Halae: Bibliopolii Orphanotrophei, 1769–74.

———. *Theodoret von Kyros, Kommentar zu Jesaia*. Edited by August Möhle. Mitteilungen des

Septuaginta-Unternehmens der Gesellschaft der Wissenschaften zu Göttingen 5. Berlin: Weidmann, 1932.

Tholuck, F. A. G. *Exposition of St. Paul's Epistle to the Romans.* Translated by Robert Menzies. Philadelphia: Sorin and Ball, 1844.

Trakatellis, Demetrios. "Theodoret's Commentary on Isaiah: A Synthesis of Exegetical Traditions." Pages 313–42 in *New Perspectives on Historical Theology: Essays in memory of John Meyendorff.* Edited by Bradley Nassif. Grand Rapids: Eerdmans, 1996.

Truitt, Danny P. "The Function of Elijah in the Markan Messianic Drama." Ph.D. diss., Baylor University, 1993.

Turner, H. E. W. "Nestorius Reconsidered," *Studia Patristica* 13 (1975): 306–321.

Urbainczyk, Theresa. *Theodoret of Cyrrhus: The Bishop and the Holy Man.* Ann Arbor: The University of Michigan Press, 2002.

Vaccari, A. "La θεωρία nella scuola esegetica di Antiocha." *Biblica* 1 (1920): 3–36.

Van Buren, Paul M. "The Church and Israel: Romans 9–11." *The Princeton Seminary Bulletin, Supplementary Issue* 1 (1990): 5–18.

———. *A Theology of the Jewish-Christian Reality. Part I: Discerning the Way.* New York: Seabury, 1980.

———. *A Theology of the Jewish-Christian Reality. Part II: A Christian Theology of the People Israel.* New York: Seabury, 1987.

———. *A Theology of the Jewish-Christian Reality. Part III: Christ in Context.* San Francisco: Harper & Row, 1988.

Van der Horst, Pieter W. "'Only Then Will All Israel Be Saved': A Short Note on the Meaning of καὶ οὕτως in Romans 11:26." *Journal of Biblical Literature* 119 (2000): 521–525.

VanderKam, James C. "1 Enoch, Enochic Motifs, and Enoch in Early Christian Literature." Pages 33–101 in *The Jewish Apocalyptic Heritage in Early Christianity.* Compendia rerum iudicarum ad Novum Testamentum. Edited by James C. VanderKam and William Adler. Minneapolis: Fortress, 1996.

Vermes, Geza. *Jesus the Jew.* London: SCM, 1973.

Viciano, Alberto. "Theodoret von Kyros als Interpret des Apostels Paulus." *Theologie und Glaube* 80 (1990): 279–315.

———. *Cristo el Autor de Nuestra Salvacion: Estudio Sobre El Comentario de Teodoreto de Ciro a las Epistolas Paulinas.* Pamplona: Ediciones Universidad de Navarra, 1990.

———. "Das Bild des Apostels Paulus im Kommentar zu den paulinischen Briefen des Theodoret von Kyros." *Zeitschrift für die Neutestamentliche Wissenschaft und die Kunde der Älteren Kirche* 83 (1992): 138–148.

Walker, Williston and Richard A. Norris, David W. Lotz, and Robert T. Handy. *A History of the Christian Church.* Fourth Edition. New York: Charles Scribner's Sons, 1985.

Wagner, M. M. "A Chapter in Byzantine Epistolography." *Dumbarton Oaks Papers* 4 (1948): 119–81.

Walsh, Jerome T. "Elijah." Pages 463–466 in vol. 2 of *The Anchor Bible Dictionary.* Edited by David Noel Freedman. 6 vols. New York: Doubleday, 1992.

Walvoord, John F. *The Nations, Israel, and the Church in Prophecy.* Grand Rapids, Mi.: Academie, 1988.

Wand, J. W. C. *A History of the Early Church to A.D. 500.* London: Methuen, 1974.

Webber, Robert and Donald Bloesch. *The Chicago Call*. Nashville: Nelson, 1979.

Webber, Robert. *Ancient-Future Faith: Rethinking Evangelicalism for a Postmodern World*. Grand Rapids, Mich.: Baker, 1999.

Weinel, Heinrich. "Die spätere christliche Apokalyptik." Pages 141–73 in Ευχαριστηριον *2: Studien zur Religion und Literatur des Alten und Neuen Testaments*. Edited by H. Schmidt. Forschungen zur Religion und Literatur des Alten und Neuen Testaments 36. Göttingen: Vandenhoeck & Ruprecht, 1923.

Wiener, Aharon. *The Prophet Elijah in the Development of Judaism*. London: Kegan Paul, 1978.

Wilckens, Ulrich. *Der Brief an die Römer*. 2 vols. Evangelisch-katholischer Kommentar zum Neuen Testament. Zürich: Benziger, 1978–80.

Wiles, Maurice F. *The Divine Apostle: The Interpretation of St. Paul's Epistles in the Early Church*. Cambridge: Cambridge University Press, 1967.

Wilken, Robert L. *Remembering the Christian Past*. Grand Rapids, Mich.: Eerdmans, 1995.

Williams, D. H., "Scripture, Tradition, and the Church: Reformation and Post-Reformation." Pages 101–126 in *The Free Church & the Early Church: Bridging the Historical and Theological Divide*. Edited by D. H. Williams. Grand Rapids, Mich.: Eerdmans, 2002.

———. *Retrieving the Tradition and Renewing Evangelicalism: a Primer for Suspicious Protestants*. Grand Rapids, Mich.: Eerdmans, 1999.

———. "Reflections on *Retrieving the Tradition and Renewing Evangelicalism*: a response." *Scottish Journal of Theology* (2002): 105–112.

Williams, Rowan. *Chrisitan Spirituality: A Theological History from the New Testament to Luther and St. John of the Cross*. Atlanta: John Knox, 1980.

Wink, Walter. *John the Baptist in the Gospel Tradition*. Cambridge: Cambridge University Press, 1968.

Wintermute, Orval S. "Apocalypse of Elijah: A New Translation and Introduction." Pages 721–53 in *The Old Testament Pseudepigrapha*. Vol. 1. Edited by James H. Charlesworth. Garden City, NY: Doubleday, 1983.

———. "Apocalypse of Elijah." Pages 466–68 in vol. 2 of *The Anchor Bible Dictionary*. Edited by David Noel Freedman. 6 vols. New York: Doubleday, 1992.

Witte, Maria Magdalena. *Elias und Henoch als Exempel, typologische Figuren und apokalyptische Zeugen: Zu Verbindungen von Literatur und Theologie im Mittelalter*. Beiträge zur Literaturwissenschaft und Bedeutungsforschung 22. Frankfurt: Peter Lang, 1987.

Wolf, Herbert. *Haggai and Malachi*. Chicago: Moody, 1976.

Woollcombe, K. J. "The Biblical Origins and Patristic Development of Typology." Pages 39–75 in *Essays on Typology*. Edited by G. W. H. Lampe and K. J. Woollcombe. London: SCM Press, 1957.

Wright, N. T. *The Climax of the Covenant: Christ and the Law in Pauline Theology*. Minneapolis: Fortress, 1991.

Young, Frances M. *From Nicaea to Chalcedon*. Philadelphia: Fortress, 1983.

———. *Biblical Exegesis and the Formation of Christian Culture*. Cambridge: Cambridge University Press, 1997.

———. "The Rhetorical Schools and their Influence on Patristic Exegesis." In *The Making of Orthodoxy: Essays in Honour of Henry Chadwick*. Edited by Rowan Williams (Cambridge: Cambridge University Press, 1989).

Zeller, Dieter. *Der Brief an die Römer*. Regensburger Neues Testament. Regensburg: Pustet, 1985.

———. *Juden und Heiden in der Mission des Paulus: Studien zum Römerbrief*. Forschung zur Bibel. Stuttgart: Katholisches Bibelwerk, 1973.

Index

Scripture References

Luke

1:17, 17, 133, 140, 142, 150
3:16, 111
7:27, 137
9:18-19

John

1:21 & 25, 18, 99, 119, 142
1:21, 133-134, 140, 150

Romans

7:24, 12
9-11, 55-93
9:5, 13
9:10-13, 5
9:33, 13
10:18-11:36, 12
11:11-24, 9
11:12, 10, 151
11:15, 10, 151
11:25-27, 8
11:26-27, 11
11:25, 10
11:26, 1, 9-10, 14-15, 17-19, 149, 151
11:26b-27, 9
11:27, 12
11:30, 12
11:33-36, 12
12:25-26, 136
15:31, 11, 12

1 Corinthians

11:25, 12

2 Corinthians

1:10, 11, 12
3:6, 12

Galatians

4:26, 12

1 Thessalonians

1:10, 11, 12

Hebrews

12:22, 12

Revelation (The Apocalypse)

3:12, 13
11, 126, 129, 132, 150
11:3-11, 123, 125
11:3-13, 18, 99, 119-121, 127, 129, 131,
      140, 142, 149
11:6, 120
11:12, 125
12:7-9, 126
12:14, 126
12:16, 126
21:2, 13